The Case for Humanism

The Case for Humanism

An Introduction

Lewis Vaughn and Austin Dacey

This book was made possible by a grant from the Institute for Humanist Studies, Albany, New York, and through the generosity and support of Robert Morse.

ROWMAN & LITTLEFIELD PUBLISHERS, INC.
Lanham • Boulder • New York • Oxford

ROWMAN & LITTLEFIELD PUBLISHERS, INC.

Published in the United States of America
by Rowman & Littlefield Publishers, Inc.
A Member of the Rowman & Littlefield Publishing Group
4501 Forbes Boulevard, Suite 200, Lanham, Maryland 20706
www.rowmanlittlefield.com

PO Box 317
Oxford
OX2 9RU, UK

British Library Cataloguing in Publication Information Available

Library of Congress Cataloging-in-Publication Data

Vaughn, Lewis.
The case for humanism : an introduction / Lewis Vaughn and Austin Dacey.
p. cm.
Includes bibliographical references and index.
ISBN 0-7425-1392-0 (hardcover : alk. paper) — ISBN 0-7425-1393-9 (pbk. : alk. paper)
1. Humanism. I. Dacey, Austin, 1972– II. Title.
B821.V38 2003
144—dc21 2003001506

∞™ The paper used in this publication meets the minimum requirements of American National Standard for Information Sciences—Permanence of Paper for Printed Library Materials, ANSI/NISO Z39.48-1992.

Contents

Foreword

As we grow up, become educated, and secure for ourselves a place within the social fabric, almost all of us acquire certain general patterns of thought that form what is commonly called a worldview. The process of acquiring a worldview occurs almost entirely unreflectively. We are consciously aware of forming many of our beliefs, but the ways in which these beliefs are arranged and structured into a global framework of understanding is a process that largely occurs subliminally and without careful examination.

However, once acquired, worldviews are triply potent within our lives. First, they provide a set of assurances about what *is true*—and especially, they include certain general and fundamental truths that provide us with a way of assessing and fitting together more garden-variety claims into a coherent picture of the world. Second, they provide the strategies and means of *explaining and understanding* the features of the world that interest us. (This may indeed be largely what "fitting together" amounts to.) Third, worldviews typically play an important role in providing us with our social identity. To a greater extent than we may realize, worldviews mark off social boundaries, distinguishing between a like-minded "we," who share a worldview, from "them," who do not. Thus a worldview can function as a kind of entrance ticket to full admission in a social group, society, or nation.

Worldviews are therefore highly prized and, ordinarily, tenacious. Much is at stake in the adoption of a worldview—and in converting from one view to another, a process that is often wrenching both socially and intellectually. Because of this, it is all the more striking (and worrying) that we often seem to drift into acceptance of an initial worldview so casually. But there is a remedy. It is the central mission of philosophy to ask the probing questions that may force us to scrutinize our beliefs to determine whether they can meet basic standards of intellectual rigor. Moreover, it is the special penchant of philosophy to ask these searching questions about *fundamental* beliefs—the sorts of beliefs that constitute the structural girders and foundation stones of worldviews.

This book by Lewis Vaughn and Austin Dacey is for those who have the courage to ask themselves such questions. It is an introduction to that cluster of ideas and issues that constitute the historical legacy and ongoing projects of a movement (or rather, group of movements) known as humanism. These ideas are characteristically framework ideas: ideas concerning the basic nature of the physical universe, the place and value of human life within it, the proper ends and goals of a life well lived, the proper places within such a life of reason, empirical knowledge, faith, desire, and action, and the nature of those social institutions that permit humans to flourish.

Where they raise methodological questions, these issues force us to think about epistemology—the study of human beings as would-be knowers of their world. What are the means by which we can come, not merely to believe, but properly to know that certain things are true? Are these means content-independent, or are they sensitive to the sort of knowledge we seek? Do they depend, for example, upon whether the knowledge in question is knowledge of the physical world, or of mathematics, or of values, or of supernatural things? And how reliable are the means we have at our disposal?

Where it raises substantive questions, the humanist tradition forces us to think about metaphysics, which concerns the most basic categories of existence—matter, minds, space-time, and qualities—about science, and about religion. It forces us to think about how the world is put together. Is the world purely the product of natural forces, or does its structure bespeak the craftsmanship of some supernatural intelligence? How do the laws of nature bear upon human behavior and ascription of moral responsibility? How, in general, is consciousness connected to bodily existence?

The special approach that Vaughn and Dacey have taken is to discuss these traditional philosophical problems in the context of an engaging journey through the history of humanistic thought. We tend nowadays to think of humanism as *secular* humanism, but it has not always been secular. What distinguishes humanism is the central role it accords to concern about human beings and the requisites for human flourishing. There have been religious humanisms as well as secular ones.

Nevertheless, humanism—secular humanism—has come to be seen, at least within the contemporary culture of the United States, as an alternative ideology. Indeed, it is considered the chief ideological rival to Christianity. Those who use the unfortunate metaphor "culture wars" to describe this rivalry tend to see modern Western culture as polarized into two opposing and irreconcilable camps, with Christian—often evangelical—theism as one contender, and secular humanism as the other. This oversimplification, which is more harmful than helpful, illustrates the need for a greater understanding of both positions and their histories. This book contributes to that goal.

The bunker mentality reflected in the culture-wars metaphor has fostered some peculiar and sometimes outlandish claims by partisans on both sides. Each party tends to see itself as a besieged minority; each claims to find evils spawned by the opposing ideology to exert pervasive influence upon modern culture. Evangelicals as a group have been accused of racism, militarism, narrow-minded jingoism, the worst sins of capitalism and antienvironmentalism, moral hypocrisy, and more. At the feet of secular humanism (and its supposed allies, Darwinism and metaphysical naturalism) has been laid responsibility for everything from the high divorce rate to illegal drug use, rejection of basic moral principles, mass murder, sexual deviance, the welfare state, and even love of rock music.

Ideas have consequences, so the saying goes, but what consequences? That is an empirical question, and those that make the sorts of claims just mentioned rarely have any good evidence to support their conclusions; often they do not even care about such niceties. Perhaps they believe that the connections between the ideas and their purported consequences are just "intuitive." The beginning of a corrective for this irresponsible naivete is to acquire an accurate and thorough grasp of the ideas themselves. That is the business of this book. The empirical studies required to both determine the degree of penetration of various ideas into our culture and establish causal connections between their acceptance and one or another social condition is a matter proper to careful sociological analysis.

This book provides an accessible but fairly comprehensive overview of humanist positions and arguments concerning the centrally disputed issues that have fueled the debate. It also provides a fair summary of major arguments from opponents of humanism. Understanding these arguments will give the reader a better basis for evaluating the culture wars and provide an excellent introduction to the broader arena of philosophical debate. It is to be hoped that some readers will be stimulated to pursue at greater length the important questions that Vaughn and Dacey raise.

Evan Fales
Professor of Philosophy
University of Iowa

1

Humanism and Philosophy

Lewis Vaughn

In the Columbia River of Washington state, an 8,400-year-old skeleton of a man is uncovered. One of the oldest ever found in the New World, the skeleton is exceptionally well preserved. Anthropologists are thrilled. "Kennewick man," as the remains come to be named, promises to contribute much to their knowledge of the migrations of early North Americans. However, to many Native Americans on whose ancestral land the find was made, this "Ancient One" is no scientific specimen, but instead a distant relative who deserves a proper burial. A coalition of five Umatilla Indian tribes files a claim under the Native American Graves Protection and Repatriation Act, a 1990 law that provides for the return or repatriation of Indian skeletons and artifacts to tribes. Eight anthropologists file a lawsuit to stop the repatriation, challenging the act.

In the controversy that ensues, Douglas W. Owsley of the Smithsonian Institution and Richard L. Jantz of the University of Tennessee, Knoxville, warn that "if a pattern of returning [such] remains without study develops, the loss to science will be incalculable and we will never have the data required to understand the earliest populations in America."[1] The Umatilla Confederated Tribes, in a statement to the press, say they are not "urging an end to science, but only that science be guided by some ethical boundaries respecting the beliefs and rights of the people they are purporting to study."

> This case is about fundamental human rights, not about science versus religion. . . . Over the years we have built relationships with museum and university scientists in the pursuit of protecting our own heritage and developing an accurate scientific portrayal of who we are. This lawsuit seeks to destroy those relationships by giving complete control over Native American ancestral human remains to those scientists. . . . All knowledge is acquired at a price and we argue that scientists may not appropriate Indian ancestors over the objections of the culturally affiliated tribes.[2]

"In their search for the missing link," observes a tribal newspaper editorial, "scientists may want to first consider their own family trees and establish the same kind of respectful, reverent relationship with their ancestors that Indians have with those who have lived and died before them."[3]

Missouri Citizens for Educational Reform (CER) has fought since 1959 for parents' rights to choose where public educational funds are spent. Advocating school voucher and tax credit programs, the organization contends that a dual system of government and non-government operated schools is essential to a free, pluralistic society. In particular, says CER founder Mae Duggan, public schools have failed society by failing to provide proper religious instruction. They are *secular* to a fault:

> [T]he good teacher should be seeking truth and seeking to impart truth and handing this down as a heritage to her students. And the starting point is a belief that God is truth.
>
> Our schools have deteriorated under the influence of John Dewey and his secular humanist philosophy. Dewey said himself he was founding a new religion that would reject the old traditional religions—Christianity and Judaism. In their place he would substitute his secular religion of science and materialism.[4]

Harriet Woods, a former lieutenant governor and state senator of Missouri, is uncomfortable with Duggan's vision of education. "I think every parent has a right to challenge the public schools. But there is a line between the right to say, 'I'm going to have my child read this,' and saying, 'I want a law to impose my solution on everyone else at whatever the cost.'" She fears that sectarian schools are "not open to challenge from the outside" and that this encourages a "narrowness" of mind "that can lead to tyranny."

In November, the Association of Los Alamos Scientists convenes to hear a lecture by a world-famous physicist. He tells them, "the reason that we did this job is because it was an organic necessity. If you are a scientist you cannot stop such things. If you are a scientist you believe that it is good to find out how the world works; that it is good to find out what the realities are; that it is good to turn over to mankind at large the greatest possible power to control the world and to deal with it according to its lights and values."[5]

The year is 1945, just three months after the United States detonated atomic bombs over Hiroshima and Nagasaki, and the speaker is Robert Oppenheimer, one of the physicists who led the Manhattan Project that developed the bomb.

Upon reflection, these stories should raise a number of questions. What is the authority of science? Of religion? Is science based in faith? Are human beings purely "material," or do they possess a spiritual nature? In what sense, if any, should public institutions be secular? How far ought we to go in the quest to investigate and manipulate nature? Such questions cut to the heart of a body of philosophical ideas and moral ideals that are often described as "humanist." These ideas—what we like to call **philosophical humanism**—are interrelated and human centered.

The stories also dramatize important points about ideas in general and humanist ideas in particular and give us an opportunity to clarify a few things. First, our stories focus on only one kind of humanism—philosophical humanism. But it is important to remember that this set of ideas is not one changeless bundle of assertions, like the Ten Commandments or the Magna Carta. At various times in the past thousand years, the content of philosophical humanism has changed. Also, humanism has taken several forms in addition to its philosophical type. It has been an educational program and outlook that reveres classical thinkers and values (the distinctive outlook that arose in the Renaissance); a movement in art and literature (focusing on mankind instead of supernatural or religious themes); and a human-centered movement in society and culture. Several modern versions of philosophical humanism place most emphasis on one or two key ideas (as in "secular humanism," "scientific humanism," "naturalistic humanism," and "religious humanism"). Also, there is no such thing as a pure set of *exclusively humanist* ideas—that is, ideas that belong to the tradition of humanism alone. *Every* idea that can legitimately be called "humanist" is shared by at least one other influential worldview, philosophy, or religious tradition.

Second, a powerful reason for dramatizing humanist ideas with a few real-life examples is to illustrate that *ideas matter*. Sometimes they matter more than any other force in our lives, whether for good or ill. Of course, many factors can alter the course of history or an individual life, not just ideas. But history itself shows that ideas are among the most potent forces in human affairs. It is also clear that in our own lives every judgment we make is influenced by our ideas about how the world is and how it should be.

We are often completely unaware of the influence ideas have on our own actions, aspirations, and society—and we can pay dearly for being in the dark. The ideas alluded to in our stories, for example, have been influential or controversial in Western civilization for hundreds or thousands of years. It is probable that at least some humanist ideas have already profoundly affected many of your choices and views without your knowledge of it. How many of these assumptions or beliefs have you carefully assessed for yourself and how many have you simply assumed to be true (or false)? How many came from your parents, your culture, your government, or your own thinking? These are crucial questions because if you merely "absorb" the ideas that help shape your life without critically examining them, they are not truly yours. Your actions and choices based on these unexamined ideas therefore cannot be truly free. This predicament is the equivalent of living your entire life according to someone else's instructions.

The influence of individual humanist ideas, like any other philosophical ideas, can be overlooked because they may show up in the thinking of people who would never consider themselves humanists. Some of the ideas may even be a part of other philosophical or theological points of view that have nothing much in common with humanism.

Then there is this fact: Humanist ideas not only pertain to interesting issues in Western thought; they relate to *fundamental* issues of human life. They are ideas that deal with the big questions of existence, the kinds of questions that are the focus of the discipline of philosophy. They concern questions about (1) how (or if) we can come to know anything about reality (what philosophers call **epistemology**), (2) the nature of God and religious assertions (theology or the **philosophy of religion**), (3) the nature and justification of morality (the field of **ethics**), (4) the nature of human beings—concepts of free will, human goodness or evil, fate, souls, mortality, and immortality (included in what philosophers call **metaphysics**), and (5) the nature and justification of institutions that have power, such as families, tribes, nations, and world governments (**political philosophy**).

So there are good reasons to pick out the humanist ideas embedded in our lives and our world, drag them one by one into the open, and determine if they are worth keeping. There are also good grounds for considering those ideas all together—that is, as a **worldview**. A worldview is a philosophy of life, a comprehensive conception of reality, a set of ideas that help us make sense of a wide range of issues in life, including most or all of the five areas mentioned above. Throughout history, ideas associated with humanism have often been taken together as a coherent set—as a worldview that furnished an approach to the pivotal issues of life. Likewise, other worldviews have sometimes provided very different answers to the same big questions. In this way, humanism has often been thought to compete with other worldviews—for example, various forms of Christianity, Judaism, Islam, Hinduism, mysticism, idealism, skepticism, fascism, postmodernism, deep ecology, and feminism (though there are occasionally many areas of agreement among worldviews).

Philosophers, theologians, and others are often preoccupied with examining worldviews because so much depends on having one that produces understanding and success. If a worldview is flawed—that is, if it consists of false, contradictory, or incoherent ideas—it can lead to a life of wasteful illusions, bad choices, and futile actions. If it is well made, it can help us not only understand the world, but also succeed in it, however we define success. What's more, when we critically examine our worldview to ensure that it is indeed well made, it becomes our own.

An interesting fact about worldviews is that we all have one, whether we want one or not. We all have certain conceptions about what exists, what we can know, and what is of value. Even the rejection of all worldviews is a worldview. So the question to ask is not whether you have a worldview, but whether your worldview is a good one. For reasons that will become clear later, we argue in this book that such evaluation of worldviews is not only possible in philosophy, but is necessary for living a fully aware and rewarding life.

In light of all of this, we should be prepared to ask tough questions about humanism just as we would of any other worldview. Does humanism as a worldview make sense? Do humanist ideas—these notions that are so much a part of so many lives—stand up to close examination? Put another way, are humanist claims about morality, God, human nature, and society worth incorporating into our own worldview?

Note that these questions are not about whether humanism has had a good or bad effect on society, or what causes people to believe one thing or another, or whether humanism has made people happy or miserable, or whether it has any political implications. Such questions almost always come up in any discussion of humanist ideas, and we will touch on many of them in this book. But the kinds of questions we are most concerned with here are not sociological, psychological, or political. They are philosophical. They are about the *justification* of ideas, not their *cause*—whether there are good grounds for accepting or rejecting certain claims about humans and the world they inhabit.

There are several reasons for this philosophical approach to humanism. First, it is sorely needed. It is needed for the reasons we have already mentioned. In addition, the intellectual battles over the validity of humanist ideas are fought again today, just as they have been at other times in the past. As always, what is invaluable in such struggles is not power and partisanship, but clear thinking, an objective stance, and sound arguments—the primary tools of philosophy.

Second, this type of approach to philosophical humanism is rare. It is rare, we think, because (1) many people have assumed that justification of philosophical positions and worldviews is impossible and (2) most of those who have addressed the issues raised by humanism have been more concerned with explaining, affirming, promoting, or rejecting humanist ideas than fairly assessing them. Humanists themselves have sometimes shown very little, if any, interest in examining the fundamental underpinnings of their philosophical positions. The rest of this book serves as a demonstration of how this philosophical methodology is possible, how it is undertaken, and why it is worthwhile.

For now, we can point out one of the more obvious reasons why humanist ideas should be examined in this way. The appeal of various humanist concepts has been waxing and waning for several millennia. During this time, philosophy itself has matured, gained new insights on ancient problems, discarded some untenable theories, learned from science, and found new tools for answering tough questions. Consequently, philosophy can now shed new light on many old humanist concepts and claims. In some cases, new developments in philosophy have strengthened the justification for certain humanist beliefs. In other cases, rigorous philosophical evaluation has undermined some ideas that have been associated with humanism in different stages of history. Humanist ideas have been interpreted differently in different eras. Recent philosophical investigation has shown that some of these interpretations are unsubstantiated or improbable. If they are part of philosophical humanism, it must be—at best—what we might call "naive humanism." In any case, we have good reason to believe that contemporary philosophical analysis of humanist ideas is worth the trouble.

We begin in this chapter by supplying a more precise statement of humanism as we use the term, offering a brief overview of humanism in its various forms, tracing the history of some humanist ideas in Western culture, and—most important—laying out the ideas that we examine throughout this book (section 1.1). We have made this last task more manageable by distilling humanist ideas into statements, or propositions, to make them easier to understand and evaluate. Statements are claims that are either true or false; they are the stuff that philosophers and other thinkers spend most of their time studying and assessing. We intend to be as inclusive as possible in our selection of such statements, including ideas from past and present, and those controversial and not. Then we explain how philosophical inquiries are carried out, how it is possible to assess competing worldviews and theories, and what the criteria are for judging the validity of important ideas (section 1.2).

SECTION 1.1

On the Trail of Humanism: A Survey of Humanist Ideas

This book purports to examine certain humanist ideas to determine if there is any justification for accepting or rejecting them. A fair question then is this: What is the justification for *that* idea? That is, what are the grounds for even thinking that humanism can be scrutinized in this way? After all, there is no universally accepted definition of humanism. In fact, there are several competing, restrictive definitions. People usually recognize the need for something like a definition because the term "humanism," like "democracy" or "realism," has been used in more senses than we would care to count. Because of this lack of a common definition, there is a temptation to think that there is no fact of the matter regarding the nature of humanism.

Furthermore, some modern humanists would claim that the very notion of breaking humanism down into distinct statements for easy analysis is wrongheaded. They might say that humanism is not a set of propositions at all, but an attitude toward life, a way of viewing the world construed in different ways in different eras. Some might even say that humanism defies analysis because it, above all, is neither creed nor dogma.

Even among those who say that humanism does have propositional content and agree more or less on what that content is, there are many differences in emphasis, focus, and implication. The picture gets even fuzzier when we consider that other perspectives that seem clearly nonhumanist share many of the ideas that we have labeled humanist.

There is more than an ounce of truth in all of these claims. So how can we even presume to assess "humanist ideas" or to trace the paths of "humanism" through history? How can we dissect a creature we cannot see?

HUMANISM OR NOT?

Actually, these difficulties are not as formidable as they may seem. First, as the following chapters show, there is indeed such a thing as a humanist attitude or way of living, which people can have without ever articulating any humanist principles. Humanism can surely engender distinctive ways of dealing with the challenges of being human, just as Catholicism, Lutheranism, Buddhism, or socialism can. For many people humanism is, more than anything else, a way of life. But it does not follow from any of this that philosophical humanism is *only* an attitude or way of life, that it can have no ideas—that is, propositional content—and therefore does not exist.

It is simply obvious that for hundreds of years people have advocated certain propositions or principles about morality, religion, existence, and society, and that these propositions have been called humanist and been advocated by those calling themselves humanists. If humanism has no propositional content, a great deal of intellectual history is hard to explain. If humanism is devoid of ideas or principles, it is difficult to see how anyone could discuss it, teach it, or promote it.

Those who deny that humanism is anything like a creed or dogma have a point. Humanism—either as a movement or a worldview—has never embraced a stone tablet of changeless, sacrosanct propositions. Not only have humanist statements been continually altered over time, they have typically been regarded as tentative and evolving, subject to new information and reasoning. It should be clear by now that a common feature of philosophical humanism is diverging views on just about everything. None of this shows, however, that humanist statements cannot be formulated, critiqued, or distinguished from other views. Humanist ideas—despite their variations—do have common threads.

As for the problem of definitions, trying to devise a universally acceptable definition of philosophical humanism is indeed a tall order, as many humanists have discovered. Most definitions of humanism are attempts to state the *meaning* of the term by selecting from the rich reservoir of humanist thought those ideas that seem to capture what is essential. Discrepancies among definitions arise when humanists disagree about what ideas to leave in or leave out or how the included ideas are to be interpreted. Sometimes this task of definition is further shaped by the need to seek consensus, which means that ideas on which there is no general agreement are left out. The work of trying to define humanism in this way is a legitimate enterprise, and disagreements are expected. But this approach can easily leave something interesting out of account—and usually does. Intellectual history has shown that the total set of humanist ideas from past and present is generally larger than the set entailed by most definitions of humanism.

Scholars generally take a different tack from those who search for humanism's meaning. They concentrate not so much on the meaning of "humanism" but its *reference*—the ideas to which the term refers. Thus they are able to examine a bigger set of ideas. They can identify this larger set because the ideas are logically and historically con-

Some Definitions of Humanism

Humanism. The tendency to emphasize man and his status, importance, powers, achievements, interests, or authority. —*The Oxford Companion to Philosophy*

Humanism, a set of presuppositions that assigns to human beings a special position in the scheme of things. Not just a school of thought or a collection of specific beliefs or doctrines, humanism is rather a general perspective from which the world is viewed. —*The Cambridge Dictionary of Philosophy*

Humanism is a democratic and ethical life stance which affirms that human beings have the right and responsibility to give meaning and shape to their own lives. It stands for the building of a more humane society through an ethics based on human and other natural values in a spirit of reason and free inquiry through human capabilities. It is not theistic, and it does not accept supernatural views of reality. —The International Humanist and Ethical Union

Humanism is a way of living, thinking, and acting that allows every individual to actualize his or her highest aspirations and successfully achieve a happy and fulfilling life. Humanists take responsibility for their own morals and their own lives, and for the lives of their communities and the world in which we live. Humanists emphasize reason and scientific inquiry, individual freedom and responsibility, human values and compassion, and the need for tolerance and cooperation. Humanists reject supernatural, authoritarian, and anti-democratic beliefs and doctrines. —The American Humanist Association

Humanism is a philosophy, worldview, or life stance based on naturalism—the conviction that the universe or nature is all that exists or is real. Humanism serves, for many humanists, some of the emotional and social functions of a religion, but without belief in deities, transcendental beings, miracles, immortality, and the supernatural. Humanists seek to understand the universe by using science and its methods of critical inquiry—logical reason, empirical evidence, and skeptical evaluation of conjectures and conclusions—to obtain reliable knowledge. Humanists affirm that humans have the freedom to give meaning, value, and purpose to their lives by their own independent thought, free inquiry, and responsible, creative activity. Humanists stand for the building of a more humane, just, compassionate, and democratic society using a pragmatic ethics based on human reason, experience, and reliable knowledge—an ethics that judges the consequences of human actions by the well-being of all life on Earth. —The Virtual Community of Humanists

nected by certain themes. They try to identify the themes and follow them to whatever ideas fit. As a result, they end up tracking a vast repertory of ideas, some contradictory, some now accepted, rejected, or debated, but all of them part of the corpus plausibly called "humanism."

The scholars' road is the one we will follow here. If our purpose is to explore the full range of humanist thinking—the whole panoply of ideas that have been part of the long historical debate we have called philosophical humanism—then a restrictive definition will not do. We need a description of humanism that points us to as much of the repertory as possible. A description that provides the definitive last word on humanism, though, is neither necessary nor possible.

Here is one scholar's attempt to articulate the constant themes of philosophical humanism:

> First, by contrast with a theological view of man (which sees him as part of a divine order) or the scientific (which sees him as part of a natural order), and in neither case central to it, humanism focuses on man, and starts from human experience. . . . [Second,] the individual human being has a value in him or herself—we still use the Renaissance phrase, the dignity of man—and that it is respect for this which is the source of all other values and of human rights. This respect is based upon the latent powers which men and women, and they alone possess: the power to create and communicate (language, the arts, sciences, institutions), the power to observe themselves, to speculate, imagine, and reason. . . . [T]hese powers enable men and women to exercise a degree of freedom of choice and will. . . . A third characteristic of the [humanist] tradition is the importance it has always attached to ideas.[6]

The scope of ideas here is vast, and that is the point. Many other more elegant, more compelling characterizations of humanism have been devised. But typically they cover less ground. For example, the entry in the *Encyclopedia of the Social Sciences* states that humanism "is characteristically human, not supernatural, that which belongs to man and not to external nature, that which raises man to his greatest height or gives him, as man, his greatest satisfaction."[7] The British Humanist Association states that humanism is "an approach to life based on reason and our common humanity, recognizing that moral values are properly founded on human nature and experience alone."[8]

Let us see if we can improve on all of these, thereby crafting our own touchstone for an exploration of humanist thinking:

> Philosophical humanism is a set of interrelated propositions that assert (1) the importance of humankind and human experience over things supernatural or otherworldly, (2) the value, dignity, and rights of individual persons, (3) the power of humans to understand themselves and the world through science, reason, and free inquiry, (4) the capacity of humans to make free choices and direct their own lives, and (5) the responsibility of humans to conduct their lives according to rational moral standards and to promote the welfare of themselves and all people.

This statement is broad enough to entail a great many interesting ideas but definitive enough to distinguish them from the ideas of several other traditions. It will serve as our guide for the chapters to come.

However, it is only a guide. We still must choose from these broad themes which ideas we intend examine. This task is complicated by the fact that humanists have sometimes differed on what specific propositions best express these themes. Reliance on the powers of reason, for example, is a constant humanist theme, but humanists have disagreed about the scope of reason. Some have thought that reason is supreme, the sole or primary source of all knowledge. Others, in various ways, have given reason a reduced status, as the philosopher David Hume did when he asserted, "Reason is and ought only to be the slave of the passions." Jean-Jacques Rousseau asserted that emotion and intuition play a larger role in human lives than reason.

Any close examination of these competing interpretations of reason would confirm that some of them are better than others. That is, some propositions expressing specific interpretations of humanist themes have solid justification—and some do not. Our main task is to use the tools of philosophy to determine which is which.

Our strategy then is to select for assessment those humanist propositions that seem to us to be both the most defensible and the most seriously challenged by other competing humanist and nonhumanist propositions. Where possible we have also preferred ideas that are controversial or relevant to fundamental philosophical issues that have always confronted humans. Converting ideas that have been variously expressed throughout history into explicit propositions is a challenge. The goal is to be clear without oversimplifying, and precise without giving the impression that there is only one way to state an idea. We will let you judge how well we have done.

We can now give a brief inventory of the propositions we intend to investigate in this book:

1. Human beings are superior to the rest of nature in their value, powers, and place in the world.
2. We are physical systems with minds, but devoid of immaterial souls.
3. This earthly life is the only one we can hope for and the only one we need.
4. Humanity is not fallen by nature and is capable of moral self-improvement.
5. We are not determined beings in a determined universe but are in some sense free to choose our own paths.
6. Humans are not controlled by fate or divine power but are sometimes free to do otherwise.
7. Morality cannot be based on the supernatural or the nonrational.
8. Morality has a rationalist or naturalistic basis.
9. We can know many things through reason and unfettered inquiry, but skepticism and faith block understanding.
10. Even in a world without God and ultimate authorities, there is such a thing as objective truth.
11. Science is a privileged source of knowledge about the world.
12. Science undermines supernatural religion.
13. There is no warrant for believing in God, as traditionally conceived.
14. There is good reason to deny the existence of God, as traditionally conceived.
15. All people have equal moral rights and deserve corresponding political rights.
16. Governments and other public institutions should not favor a religious faith or religion in general.
17. A good society nurtures freedom of conscience, toleration, and open, critical dialogue.

Now, let's acknowledge right off that such a tidy list may indeed help us focus our investigation, but it can also be misleading on several counts. First, it might lead you to think that these propositions are *exclusive* to the humanist tradition, that other traditions (religious, cultural, or philosophical) have no claim on them. This assumption is false. All of these statements belong to the humanist tradition—but they are not necessarily exclusive to that tradition. The notions of free will, personal autonomy, objective truth, human rights, and tolerance, for example, are crucial elements in many nonhumanist worldviews. What's more, some modern humanists would almost certainly take exception to at least some of the propositions.

Second, you might conclude from this list that humanism—*true* humanism—must embody *all seventeen of the propositions.* But such an inference would be mistaken. There is no fact of the matter as to how many of these ideas (or any other set of ideas) are required to comprise the worldview known as humanism as we have defined it. Clearly, philosophical humanism must embody at least *some* of these ideas, and a worldview that incorporates a *majority* of them (without entailing any contradictions) could hardly avoid a humanist label. But beyond such wide parameters, there is considerable ambiguity and no humanist litmus test at all.

Third, you might assume that we intend to establish all seventeen of these propositions through philosophical argument. That is not the case because *we think that there is good reason to reject some of them,* at least as many contemporary thinkers interpret them. Whether we are justified in rejecting them is an issue that we invite the reader to assess—for judging the grounds for certain positions is very much the point of this book.

How did the ideas behind these philosophical propositions arise? What traces have they left in the strata of time—and on our current perspective on the world? The remainder of this section provides a brief answer to these questions.

IDEAS IN THE MAKING

One way to appreciate the power and worth of certain ideas is to look back into history to the time when the ideas were new—before many of them soaked into civilization so deeply that they became almost invisible.

If we take this backward look at the first glimmers of various humanist ideas, we find ourselves focusing on many of the conceptual sparks that lit up Western civilization. We should not presume, though, that humanism is a purely Western invention, even though in this book we concentrate mainly on humanism in the West. In the East, for example, humanist ideas showed up in the godless philosophy and secular moral system of Confucius and the human-centered concerns and code of conduct found in the teachings of Buddha. Arabic philosophy began around the eighth century and articulated several humanist ideas derived from the ancient Greeks.

The Greek Miracle

The outlines of Western civilization were first a dream in the minds of the ancient Greeks, and so were many humanist ideas. Certainly, long before the Greek dream began, there were other great civilizations in Egypt and Mesopotamia. They had knowledge and skill, but they never experienced the kind of explosion of new ideas that reverberated from Greek civilization. They did not, for example, invent philosophy, science, drama, and the liberal arts as the Greeks did. In fact, to this day there has never been anything like the intellectual critical mass that happened among the Greeks over twenty-five-hundred years ago. Their creations in philosophy, science, and the arts set the standards by which much of Western civilization is now judged.

In the sixth century B.C.E., the old feudal order that had dominated the Greeks was collapsing, the traditional assumptions were losing their influence over many, and new outlooks on the world arose as the city-states did. Early Greek thinkers questioned the old mystical and re-

Confucian Humanism

The English term "Confucianism" embraces a variety of East Asian traditions inspired by and developed from the thought and practice of the Chinese sage Confucius, or K'ung Fu-tzu (551–479 B.C.E.). It is a text-based system of religious, philosophical, and ethical thought as well as a body of practices and rituals. Some central concerns of Confucian teaching are personal virtue and self-discipline and the realization of a humane civilization. Although Confucius himself accepted the traditional belief in the Lord-on-high—a supreme, personal deity—Confucianism represented a departure from the supernaturalism of earlier Chinese religion. Confucian ethics is preoccupied with the universal virtue of *jen*—humaneness, love, or altruism—which is linked with natural benevolence and social reciprocity rather than with one's relationship to the divine or transcendent:

> Jan Jung asked about goodness. The Master said, Behave when away from home as though you were in the presence of an important guest. Deal with the common people as though you were officiating at an important sacrifice. Do not do to others what you would not like yourself. Then there will be no feelings of opposition to you, whether it is the affairs of a state that you are handling or the affairs of a family.*

* Analects, XII, *The Original Analects*, translated by E. Bruce Brooks (New York: Columbia University Press, 2001).

ligious explanations for phenomena of all kinds and sought new explanations. The most important (and astounding) aspect of this quest was the Greek philosophers' tendency to ask general questions—questions that had never been seriously asked before. What is the nature of the universe? What is it made of and how does it work? Is reality made of only one kind of stuff, or is it composed of a pluralism of things? What can we know through reason or the senses? What is the meaning of right, wrong, virtue, vice, and duty? How should we live our lives? What is the proper role of the state? In the course of asking such questions and attempting answers, the ancient Greeks created the philosophic and scientific enterprises.

Before long, the early Greek philosophers—the so-called pre-Socratics—devised brilliant theories to explain various aspects of nature, and some of these ideas are still, after two and a half millennia, thoroughly modern. Thales (c. 640–546 B.C.E.), often regarded as the first philosopher, set the goal for both science and metaphysics when he tried to explain the complexities of the world by positing a much simpler reality that underpins everything. He was one of several early Greek philosophers who asked, perhaps for the first time in history, the extraordinarily simple but profound question: Is there some basic stuff out of which everything existing is made? He and other pre-Socratics gave various answers that may sound strange at first (for example, Thales' answer was *water*), but behind the weirdness often lurked important insights.

Anaximander (c. 611–547 B.C.E.), the first mapmaker, was one of those bold thinkers. He reasoned that the world must be made of one kind of stuff that is ageless and infinite—a notion not far removed from modern physics. He also was the first evolutionary theorist, inferring from some simple observations that humans must have evolved from an animal and that this evolution must have begun in the sea.

The philosophers Leucippus (mid-fifth century B.C.E.) and Democritus (460–370 B.C.E.) theorized that all things are composed of atoms—tiny physical particles that are indivisible, indestructible, uncreated, and eternal. These atoms combine in various ways to comprise all the objects in the world, moving ceaselessly according to natural laws. Thus the atomist philosophers offered a view of the universe that would seem familiar to citizens and scientists of the twenty-first century.

The pre-Socratics were the first to assert, and often to put into practice, the fundamental scientific idea that knowledge of the world can be gained through observation guided by reason. Empedocles (c. 495–435 B.C.E.), for example, discovered through experimentation that air and water are separate substances. He also knew how solar eclipses worked, that the speed of light is finite, and that the light of the moon is indirect. (On the poetic side, he wrote a poem that told the story of mankind's Fall, a tale very much like the Judeo-Christian account of the Fall of man and Original Sin.)

Early Greek thinkers were the first to study "human nature" as separate from nature as a whole and the first to systematically inquire into what being human means. The first great philosopher to make human concerns his primary subject was Socrates (469–399 B.C.E.). He claimed to know nothing, but through critical reasoning and questioning he arrived at several unsettling and illuminating conclusions about the experience of being human, especially in the field of ethics. He asserted that the Good is knowledge, the greatest cause of evil is ignorance, virtues are forms of knowledge, and the only way to live a worthwhile life is to rationally assess its worth. As he put it, "The unexamined life is not worth living." (Centuries later, Christian ethics would put the emphasis not on knowledge but on a pure heart.) As with other ancient Greek philosophers who thought about human conduct, Socrates' ethical theorizing suggested a radical idea: Morality must have a rational justification regardless of what tradition and authority say. He and other Greek philosophers rejected the notion that morality must have a religious foundation.

Perhaps more important than any of these ideas was the technique that Socrates used to search for truth. Now called "the Socratic method," or dialectic, it is a dialogue, a question-and-answer discussion in which a proposition is put forth and then systematically dissected through penetrating queries until the truth of the matter is revealed. There are two profound implications here: (1) The search for knowledge is a human endeavor requiring only human faculties to succeed, and (2) to find the truth, we must give our minds free rein to go wherever reason leads. These notions were assumed by all of the great Greek philosophers, including the two philosophical giants who followed Socrates—Plato (c. 427–347 B.C.E.) and Plato's famous pupil, Aristotle (384–332 B.C.E.). Their work is a monumental validation of the power of the human mind to acquire knowledge and uncover error—a demonstration that is all the more compelling because their achievements ranged over such broad conceptual terrain. Aristotle, in particular, added to the world's knowledge in almost every subject of the times—all the major areas of philosophy, plus psychology, physics, biology, politics, and more.

Among the early Greeks there also arose an idea that is as humanistic as they come: The highest goal in life is human excellence, or being the best human possible in every way. This means humans should fully develop their capacity for reason, for virtue, for the good life, for citizenship. The essence of this idea is captured in the now popular cliché: Be all that you can be.

A great deal of ancient philosophy is an attempt to define what the development of human excellence entails. Aristotle thought that our highest good is whatever is natural (that is, in accordance with human nature), which happens to be happiness. The most important component of happiness, he thought, was the exercise of reason.

Epicureanism, the philosophy of Epicurus (341–270 B.C.E.), stressed the idea that the good life is indeed the pursuit of happiness but—contrary to Aristotle—claimed that happiness is equivalent to pleasure. Today Epicureanism is sometimes thought to be a synonym for wild living—for gluttony, drunkenness, and sexual excess. Epicureanism, however, does not advocate the satisfaction of just any desires, but only those considered natural. Excessive desires—such as those that lead to the "extreme" behavior just mentioned—are to be avoided. Epicurus actually led a life of moderation, repose, and avoidance of extravagant pleasures. He was also adamant about one other point: the good life can be achieved even though there is no such thing as an afterlife. He advocated living fully in the here and now and not worrying about the prospect of death. As he put it, "Death, the most terrifying of ills, is nothing to us, since so long as we exist, death is not with us; but when death comes, then we do not exist."[9]

Stoicism, a school of thought founded by Zeno of Citium (334–262 B.C.E.), was a very influential worldview that spread among both Greeks and Romans. Its central idea was that the greatest good is acting according to Nature in the broadest sense. To a Stoic this means aligning our desires with reality—that is, coming to desire not what Nature denies us, but what Nature will allow us to have. In other words, don't want what you can't have—and thus become serenely indifferent to death, dearth, and pain. As many in the ancient world discovered, Stoicism is a very useful philosophy to have in troubled times.

The ancient Greeks believed that human excellence is something that can be taught. In fact, the very idea that it is possible to mold the human personality through education is a Greek creation. Upon these ideas (and a few others), the Greeks invented Western education, which they viewed as a way to teach humans how to be better humans.

At the heart of this educational program is what the Greeks called *paideia,* a course of education that came to include philosophy, drama, logic, grammar, rhetoric (argumentation), mathematics, and astronomy. These are the original "liberal arts," or humanities, the historic cornerstone of university education for centuries. The Romans adopted the *paideia* as their own, giving it the equivalent Latin name *humanitas.* The Latin term was the inspiration for the noun "humanism," which appeared for first time in the nineteenth century. In all of these usages, the core idea is still humans excelling at being human.

The Renaissance

Just two hundred years after the brilliant Greek explosion of thought and culture began, its light started to fade, just as a new phase in Western civilization was starting—the Hellenistic period. The Hellenistic age was the era in which Alexander the Great (one of Aristotle's students) and his generals ruled the known world and expanded Greek influence. It lasted from about the time of Aristotle's death to the defeat of the Greek generals some one hundred and fifty years later, about 190 B.C.E.

The victors were the Romans, whose emerging Empire would redefine Western civilization and last for three-fourths of a millennium, until almost 500 C.E. Besides being masters of military matters, the Romans were genius builders, administrators, and legal experts, but they derived most of their literature, art, and philosophical ideas from the Greeks. It was the Greek ideas—ideas of liberation and enlightenment—that outlasted not only Greek imperial power but Roman imperial power as well. The Romans, though, knew a good thing when they saw it and adopted or imitated Greek philosophy and literature, preserving a humanist perspective in the process.

Rome was sacked in 410 C.E. by the Visigoths, but the Empire struggled along until the last Roman emperor of the West was deposed by a German chieftain in 476 C.E. After the Empire fell, the Middle Ages began. This period spanned as much as a thousand years, from the Fall of Rome to the thirteenth, fourteenth, or fifteenth century. (The Middle Ages lasted longer in some parts of Europe than in others.) During this time virtually the whole of Europe went into a general cultural and intellectual decline. The philosophical and humanist ideas from the Greeks and Romans were on the verge of vanishing. As Roman roads and aqueducts slowly crumbled, so did the knowledge of classical sources. As time went on, classical manuscripts became harder to find, with remnants of them scattered in a few monasteries.

After Rome imploded, there was no unified empire left to hold the multicultural pieces of Western civilization together. Europe then should have shattered into a million worldviews with none dominant for the duration. Instead, most of the West became—intellectually and socially, at least—more monolithic than ever. The new rising order was Christendom, a church-state system that spanned the Continent and beyond. The secular authorities minded secular affairs, and ecclesiastical authorities dominated spiritual matters, with both sides trying to exert control in the other realm. In large measure, the church assumed ownership of ideas, taking over philosophy and using it to protect orthodoxy, becoming virtually the only source of literacy; it also took charge of whatever pieces were left of the classical past and guarded church dogma by persecuting heretics. Philosophers worked to reconcile church teachings with the Aristotelian science of the day. This tradition of scholasticism created the institutions from which modern universities developed.

Then came the Renaissance, a bright light somehow arising from the Middle Ages. It was a period of intellectual, literary, and cultural rebirth that lasted for about two hundred and fifty years. The spirit of the Renaissance manifested itself in many different ways, but it was primarily a resurgence of humanist ideas that had been the legacy of ancient Greece and Rome. The force behind this resurgence was a rediscovery of, and renewed interest in, classical learning. At first this inclination toward humanism showed up as an educational program. Scholars studied and taught the Greek *paidiea,* or the *humanitas,* the curriculum designed to produce the maximum development of virtue and potential in human beings. In Italy, where the Renaissance began before spreading throughout the rest of Europe, the men who taught the "humanities" were called "humanists." Humanism, however, gradually went from embodying an educational program to being a movement among the thinkers of the day.

Renaissance humanism in this broader sense entailed themes that were considered new, revolutionary, or even heretical at the time, but they were as ancient as Socrates and Epicurus. Renaissance humanists asserted that direct experience was at least as good as received wisdom; preconceived notions and pronouncements of authority should never be accepted blindly but must be critically assessed; the experience of the individual can be inherently noble, even heroic; there is dignity in humans and in earthly human pursuits; peo-

Islam and the Making of Modern Science

In ninth-century Baghdad, a diverse network of thinkers based at the "House of Wisdom" sparked an intellectual revolution when they embarked on the most ambitious scholarly project history had ever seen: collecting, cataloging, and translating documents from the Greeks and others throughout the known world. For almost five hundred years, the fields of optics, vision, anatomy, medicine, astronomy, mathematics, geometry, and philosophy would be centered in the Arab world, dominated by such figures as al-Khwarizmi, al-Haytham, al-Biruni, Ibn Sina, Ibn Rushd, and al-Tusi.

Historians cite many factors in the rise of Islamic learning. Some are economic and material, such as the important technology of papermaking—acquired from the Chinese in the eighth century—the commercial wealth of the caliphs, and the shared scholarly language of Arabic. Others factors related directly to the theology of the period, which saw the enterprise of rational, scientific investigation as consonant with or even following from one's religious duties. According to the medical writer Abu Bakr Muhammad ibn Zakariyya al-Razi (850–925), known in Europe as Rhazes, "The Creator, praised be his name, bestowed upon us reason and gave it to us in order that we might thereby attain and achieve every benefit that it lies within our nature to attain and achieve, whether in this world or the next."

It is somewhat misleading to say that the Islamic intellectual tradition declined following the thirteenth century, although the centers of learning and research undeniably began a permanent shift from East to West. It is clear that important social preconditions, such as wealth and communication among communities of scholars, were degraded by the military and economic decline of the Arab empire, and today Muslims represent 15 percent of the world's population, but only 1 percent of the world's scientists.

In one sense, however, the modern scientific tradition that emerged in Europe in the sixteenth and seventeenth centuries was continuous with the preceding tradition of Arabic scholarship, which from the beginning had involved Christians, as well as Jewish and Muslim thinkers. It is sometimes suggested that the Islamic tradition "carried the torch" of Greek knowledge until it could be passed to the West by way of the conquest of Spain. But this misrepresents its creative contributions and lasting influence. For example, Ibn Sina (980–1037) authored a vast medical encyclopedia that remained a part of European training and practice well into the seventeenth century.

ple should never blink from critiquing human error and foolishness; ecclesiastical authority can have no hold on a free mind; the church is not the primary source of intellectual or moral wisdom; free inquiry is better than dogma; a questioning attitude is better than humble acceptance; the best society is a free society; and philosophy should address the big questions of human life and resign from the post of defender of the church.

Throughout the Renaissance, intellectuals, artists, and common people struggled to reconcile the old medieval order with the changing times. Not surprisingly, the great minds of the day expressed a diverse, sometimes conflicting, assortment of ideas that were both humanist and antihumanist. Often this intellectual tension arose within the same person. Those affected most by the new humanist/classical ideas were themselves a diverse group—courtiers, officials, aristocrats, writers, librarians, merchants, princes, and priests.

Among these we have Petrarch (1304–1374), the greatest man of letters in his century. He was both a Christian and an admirer of the classics, a man who wanted to believe that these two parts of himself could be mutually supporting. Ultimately he leaned closer to the ancient wisdom than to Christianity and revealed a strong humanist bent throughout his art and life. He concluded that the individual human had value and potential that was superior to any allegedly transcendent reality; that human concerns were valid subjects for philosophy; and that life and art were good for their own sake, not just for God's sake. From the Netherlands came Erasmus (c. 1466–1536), the great scholar known as the "prince of humanists" because of his mastery of classical literature. He never departed from the core of his Christian heritage, and he was unsympathetic to the Reformation. But he combined his faith with the ancient wisdom and wrote scathing criticisms of both mankind and the institutions and officials of the church. He devised an approach to life that was a kind of Christian Epicureanism (the search for "true pleasure" in righteousness, reason, and moderation) and gave intellectual fuel to the fire of the Reformation. The Englishman Sir Thomas More (1478–1535), also a Christian humanist in the same sense that Erasmus was, wrote of an ideal society in his book *Utopia*. This new world was guided not by piety but by reason and nature. Its government was radical, for its purpose was not to serve some preordained hierarchy of power, divine or secular, but to ensure the happiness of the governed.

The Enlightenment and Beyond

The Renaissance and some of the humanistic projects it spawned (for example, criticism of the church and more objective study of the Scriptures) helped spark the sixteenth-century Protestant Reformation as well as the Counter-Reformation (or Catholic Revival) of the same era. In the seventeenth century, following this massive reevaluation of religion in the West, there was a religious resurgence of commitment to both Protestant and Catholic dogma.

Later in the century, though, traditional faith began to erode as doubts crept in from many directions—from the rise of modern science as articulated by Francis Bacon (1561–1626), Galileo Galilei (1564–1642), and Isaac Newton (1642–1727); the spectacle of religious wars and intolerance; the mathematical and rational achievements of René Descartes (1596–1650) and Benedict Spinoza (1632–1677); and the new critical and skeptical spirit that had crept into philosophy. Under pressure from all of these elements and more, the eighteenth century took a different turn. It saw the rise of an intellectual movement known as the Enlightenment.

Philosophers, scientists, and writers from all over Europe propelled the Enlightenment. In France there were the intellectuals called philosophes—Voltaire, Montesquieu, Condorcet, Diderot, Rousseau, Wollstonecraft, and others. From Britain came the philosophers John Locke, David Hume, Thomas Reid, and Adam Smith. From Germany, the philosopher Immanuel Kant. From America, the statesmen-inventors Thomas Jefferson and Benjamin Franklin.

Enlightenment thinkers elaborated and defended many of the same humanist ideas that the ancients had embraced, though there were few doctrines common to all of the leading Enlightenment figures. At the top of the list was the notion that reason was not only the key to knowledge, but the instrument with which people could shape their lives, their values, and their society. Trying to ascertain God's will was not mankind's main purpose of life, but fashioning the good life by wielding the power of rational thought. In a post-medieval world in which faith, authority, and tradition were still powerful forces, humanists of the Enlightenment declared the shocking proposition that reason could do the job that these revered instruments had done—and could do it better. Kant (1724–1804) summed up the view of many when he said, "Have courage to use your own reason—that is the motto of the Enlightenment." Enlightenment humanists surpassed their Renaissance counterparts in their confidence in reason as a force for truth and human happiness. Their emphasis on mankind's rational faculty, however, did not exclude the emotional or artistic side of life. They found no contradiction at all in the fact that they applied their powers of reason with a passion.

Enlightenment theorists were inspired and impressed by the rise of a novel intellectual and social force that they themselves had helped create: modern science. Probably more than anything else, the new scientific outlook marked the transition between the classical-medieval view of life and attitudes peculiar to the modern world. From antiquity, Western thinkers had inherited the Platonic notion that figuring out how the universe worked was mostly a matter of logical deduction from mathematical truths, not observation and empirical testing. From Aristotle, they got the idea that understanding a material phenomenon meant discovering its "essence," a process that relied only slightly more on direct observation than did Plato's method. But scientists of the seventeenth and eighteenth centuries chose another way. They began to search not for essences but for the physical causes of phenomena. They tested their conclusions through careful experiments and observations. They ultimately treated their ideas about nature as working hypotheses subject to verification through empirical evidence—not as inferences from self-evident truths. From the results and methodology of the new science arose a picture of the universe as a great ticking machine operating by laws that could be fathomed by the human mind. This machine moved in ways that scientists could predict. This machine was complex, but it did not seem to require a divine mechanic to keep things running, though that mechanic may have set the gears turning eons ago. This mechanistic view of the universe was dominant among scientists until the twentieth century, when quantum physics ushered in a radically different conception of the world.

The very idea that one should question the assertions of revered, learned, or powerful people, that one should examine the basis of such propositions or test them empirically—this was a staggering notion at the time though it seems the most basic presupposition now. A large part of the Enlightenment program, then, was skepticism toward claims of all kinds and a critical bent that was used to expose folly, error, and injustice in society. Enlightenment thinkers thought that the radical use of reason would make life better and, above all else, would set men free. Kant put it this way:

> Enlightenment is man's release from his self-incurred tutelage. Tutelage is man's inability to make use of his understanding without direction from another. . . . Laziness and cowardice are

> the reasons why so great a portion of mankind . . . nevertheless remains under lifelong tutelage, and why it is so easy not to be of age. If I have a book which understands for me, a pastor who has a conscience for me, a physician who decides my diet, and so forth, I need not trouble myself. I need not think, if I can only pay—others will readily undertake the irksome work for me.[10]

If for Socrates the unexamined life is not worth living, for Kant it is a kind of slavery. Reason, though, was hailed as the great liberator not only because it allows everyone to suspend the external tutors but because its objective character helps people step back and examine their own worldviews, breaking out of them if need be.

The humanists of the time thought they had good grounds for believing that mankind could change the world. They saw the natural universe as governed by rational laws that rational beings can understand and use to good purpose. It was science—the systematic methods of experimentation and observation guided by reason—that could peel back nature to uncover those laws. Science and the technology that sprang from it would harness nature to benefit humans, to sweep away superstition, and open up a future that could be far better than the present. To the Enlightenment mind, science was the best reason of all to believe in the revolutionary ideas of unlimited human progress and the perfectibility of mankind. Benjamin Franklin, an Enlightenment scientist himself, could not suppress his optimism about the future. He wrote, "The rapid Progress *true* Science now makes, occasions my regretting sometimes that I was born so soon. It is impossible to imagine the height to which may be carried, in a thousand years, the power of man over matter."[11] Renaissance thinkers looked back to the good old days of the classical period. Children of the Enlightenment, though, looked to the future as no one had ever done before.

To the philosophes and others who championed Enlightenment ideas, reason was more than just analytic and revealing—it was subversive. They used it against established order of all kinds: against old-school philosophy that built towering, abstract systems out of thin air (what they disdainfully called "metaphysics," a term with a different meaning today), against all that threatened human freedom and well-being (tyranny, prejudice, and ignorance), and against religious superstition and authority. Of all these, the last drew the most attention from the Enlightenment theorists.

The target was not just religious dogma and superstition, but heinous acts performed in the name of religion throughout Europe at the time. The humanists took note of the persecution of dissenters, the censorship of heretical ideas, the restrictions on basic freedoms (what would now be called violations of human rights), and the many other crimes that sprang from religious fanaticism. Enlightenment thinkers now had better weapons than ever—critical reason and successful science—to launch assaults on the church.

Voltaire (1694–1778) was the most outspoken of all the philosophes against supernatural religion and the abuses it was thought to entail. He was a master at argument and satire and used them more sharply than anyone of his day. "May the great God who is listening to me," he wrote, "this God who surely cannot have been born of a virgin or have died on the gallows or be eaten in a piece of dough or have inspired these books [the Old Testament] filled with contradictions, madness and horror—may this God, creator of all the worlds, have pity

Critics of the Enlightenment

Enlightenment ideas and values have been critiqued from the eighteenth century to the present day. In fact, the Romantic movement, which came to fore between the late 1700s and early 1800s, was in part a reaction to the Enlightenment emphasis on rationality and analysis.

Early critics included the British thinker **Edmund Burke** (1729–1797), who asserts that men should be guided not by a tyrannical reason, but by feelings, tradition, custom, and respect for traditional religion. He scorned the Enlightenment's preoccupation with abstract thought, including the notion of political structures and ideals established through theoretical or rational considerations. He thinks that societies are not held together by rational constructs (such as social contracts or individual rights)—but by communal feelings such as love and loyalty. He thinks that humankind's faculty of reason is tiny and that social and political problems arise because people pretend that our powers of reason are unlimited. It is far better, he says, that people know their place in creation and understand that God has "subjected us to act the part which belongs to the place assigned to us."

Later criticism was spearheaded by the historian **Carl Becker** (1873–1945), who sees the Enlightenment as a misguided utopianism, a hazardous search for human perfection on Earth, similar to the old Christian yearning for paradise in the world to come. He maintains in his book *The Heavenly City of the Eighteenth-Century Philosophers* that the Enlightenment destroyed the traditional, religious order—then replaced it with a Frankenstein order pieced together from parts of the old:

> [The Philosophers] denounced Christian philosophy, but rather too much, after the manner of those who are but half emancipated from the "superstitions" they scorn. They had put off the fear of God, but maintained a respectful attitude toward the Deity. They ridiculed the idea that the universe had been created in six days, but still believed it to be a beautifully articulated machine designed by the Supreme Being according to a rational plan. . . . They renounced the authority of church and Bible, but exhibited a naïve faith in the authority of nature and reason. . . . They defended toleration valiantly, but could with difficulty tolerate priests.*

Historian of science **Carolyn Merchant** decries the mechanistic worldview of the Scientific Revolution and the Enlightenment reverence of progress and technology. The result of this perspective, she says, has been the insidious exploitation of nature and human beings, especially women. One inevitable consequence is world pollution:

> The pollution "[of Earth's] purest streams" has been supported since the Scientific Revolution by an ideology of "power over nature," an ontology of interchangeable atomic and human parts, and a methodology of "penetration" into her inner-most secrets. The sick earth, "yea dead, yea putrified," can probably in the long run be restored to health only by a reversal of mainstream values and a revolution in economic priorities. In this sense, the world must once again be turned upside down.†

* Carl Becker, *The Heavenly City of the Eighteenth-Century Philosophers* (New Haven, Conn.: Yale University Press, 1932), 31–32.

† Carolyn Merchant, *The Death of Nature: Women, Ecology, and the Scientific Revolution* (New York: Harper & Row, 1980), 295.

on this sect of Christians who blaspheme him." Like other Enlightenment thinkers he wanted religion removed from public life where it was apt to trample on people's rights. He ended all of his letters with the motto "Wipe out this Infamy."

As Voltaire and the other philosophes railed against the sins of the church, they also called for religious tolerance. In particular they wanted Christians to halt their persecutions of those they disliked. In his famous "A Letter Concerning Toleration," John Locke (1632–1704) declared, "The toleration of those that differ from others in matters of religion, is so agreeable to the Gospel of Jesus Christ, and to the genuine reason of mankind, that it seems monstrous for men to be so blind as not to perceive the necessity and advantage of it in so clear a light."[12]

Among Enlightenment intellectuals there were some atheists and agnostics. Many others, however, found an alternative stance that they thought did justice to both science and divinity. In place of "revealed" religion, many Enlightenment theorists called for a type of "natural religion," that is, one that can be established through reason instead of revelation. Their natural religion was **deism**, the notion that God exists, created the universe, but has no interest in the affairs of humans. This is the absentee-landlord God who made the world and left it alone. As the deistic saying goes, "God created the world in six days and has rested ever since." In deism there is no place for prayers, rituals, dogma, revelation, priests, or persecutions, but there is an insistence on tolerance. Voltaire was a deist, as were many of the philosophes and the founders of the United States.

Echoing and extending ideas first put forth by the Epicureans, Stoics, and other ancients, Enlightenment thinkers embraced some radical notions about the nature of human persons. Essentially they severed the concept of personhood from the realm of the divine and found new reasons to elevate persons in the order of the universe. They thought that humans had dignity and worth not because of some relationship with God, but because of the human capacity for reason and autonomy. The purpose of humankind, then, was self-creation and self-development, not the submission of the human will to God's will.

This view of mankind was accompanied by the idea that humans were not inherently depraved—but inherently good. The doctrine of Original Sin was replaced by a notion of Original Goodness. If people were wicked, it was society that made them that way. Along with this notion of basic goodness came the belief that people had "natural rights"—rights by virtue of being a human being. People had these rights whether there was a God or not, whether authorities approved or not.

So in the Enlightenment era the individual acquired a status that was unthinkable in the past. The interests of the individual person were thought to be more important than the interests of either church or state. Self-interest—including the striving for one's own happiness or fulfillment—became for humanists of the day a legitimate goal. As Thomas Jefferson asserted, each person has the right to "life, liberty, and the pursuit of happiness." Church and state could no longer sanction a moral or social order and expect that individuals would conform.

These humanist ideas about persons lead naturally to humanist premises about government and society. If humans have rights and are autonomous, rational, and valuable, then the purpose of government should be to respect and preserve these aspects of humanity. Taking their cue from John Locke and echoing the ancient Greeks, Enlightenment theorists maintained that governments are supposed to be established by autonomous persons to serve autonomous persons. Free individuals (which at the time meant white male property owners) set up governments through a contractual relationship. The governments in turn help ensure that the individuals' natural rights are protected and that peace and tolerance are

Challenges to Enlightenment Models of Knowledge: Truth and Evidence

One important legacy of the Enlightenment is the idea that science and philosophy help put us in touch with *reality*. When successful, they present us with a true representation of the way the world really is, and not simply the way that it may appear to this or that person. In contemporary philosophy, these ideas are expressed in the doctrines of *scientific realism* and the *correspondence theory of truth*. In recent years, both have been attacked from a number of directions, perhaps most famously by American philosopher Richard Rorty:

> All human beings carry about a set of words which they employ to justify their actions, their beliefs, and their lives. . . . I shall call these words a person's "final vocabulary." . . . [I]ronists do not see the search for a final vocabulary as (even in part) a way of getting something distinct from this vocabulary right. They do not take the point of discursive thought to be knowing, in any sense that can be explicated by notions like "reality," "real essence," "objective point of view," and "the correspondence of language of reality." They do not think its point is to find a vocabulary which accurately represents something, a transparent medium. For the ironists, "final vocabulary" does not mean "the one which puts all doubts to rest" or "the one which satisfies our criteria of ultimacy, or adequacy, or optimality." They do not think of reflection as being governed by criteria. Criteria, on their view, are never more than the platitudes which contextually define the terms of a final vocabulary currently in use.*

Rorty argues that despite centuries of philosophical reflection, no one has succeeded in making sense of the notion of correspondence presumed by the Enlightenment model of knowledge.

Another notion articulated by Enlightenment thinkers is that beliefs are rational to the degree that they are supported by *evidence*. The demand for evidence was brought to bear rather strikingly on religious belief, such as the belief in the God of Western monotheism. Alvin Plantinga, Nicholas Wolterstorff, and William Alstoy have developed powerful criticisms of this way of thinking about the rationality of religious belief. In the process, they have defended a sweeping rejection of the epistemological traditions they call "evidentialism" and "classical foundationalism." In their place, Plantinga proposes a "Reformed epistemology," named for its pedigree in certain insights of the Protestant reformer John Calvin. (See chapter 7 for further discussion of this view.)

* Richard Rorty, "Ironists and Metaphysicians," in *The Truth about the Truth*, ed. Walter Truett Anderson (New York: G. P. Putnam's Sons, 1995), 100–103.

preserved. Individuals could then freely pursue self-creation and self-development because the new order ensured that everyone had an equal opportunity to succeed. The idea that the state was established to serve God and king was an old proposition that humanists sought to bury, and bury it they did through the American Revolution and the Enlightenment-inspired government that followed.

By the end of the Enlightenment era, the main ideas of philosophical humanism—ideas first voiced hundreds of years earlier—had been articulated in one fashion or another. In the following two centuries, they would be fleshed out in greater detail, given new twists, and debated as hotly as they had been in the past.

All of the humanist ideas mentioned above have been rejected or resisted by numerous critics, and many strands of humanist thought are controversial to this day. Today commentators have denounced the humanist and Enlightenment idea of the autonomous, free individual or person. They offer, instead, a view of persons as "socially constructed" and indistinguishable from the cultures and traditions that created them. They tend to emphasize not individual rights, but the rights of the group. Some have asserted that the humanist emphasis on reason and science has been a disaster, leading to coercion and domination in the name of rational progress, just as the "enlightened" French Revolution soon yielded intolerance against the "unenlightened" and, in the Enlightenment's darkest hour, the Reign of Terror. Reason is thought not to help humanity, but to rationalize inhumane acts. Some modern thinkers have attacked the very foundations of reason and science, insisting that the acquisition of objective knowledge through science is a myth, that science is no better than any other "narrative" in understanding the world, and that all truth is relative to cultures or "conceptual schemes." Others believe that the humanist insistence on secular values and institutions has helped rob modern society of morality, meaning, and divinity. For many, humanism is next to nihilism.

Many humanist ideas are criticized on social or psychological grounds—that is, based on the perceived harm done to individuals or society. Others are condemned on philosophical grounds—on the truth or falsity of certain propositions. Both these tacks are legitimate; there are times when we want to know the effects of an idea, and times when we want to know its validity. In the following chapters, though, we concentrate on the latter. In chapter 5 we explore in more detail the cases for and against realism, correspondence, and evidentialism.

SECTION 1.2

How to Make Up Your Mind: Testing Ideas through Philosophy

Why philosophy? Why bring the discipline of philosophy to bear on humanist ideas when we could easily enlist the methods and perspectives of, say, psychology, sociology, history, anthropology, or semantics? Instead of asking if humanist propositions are justified, why can't we just concentrate on what they mean, how they arose, how they affect society, or whether they make people happy or miserable? For that matter, why bring in any academic discipline at all? Why not evaluate such important claims using the concepts and criteria at hand—those derived from our own society, traditions, culture, habits, or upbringing?

In part, the answer is that our purpose here, as we have said, is to examine the meaning and justification of humanist ideas, and philosophy is the best tool we have to do that. Philosophy goes deep—deeper, in an important sense, than all of the above paths to understanding. Philosophy penetrates to the fundamental assumptions or principles that structure academic disciplines, underpin social institutions, and shape our lives. A physiologist may want to know how our brains work, but philosophy asks if the brain is the same thing as the mind. Are we computers with really good chips inside? If the brain is not identical with mind, what is mind? Is mind an immortal soul? An astrophysicist may want to understand the origin of the universe, but philosophy asks whether science can prove that God is or is not the creator of everything. Is the universe a machine that runs itself and needs no god to turn the crank? Are there immaterial things in the universe like spiritual entities? You may wonder if lying to your best friend yesterday was right or wrong, but philosophy asks what it *means* for an act to be right or wrong. What moral principles, if any, can guide you in situations like that? Are moral principles objective and universal—or are they subjective and relative to whatever people and societies happen to believe?

Such questions may at times seem far removed from your everyday world, but they have a way of being unavoidable and unexpectedly relevant to our "real" lives. This process can be both agonizing and liberating. Here's how one philosopher describes it:

> The primary problems of philosophy are those to which everyone has an answer, whether he knows it or not, and which everyone can understand whether he has tried to or not. A man's private behavior makes clear whether he believes morality to be just a system of conventions, art a matter of taste, and God a myth; and the questions whether he is right in these beliefs are three of the primary problems of philosophy. Although he may never discuss these issues in his lifetime, he does not hereby avoid them; and they are the first questions he raises if he has an inquiring mind and a desire to justify his behavior or understand the most penetrating puzzles about his world. Even for those who dismiss philosophical speculation with disdain for many years, there often comes a day when they are tormented by deep questions: Why did this terrible thing have to happen? How can you be so *sure* this is the right thing to do? What have I done to deserve this? Why are any of us here at all? Such questions—not themselves primary problems—exhibit vast philosophical assumptions which are answers to the primary problems. . . . And they illustrate the sense in which the primary problems of philosophy are the primary problems of life. We cannot choose whether to answer them, for to live requires that we answer them in our lives. We can only choose whether to think about them.[13]

So philosophy examines the unexamined—the beliefs that we usually take for granted, even though they guide our actions and chart our plans, the ideas that were handed to us because we happen to be born into a particular niche of the world. Philosophy helps us rise above the everyday details of life to see the larger landscape. In this sense, the inadvertent result of doing philosophy is transcendence.

Philosophy has a reputation among nonphilosophers as a trifling endeavor—a lot of intellectual nitpicking and pretentiousness generated from very small matters. But it should be evident by now that philosophy concerns itself with very important matters indeed. (Whether trivial issues consume certain philosophers is another story.) Whether the philosophical approach ever produces anything worthwhile regarding these important concerns is something you can judge for yourself after reading this book. But the primary aim of philosophy should be clear: to achieve understanding of the fundamental or general nature of the world. So if understanding important things matters, philosophy should matter.

Philosophy cuts across all disciplines, examining the basic presuppositions that various fields of study use in their work. Thus we have multiple subspecialties in philosophy—the philosophy of science, of law, of history, of religion, and many more. So philosophy—this critical and wide-ranging search for understanding—is well suited to assessing ideas that are as diverse as those of philosophical humanism.

Because the job of philosophy is not to confirm our prejudices, but to help us rise above them, doing philosophy can be unsettling and revolutionary. Both the pleasure and the pain of doing philosophy is discovering that the world is not as we thought it was. Philosophy, as Aristotle said, begins in wonder. But it can end in either doubt or discovery—usually both.

Is Progress Possible in Philosophy?

Here is a common complaint about philosophy: It never seems to get anywhere. That is, philosophers debate the same old questions discussed hundreds of years ago without any headway, without any resolve, without arriving at any definite answers. In contrast, science makes progress, for after debate and investigation, scientists often reach consensus about the facts. Philosophy, though, never comes to any consensus about anything.

There is some truth to these charges—but not much. Philosophers often do ponder questions that have been around for generations. But this fact alone is not evidence that progress is never made in philosophy. Moreover, the allegation is often based on misconceptions about philosophy and the notion of progress itself.

First, it simply does not follow from a lack of consensus on an issue that no definite answers can be given. If that were so, we would have to conclude that science itself can make no progress in answering certain questions. For example, after hundreds of years of debate there is still no consensus among physicists about what matter is. In addition, we must be careful to distinguish between *justification* and *persuasion.* A group of people may reach general agreement on an issue, but that may be because they were effectively persuaded to do so. Whether people are persuaded is a separate concern from whether there is any good reason to accept a particular view. Sometimes the minority view is correct.

Second, the impression that philosophers never seem to agree on anything is probably strengthened by a simple fact: Once general agreement is reached on a philosophical question, philosophers tend to abandon the inquiry and move on to areas where there are more problems to be solved. As a general rule, then, philosophy usually concerns itself with the most difficult questions. In fact, philosophy concentrates on the toughest questions imaginable. The scientific question of how neurons in the brain affect muscle coordination, for example, seems manageable compared to related philosophical questions—What is the mind? Is it the same thing as the brain or is it something else? Do we have a soul that will survive the death of our bodies? Do humans have free will or are their choices and actions determined by a chain of physical causes? How can we tell the difference between good science and bad science?

Third, there are other legitimate indicators of progress in philosophy besides producing definitive answers to big questions. Often philosophers are able to clarify questions, resolve confusions, abandon flawed theories, and uncover mistakes in previous lines of thought. These are all signs of progress.

The best way to see progress in philosophy is to examine the philosophical arguments that purport to be examples of genuine progress. One of the goals of this book is to provide such examples so you can judge for yourself. In the meantime, we can register our complete agreement with one philosopher's assessment of the question: "[I]t seems possible to give and justify definite answers. Certainly the attempt should be made; and if it fails, it must be made again and again."*

---

* Michael Scriven, *Primary Philosophy*, (New York: McGraw-Hill, 1966), 2.

PHILOSOPHY AT WORK

Philosophy, more than anything else, is a process, and "doing philosophy" means implementing the process. The process consists primarily of the systematic use of critical reasoning to clarify the meaning of concepts and to evaluate arguments. The subject matter to which the process is applied can be, as we have seen, any area of interest that provokes fundamental questions.

The elucidation of the meaning of concepts is important because we cannot assess the grounds for a proposition unless we are clear about what is being claimed—and people are often confused about meanings. The larger—and in a sense, deeper—part of philosophy, however, is the assessment of arguments. In philosophy, an argument is a group of statements consisting of (1) a claim, or conclusion, and (2) other statements called "premises" that offer reasons for accepting the conclusion. The premises are supposed to provide justification for believing that the conclusion is true. In any kind of rational discourse, accepting a conclusion without good reasons, or justification, is the most basic error. Accepting a conclusion only if it is justified increases the chances that it is true.

So when we do philosophy, we are mostly trying to either construct good arguments to support propositions or examine arguments to see if they really are good. If we are honest and careful in this work, we may find that one of our cherished ideas has no rational justification, or that an idea that we dislike does have solid justification, or that we must suspend judgment because the justification or the idea itself is unclear. Sometimes we might even discover that a widely held belief has no arguments in its favor at all. The proposition has simply been accepted as true—out of habit, tradition, social pressure, or some other factor that cannot constitute a good reason.

Since philosophy is a process, observing the process in action should be helpful. That is why the following chapters are filled with arguments and criticism of arguments relating to humanist ideas. In the true spirit of philosophical inquiry, you should accept none of the conclusions or premises at face value. Read the arguments critically, decide if you agree or disagree with them, draw your own conclusions, and—most of all—make sure those conclusions are backed by good reasons.

PHILOSOPHY RESTRAINED

Philosophy and Not Philosophy

Philosophy does have its limits, but they are not the kind that many people expect. As we have seen, philosophical inquiry can increase your understanding of the big questions in life—but it cannot supply you with a ready-made worldview. It may help you develop a coherent and comprehensive view of the world and thus enable you to achieve the Socratic ideal of an "examined life." But the hard work is yours; philosophy just supplies the tools.

As Socrates himself recognized, there is more to life than philosophy. There are, for example, things like love, desire, pleasure, pain, devotion, and meaning. Philosophy may inform these aspects of humanity, but it is no substitute for them. In fact, the philosophical quest is possible only because these other aspects of life exist.

Philosophy may yield insights into concepts and presuppositions used in the fields of history, psychology, sociology, poetry, art, medicine, and many others. But what these areas provide—detailed empirical knowledge or experience—philosophy cannot give.

Thinkers in the Enlightenment—the so-called Age of Reason—recognized that there was more to living than the exercise of the rational faculties. They established a revered place in the life of reason for the passions, creativity, and transcendence through the arts.

When Philosophy Is Crippled

These limitations seem harmless enough, but there may be others that are more troublesome. For centuries, people have been putting forth various theories that imply that the philosophical enterprise is not nearly as fruitful or useful as most philosophers would have us believe. The idea is that philosophy is somehow crippled. The "crippled" theories allege that our ability to acquire knowledge (including the kind of knowledge that philosophy is supposed to yield) is seriously impaired or deficient.

We discuss many of these theories in later chapters. For now we will just mention a few that seem particularly popular these days and hint at reasons why they may not pose as great a threat to philosophical inquiry as some would think.

Skepticism is the view that either we know a great deal less than we think we do or we know nothing at all. Skepticism has a long tradition in philosophy, going back as far as the ancient Greeks. The basic claim of skeptics is that because of the possibility of error, delusion, or other doubt-producing factors, our claims to know things are suspect. We just do not know what we think we know. Over the centuries philosophers have answered the charges of the skeptics and fine-tuned their understanding of epistemological concepts in the process. We provide an answer to traditional skepticism in chapter 5, so we won't let it detain us here. You should be aware, though, that skepticism historically has been the most serious and persistent challenge to the idea that knowledge is possible and that philosophy is feasible.

Our guess, however, is that skepticism does not loom nearly as large in young minds of the twenty-first century as **relativism** does. In its crudest form, relativism is the view that one person's opinion is as good as any other person's. To some people, this notion seems to be especially relevant in philosophy. Philosophy is just opinions, they think, and the opinions are all equally valid, just as personal preferences regarding flavors of ice cream are equally valid. Obviously, if relativism is right, any attempt to determine which ideas or worldviews are objectively true is doomed.

Relativism is a theory about what truth is. Stated not so crudely, it says that truth depends—not on the way things are—but solely on what someone believes, or on what someone's society believes, or on a person's "conceptual scheme" for organizing ideas about the world. Truth, in other words, is relative. Truth is a matter of what a person or society believes or what their conceptual scheme is like—not a matter of how the world is. This means that a proposition can be true for one person or society, but not for another. If you believe that abortion is wrong, then it is wrong (for you). If someone else believes that abortion is right, then it is right (for him or her).

Relativism, however, has some odd implications that render it implausible. We can perhaps see these problems best in the case of personal relativism (truth is relative to individuals). First, if we could make a statement true just by believing it to be true, we would be infallible. We could not possibly be in error about anything that we sincerely believed. We could never be mistaken about where we parked the car or about our views on morality or science or anything else. Personal infallibility is, of course, absurd, and this possibility weighs heavily against relativism. Second, if we each make our own truth, disagreeing with one another would be virtually impossible. We disagree with others when we think they are mistaken. But according to personal relativism, no one would be mistaken. Third, personal relativism undermines itself in a strange way. If personal relativism is true, then the belief that it is false would be just as true as the belief that it is true. As long as there is one person

Philosophers on Philosophy

[Philosophy] is rationally critical thinking, of a more or less systematic kind about the general nature of the world (metaphysics or theory of existence), the justification of belief (epistemology or theory of knowledge), and the conduct of life (ethics or the theory of value). —*The Oxford Companion to Philosophy*

Philosophy asks the simple question, What is it all about? —Alfred North Whitehead

Life involves passions, faiths, doubts, and courage. The critical inquiry into what these things mean and imply is philosophy. —Josiah Royce

The relation of philosophy to theology is of exactly the same sort as that of science to theology. Theology takes as its starting point a revelation as embodied in some sacred book. Science and philosophy, on the other hand, regard themselves as bound by no book or set of dogmas. They insist that, for their purposes, the only relevant authorities are facts verifiable by man, and the inferences which can be drawn from those facts by strict processes of deductive or inductive reasoning. —C. J. Ducasse

Philosophers rule the world—five hundred years after they are dead. —Archbishop Temple

Science is logically dependent on philosophy. If philosophy succeeded in showing, as Hume and Carnap thought it had, that reference to a nonsensible existent was meaningless, the physics that talks of electrons and photons would either have to go out of business or revise its meanings radically. If philosophy succeeded, as James, Schiller, and Freud thought it had, in showing that our thinking is inescapably chained to our impulses and emotions, then the scientific enterprise, as an attempt at impartial and objective truth, would be defeated before it started. Philosophy does not merely put a bit of filigree on the mansion of science; it provides its foundation stones. —Brand Blanshard

The most important and interesting thing which philosophers have tried to do is no less than this; namely: To give a general description of the whole Universe, mentioning all of the most important kinds of things which we *know* to be in it, considering how far it is likely that there are in it important kinds of things which we do not absolutely *know* to be in it, and also considering the most important ways in which these various kinds of things are related to one another. —G. E. Moore

who holds that relativism is false, it is false. Or if someone holds that it is true, it is true. Other forms of relativism are also burdened with such absurdities.

These problems for relativism seem small compared to this one: It is self-defeating. In all its forms, relativism defeats itself because its truth implies its falsity. The relativist says, "All truth is relative." If this statement is objectively true, then it refutes itself. If it is objectively true that "all truth is relative," then the statement itself is an example of an objective truth. So if "all truth is relative" is objectively true, it is objectively false. To get around this problem, the relativist might claim that the statement "all truth is relative" is not objectively true but *relatively* true—that is, true relative to him, his society, or his conceptual scheme. But this just means that the relativist thinks relativism is true. He thus provides no objective evidence for accepting relativism. Relativism, then, is self-defeating, and anything that is self-defeating cannot be true.

When evaluating humanist ideas and their alternatives, skepticism and relativism often crop up. Both these theories have been used as shields against rational criticism. There is another theory, though, that threatens a different kind of radical attack on rationality and logical argument. It is the primarily Protestant idea that human reason itself is unreliable because humans possess fallen and corrupt faculties. Faith and revelation are thought to be superior to reason on religious matters. Martin Luther himself disdained what he called "the harlot of reason," though he put reason to good use in his reform efforts. The theologian Karl Barth (1886–1968) was just as explicit about the depravity of reason. (The Catholic theologian Thomas Aquinas (c. 1225–1274), on the other hand, thought that reason and faith complemented each other.) This pessimism about the efficacy of reason has often collided with humanist views, especially those regarding religious matters.

We assess the merits of faith and revelation as sources of knowledge in chapter 5. In the meantime, we should point out that the rejection of reason on the grounds that it is flawed can also lead to absurdities. If people argue that reason is corrupt and therefore religious truths cannot be supported by reason, then they are contradicting themselves. If reason is corrupt and religious ideas cannot be rationally supported, then they cannot argue that reason is corrupt and religious ideas cannot be rationally supported. Worse still, if reasoning is a pointless exercise, then they cannot reflect on the tenets of their faith, their decisions and actions, or anything else. Reflection, assessment, deliberation—all these require the use of our rational faculties. In fact, all thought and communication depend on the existence of basic principles of logic. Whether we like it or not, all of us—including those who reject the authority of reason—must presuppose fundamental principles of reason.

SUMMARY

Philosophical humanism is a set of interrelated ideas that assert the importance of human experience, the dignity and rights of persons, personal freedom, reason and science, and ethical principles that promote human welfare. It is a worldview just as Christianity and postmodernism are. Many of these ideas arose among ancient Greek thinkers and were extended and clarified in the Renaissance and Enlightenment periods. Humanist ideas have been both embraced and challenged by many. Modern humanists accept all or most of the ideas identified as philosophical humanism. They also tend to be more skeptical of religious or theistic claims than humanists of earlier periods.

Philosophical humanism can be—and should be—examined with the tools of philosophy. Philosophy is, more than anything else, a process, and doing philosophy means implementing the process. Progress is possible in philosophy even while philosophers seem to debate the same issues repeatedly. Doing philosophy can also be hampered by certain theories about inquiry itself. These include skepticism and relativism.

STUDY QUESTIONS

1. What is philosophical humanism?
2. Were there some humanistic elements in ancient Greek philosophy? If so, what were they?
3. In what ways was the Renaissance humanistic?
4. What were some of the main humanistic ideas or themes articulated by Enlightenment thinkers?
5. What is deism?
6. How could skepticism "cripple" the process of philosophy?
7. How is progress possible in philosophy?

DISCUSSION QUESTIONS

1. What are some of the criticisms that have been lodged against Enlightenment ideas? Are these criticisms valid?
2. Are you a relativist? If so, how would you respond to the major criticisms of relativism? If not, why not?
3. Are humanist ideas compatible with socialism? Communism? Islam? Mysticism?
4. How many of the humanist propositions listed in this chapter do you agree with? Disagree with?
5. How many of the humanist propositions listed are likely to be accepted by a religious humanist?

FIELD PROBLEM

The original framers of the U.S. Constitution were influenced heavily by Enlightenment ideas. Do research on the Internet to determine how many of these ideas were incorporated into the Constitution.

SUGGESTIONS FOR FURTHER READING

Fowler, Jeaneane. *Humanism: Beliefs and Practices*. Portland, O.R.: Sussex Academic Press, 1999.
Kramnick, Isaac, ed. *The Portable Enlightenment Reader*. New York: Penguin Books, 1995.
Lamont, Corliss. *The Philosophy of Humanism*. Amherst, N.Y.: Humanist Press, 1997.

NOTES

1. Andrew L. Slayman, "A Battle Over Bones," *Archeology* 50, 1 (January/February 1997).

2. Confederated Tribes of the Umatilla Indian Reservation, "Press Statement Following Federal Court Hearing," 21 June 2001.

3. "Three Years Later, Ancient One Still Unearthed," *Confederated Umatilla Journal* (5 August 1999).

4. From John Davidson Hunter, *Culture Wars: The Struggle to Define America* (New York: Basic Books, 1991), 21–28.

5. Richard Rhodes, *The Making of the Atomic Bomb* (New York: Simon & Schuster, 1984), quoted in Roger Shattuck, *Forbidden Knowledge: From Prometheus to Pornography* (New York: St. Martin's Press, 1996), 184.

6. Alan Bullock, *The Humanist Tradition in the West* (New York: Norton, 1985), 155–56.

7. Edward P. Cheyney, "Humanism," *Encyclopedia of the Social Sciences* (New York: Macmillan, 1930–1935).

8. British Humanist Association, www.humanism.org.uk.

9. Epicurus, "Epicurus to Menoeceus," *Epictetus: The Discourses*, vol. II, trans. W. A. Oldfather (Cambridge, Mass.: Harvard University Press, 1925).

10. Immanuel Kant, "What Is Enlightenment?" *The Portable Enlightenment Reader* (New York: Penguin Books, 1995).

11. Benjamin Franklin, "Letter to Joseph Priestly," *The Portable Enlightenment Reader* (New York: Penguin Books, 1995).

12. John Locke, *A Letter Concerning Toleration*, 1689–1693 (Amherst, N.Y.: Prometheus Books, 1990).

13. Michael Scriven, *Primary Philosophy* (New York: McGraw-Hill, 1966), 1–2.

2

Human Nature

Austin Dacey

As a young child, you may have thought that the world revolved around you. In one sense you were naively mistaken. Plenty of people, objects, and processes were totally insensitive to your existence. In another sense, you were correct. Your immediate surroundings, such as your dwelling, were arranged with you in mind, and your caretakers probably regarded you as among the most important things in life.

What are we to say about human beings and our world? We now know that the world does not literally revolve around us. The heliocentric, or sun-centered, theory of the universe was developed in the modern period by astronomer Nicolaus Copernicus (1473–1543) and made palatable to the scientific community a century later by Galileo Galilei (1564–1642) with the help of his invention, the telescope. Copernican astronomy turned inside out the centuries-old view, affirmed by the church, that the sun, the planets, and other celestial bodies orbit around the earth, which remains stationary at the center of the universe.

The modern scientific outlook was on the rise, and with it came mechanism, the idea that nature operates, like a machine, by lots of parts acting on each other in regular and predicable cause-and-effect relationships. Inspired by the growth of mechanistic science, early modern philosophers such as Thomas Hobbes and Pierre Gassendi began to describe how human beings might also be nothing but sophisticated machines. Hobbes asked his readers, "For what is the *heart* but a spring; and the *nerves,* but so many strings; and the *joints,* but so many *wheels,* giving motion to the whole body, such as was intended by the artificer?"[1] It was the beginning of the modern **physicalist** understanding of human nature, according to which the mind is, like the rest of the cause-and-effect world, a product of physical processes or substances.

In 1838, a British naturalist named Charles Darwin hit upon a simple scientific explanation for the origin and diversity of all life. In 1859 he published his idea in *On the Origin of Species*, which was later to be called the most influential book in Western history next to the Bible. Darwin's account of evolution held that all species developed out of gradual modifications to previous species, which developed out of previous species, and so on back to a common primordial ancestor. As a result, there are no sharp discontinuities between humans and other sorts of living things. Furthermore, because random variation and the lawlike, unthinking mechanism of natural selection generate evolutionary change, there is no reason to think that evolution proceeds deliberately from "lesser" to "greater" beings, starting in single-celled bacteria and culminating in homo sapiens. As Darwinism would have it, humanity has lost its favor. We are just one species among many.

What might these developments mean for the specialness of humanity, the existence of the soul, or our moral status? Various humanist ideas have staked positions on each of these issues. This chapter explores the meaning of some of these positions and examines whether they are philosophically and morally superior to their alternatives. Section 2.1 considers the humanist ideas on our place in the world. Section 2.2 looks at the physicalist picture of the mind and behavior. Finally, section 2.3 investigates a humanist perspective on evil, imperfection, and redemption. Although these various humanist ideas can be combined into a more-or-less comprehensive view of human nature, they can also stand or fall separately. As we will see, some are more plausible than others.

SECTION 2.1

Where in the World Are We? The Descent of Humanity

Most parents think that their own children are special, and most cultures have held that humanity itself is special. They have asserted the uniqueness and importance of humanity's place in the universe. As we saw in the previous chapter, philosophical humanism historically has affirmed the worth of humankind and human experience over things supernatural or otherworldly. Furthermore, humanisms of various stripes have elevated the value, capabilities, and status of human beings above the rest of nature. For example, many Renaissance humanists elaborated on the alleged beauty, perfection, and valor of the species. This attitude is expressed in that famous passage of Shakespeare's *Hamlet,* act 2, scene 2: "What a piece of work is man! How noble in reason! how infinite in faculties! in form and moving, how express and admirable! in action, how like an angel! in apprehension, how like a god! the beauty of the world! the paragon of animals!"

Humanism in the Enlightenment placed tremendous confidence in the power of reason to direct human destiny. Eventually, some rationalists such as Auguste Comte (1798–1857) would even prophesy the decline of supernatural religion and its replacement by a religion of humanity (Comte was to be Pope). As the divine came to seem less and less important to such people, people came to seem more and more divine. We can sum up this thread of humanism by returning to one of our propositions from chapter 1:

1. Human beings are superior to the rest of nature in their value, powers, and place in the world.

Of course, this humanist self-admiration was in part an outgrowth and modification of the Western monotheistic notion that we occupy a privileged place in the Creation. Being made in the "image of God" often meant possessing a soul, or mental and moral powers modeled after His own. This radically and fundamentally sets us apart from other living things. John Calvin wrote: "[W]e may gather that when [God's] image is placed in man a tacit antithesis is introduced which raises man above all other creatures and, as it were, separates him from the common mass."[2] Furthermore, we enjoy a unique relationship with

God. We stand at the center of God's plan and, therefore, the center of the created universe itself. Christian humanists like Shakespeare retained their faith's insistence on the centrality of humanity, but began a retreat from its theological corollary, inherent and humanly irredeemable sinfulness, which we examine in a subsequent section.

As we next suggest, the anthropocentric strand of humanism has not fared well philosophically. The case against anthropocentrism is somewhat complex. It relies not on one simple argument but rather on the cumulative effect of several lines of scientific and everyday evidence, as well as philosophical reflection. In particular, the case for nonanthropocentrism depends on a clear understanding of biological evolution, which undermines some key assumptions.

FOUR VARIETIES OF ANTHROPOCENTRISM

There are many different ways one might magnify the uniqueness and importance of humanity's place in the universe. Most broadly, we can distinguish among four categories of anthropocentrism according to the scale and area on which they focus: cosmological, biological, psychological, and moral.

Cosmological Anthropocentrism

Perhaps humanity is unique and important at a cosmological scale. Perhaps the universe itself has something to do with us, or more precisely, the existence and nature of humanity is crucial to the existence and nature of the universe. The fact that we are here is crucial to explaining why the universe is here and why it has the features it does. This is **cosmological anthropocentrism**.

The great Western monotheisms are committed to cosmological anthropocentrism. They posit a divine creator whose plan for the entire universe is, like the blueprint of a building, laid out with people in mind. The centrality of humanity to the universe is reflected in the actual organization of the planets, celestial objects, and physical principles.

The belief that Earth is literally and astronomically at the center of the cosmos was gradually overturned in the seventeenth century following a brilliant defense of heliocentric astronomy by Galileo. Interestingly, at that time the most influential evidence was Galileo's discovery that the moons of Jupiter are made of stuff that is similar to the Earth and its moon. This contradicted the prevailing scientific view, derived from Aristotle, that terrestrial objects and celestial objects are totally distinct in nature.

Advances in twentieth-century astrophysics have further eroded cosmological anthropocentrism. We have discovered that the very scale of the universe is in a sense totally inhuman. When we look at the entities that really make the cosmos tick, from neutrinos and quarks to nebula and galaxies, we find that they are either so tiny that they can pass through us as though we are not here at all, or so huge that we could never pass through them. We all live and die in a sliver-thin layer of gas on one planet near a medium-sized star in a galaxy of at least one hundred billion stars, which is itself one among at least two hundred billion galaxies. And despite these trillions of stars, the universe is mostly a cold vacuum of space. Some estimate that only 5 percent of the universe is made of matter.

The time-scale in the universe is also in a sense completely alien to us. In our experience, five years can seem like a long time, and eighty years like a lifetime. Yet as famed astronomer

Carl Sagan (1934–1996) liked to point out, if the lifetime of the universe were plotted onto a twelve-month calendar to make a "cosmic year" (with origin of the universe on January 1, the formation of the Earth on September 14, and the reign of the dinosaurs during December 24–28), the entire history of the human species, from our first appearance on the plains of Africa to the present, would represent only the last half hour of the last day of the last month![3]

In recent decades, a number of scientists and theologians have produced evidence for the conclusion that the universe is "fine-tuned" for the emergence of biological life. This raises the possibility that natural laws were designed with us in mind. Indeed, it can be generally said that if a divine being created nature and gave us a preeminent place, then it is true that we have a preeminent place in nature. The continuation of this discussion will have to wait until chapter 7, in which theism will be explored at length.

Biological Anthropocentrism

One might claim that humanity is uniquely important within the phenomenon of life. This is **biological anthropocentrism**. Biological anthropocentrism is often combined with cosmological anthropocentrism, but in principle they are separable and their merits can be examined independently. Even if one denied that humanity and its home occupy the center of the universe, one could still claim that humanity is the pinnacle of life on Earth.

One version of biological anthropocentrism is the view that human beings are the best or most advanced form of life. Throughout history there has been widespread belief in a notion that historian A. O. Lovejoy named the "Great Chain of Being." The basic idea is that living things can be ordered on a spectrum from least to greatest. Human beings hold a place on the scale above all other animals, below gods and demigods such as angels. While this view was scientifically plausible before the late nineteenth century, it was exploded by the implications of Darwinian evolution, or evolution by natural selection.

Natural selection occurs when random, heritable variations among the individual organisms of a population are on average more successful at reproducing themselves than other variations. As a consequence, the frequencies of variants in the population change over time. Some enduring features of the organisms' environments (natural or social) present specific obstacles to superior reproduction, what are often called "adaptive problems." Those variants that reliably out-reproduce the alternatives do so because their structural features allow them to better overcome these obstacles. Thus, over generations, natural selection produces organisms whose features—eyes, lungs, memory, emotions, and so on—appear to solve the adaptive problems that confronted their ancestors. When a variant has been molded by selection and other factors to the point that it can no longer successfully reproduce with other variants, it has become a new species, an event called "speciation." These processes of natural selection, adaptation, and speciation constitute "evolution by natural selection."

By pointing out the significance of adaptation to local environments, evolutionary science attacks the very notion of a Great Chain of Being. Darwin's notes include a reminder to himself to "never say higher or lower in referring to organisms." He did not mean that there are no differences between us and other beings. Indeed, his whole project was to make possible the systematic description and explanation of the differences among species. What he meant is that there is no biological basis for believing that any one successful species is more advanced than others. The only biological criteria for evaluating success are adaptation and reproduction. If two species have adapted to their environments so as to ensure a future of reproduction, then they are on a par. That one adapts by simple techniques and the other adapts by complex techniques is irrelevant, biologically speaking.

The Darwinian outlook shatters the Great Chain of Being in another way. If every species has been generated out of incremental modifications to preexisting species, then there are no fundamental, metaphysical gaps between them. The proliferation and spread of life from the first primordial cells to the readers of this book has been a single continuous stream, with a seamless interconnection at the base of every branching channel. Life is not a chain with discrete links, and so it isn't a chain at all.

It must be pointed out that while the Great Chain of Being lays claim to our superiority, it is not just about our superiority *as biological systems*. It also implies that our *value* surpasses that of other beings: People are not only more advanced, they are also more valuable. Biological science alone is incapable of resolving this issue, so we make a brief foray into ethical theory in a subsequent section, although a detailed discussion of morality is reserved for chapter 4.

Suppose we reject the Great Chain of Being idea, as do many contemporary thinkers. We might still believe that evolution has been a process culminating in human beings. Like an enormous assembly line, evolution has conveyed species through time and countless modifications in order to attain an end product, humanity. In fact, this story is part of the pervasive, commonsense understanding of evolution. Nevertheless, this story is based on a complete misunderstanding of evolution, which Darwin struggled in vain to overturn in his own day.

In everyday English, "evolving" is a synonym for "developing" or "progressing." Therefore, it is tempting to think that evolution is evolution *toward* some end or goal. Philosophers refer to this state of being oriented toward an end or goal as a **teleology**, from the Greek word *telos*, for "end." The fact that humans appeared late in natural history makes it easy to imagine that we are the telos of evolution. If not humanity as such, it seems that evolution aims at ever-increasing complexity, and humans, with our massive brains, just happen to be the most complex thing around. However, this ordinary usage of "evolution" is seriously misleading when applied to biology. It is not just that evolution has no directionality toward humanity. There is not even a general trend toward greater complexity within the process of evolution. Stephen Jay Gould, professor of zoology and geology at Harvard University, explains: "Evolution is a process of constant branching and expansion. Life began three and a half billion years ago, necessarily about as simple as it could be, because life arose spontaneously from the organic compounds in the primeval oceans. . . . And since there's no way of getting any simpler, as life expanded every once in a while you get something more complex because that's the only direction open."[4]

Gould presents the following analogy. As a drunk person staggers along the outside wall of a bar, any random deviations in his course will take him away from the wall. But there is no inherent trend here, only the fact that there is no other direction to stagger! Similarly, evolution has necessarily begun at a wall of "maximal simplicity," a borderline of biological structures that are just barely capable of reproduction and death. Beyond this limit of simplicity, evolution cannot even operate because it operates on things that can reproduce and die. Therefore, any evolutionary stray from the wall aims in the direction of complexity. But this is so as a result of the logic of the situation, not any intrinsic goals of evolution.

Furthermore, if we take an unbiased look at the actual relative proportions of highly complex organisms such as ourselves, we find that they represent a rare exception to the rule. Most life throughout the history of the Earth has remained up against the wall of maximal simplicity, Gould explains:

> What you see is that the most outstanding feature of life's history is a constant domination by bacteria. In fact, this is not the age of man as the old textbooks used to say, or the age of mammals, or even the age of insects, which is more correct. . . . This is the age of bacteria. Bacteria have always been dominant. The bacterial mode, the mode being the most common form of life, is never altered in 3½ billion years. We don't see it that way because bacteria are tiny and they live beneath us, but bacteria live in a wider range of environments. There are more E-coli cells . . . in the gut of every human being than there have ever been people on earth. So this is a bacterial planet.[5]

The preeminence of simple things should not surprise, given the fundamental conservatism of the evolutionary process. Complex additions and modifications are risky and they consume time and energy, so selection favors those who can adapt to their environment with the least possible effort. Becoming more complex is only one way to adapt to an environment. Sometimes the best way is to *lose* complexity or to move to a different environment altogether. And if you can adapt without becoming more complex, why bother? Sometimes simplicity works.

At an even more basic level, evolution by natural selection is incompatible with the existence of any telos in natural history. Unlike the process of breeding animals, in which some variations are *intentionally* selected with some goal in mind, evolutionary change under natural selection is caused by differences in reproductive success resulting automatically from random variations. There is simply no mechanism within the causes of evolutionary change that could provide for any long-term directionality.

Once again, we should acknowledge that the truth or falsity of theism is relevant to evaluation of the above Darwinian arguments about contingency, teleology, and so on, including the evolutionary principles they presuppose. For example, consider the following claims: (1) living things were designed by a deity; (2) living things were generated by iterated processes of random variation and natural selection. One reasonably might think that the plausibility of the first claim bears on the plausibility of the second.

Psychological Anthropocentrism

A third manifestation of the idea that humanity is preeminent is the most narrowly focused. We may not be the center of the universe. We may not even be the pinnacle of evolution. But we have something magnificent that no other animal has: consciousness, rationality, a soul. French philosopher René Descartes gave a radical formulation to this kind of anthropocentrism in the seventeenth century when he argued that nonhuman animals have no more of an inner life than a windup toy. According to **psychological anthropocentrism**, our mental nature sets us above and apart from the rest of nature.

Once again, the basic evolutionary concept of descent from common ancestors with incremental modifications stands in the way of anthropocentrism. Given this basic concept, it would be extraordinary if human mentality were radically different from the

The Well-Cultured Primate

It has long been assumed that only humans have cultures; that is, sets of behaviors and information that are spread through nongenetic means such as imitation. In the last few years, however, some primatologists have begun to challenge that assumption. Recently, a long-term comparative study of seven chimpanzee groups has uncovered thirty-nine such behaviors that are passed through nongenetic means, like clasping hands with a grooming partner or tearing leaves noisily to attract potential mates. The traits vary among groups and change over time within groups, not unlike table manners and styles of dress among humans.

Why has no one noticed this before? Dutch-born zoologist Frans de Waal speculates that Western science in particular has been in the grip of an anthropocentric, us-versus-animals worldview: "It can hardly be coincidental that the push for cultural studies on animals initially came . . . from primatologists untrained in the sharp dualisms of the West." For instance, de Waal claims, "the Japanese did not hesitate to give each animal a name or to assume that each had a different identity and personality. Neither did they feel a need to avoid topics such as animal mental life and culture."*

* Frans de Waal, *Good Natured: The Origins of Right and Wrong in Humans and Other Animals* (Cambridge, Mass.: Harvard University Press, 1996).

mentality of other primates and mammals. Instead, we should expect to find a subtle gradation between the organization and functioning of the central nervous system across species.

In fact, that is just what we do find. For example, recent studies of primates and other mammals reveal forms of memory, belief, spatial cognition, symbolic communication, tool use, strategic planning, social norms, and cultural transmission that are all qualitatively similar to our own.

Still, it might be argued that some features of the human mind, such as self-consciousness or freedom of choice, are unprecedented in nature. Supposing that the human brain emerged gradually from the brains of nonhuman animals, it might be that once it achieved a certain level of complex organization, it unexpectedly took on mental properties that were fundamentally different from those that went before. In section 2.2 we explore the contrasting theories of the mind that inform such views of human nature.

But suppose it is granted that we have some abilities, such as self-awareness or the use of abstract conceptual language, that are utterly unique. If this is all that the doctrine of anthropocentrism comes to, it is no longer terribly significant. Once one admits that the universe is in no sense constructed for us, and that we are an otherwise unremarkable result of the thoughtless, nonteleological process of evolution, the fact that we have some cognitive abilities lacked by other animals hardly gives us a preeminent place in the universe. After all, many nonhuman animals have cognitive abilities that we lack. For instance, some sharks have special organs that detect electromagnetic radiation and precisely pinpoint its source, allowing them to "see" the invisible energy emitted by their prey. Surely this is no evidence for "chondrichthyecentrism"![6]

Moral Anthropocentrism

A fourth and final way in which humanity can be elevated above the rest of the world concerns our moral worth. It is sometimes alleged that, just as we recognize the equal worth of all people (though they may differ in their abilities and merits), we should recognize the equal worth of all living things, or *all species*: "Rejecting the notion of human superiority entails its positive counterpart: the doctrine of species impartiality. One who accepts that doctrine regards all living things as possessing inherent worth—the same inherent worth, since no one species has been shown to be either 'higher' or 'lower' than any other."[7] However, this species egalitarianism is difficult to maintain. The problem is that whichever features one judges to be morally important, it is often the case that humans possess these features *plus* other features judged to be morally important.[8] For example, suppose, as seems plausible, that the ability to suffer is morally important. This is obviously a feature possessed by many nonhuman animals. Yet it is at least as plausible that the ability to form and pursue projects is morally important as well, and this feature arguably is not possessed by nonhuman animals. However, normal human beings are capable of suffering *and* pursuing projects. So, even if one is unsure about the comparative importance of suffering versus project-pursuit, and even if one agrees that nonhuman animals are morally considerable to some extent, and it is hard to deny that humans are morally considerable to that extent, *and then some.*

Yet there is a more modest version of species egalitarianism, which ethicist Peter Singer has persuasively defended in a series of influential writings. He has called attention to a critical error in ethical reasoning, which he calls **speciesism**. A judgment or action is speciesist when it applies different ethical standards to members of another species *simply because they are members of a different species,* and despite there being no *morally relevant* difference between them. If we judge that some feature is morally relevant, then that feature is morally relevant whether it is found in a human being or a nonhuman being. For example, if suffering is, all things considered, morally bad when experienced by a human person, then it is similarly morally bad when experienced by a dog or a chicken. Insofar as the humanist idea is guilty of speciesism, it is problematic. In subsequent chapters we turn to the general questions of whether humanist ideas about morality can be vindicated.

CONCLUSION

Nothing in the previous section should be taken as a denial that some thinkers identified with humanism, such as Bertrand Russell or Carl Sagan, have adopted a thoroughly nonanthropocentric outlook. The point is that in doing so they were departing sharply from the humanist tradition that in other ways they carried on in a more-or-less unmodified form. More recently, humanists have attempted to work through the implications of humanist naturalism for humanist anthropocentrism in its several varieties, especially the moral variety. Philosophical humanism has historically affirmed the superior value, powers, and place of humans in the world. From cosmology to evolutionary biology, the history of science (and philosophical reflection on its results) has bankrupted this anthropocentrism in various ways, and forced a descent of humanity. The suggestion that the human mind in particular nonetheless represents a radical departure from the rest of nature is examined at length in the next section.

SECTION 2.2

Lost Souls: What Happened to Mind and Body

Do you have a soul? Most people think that they do. It is the part of them that thinks and feels, the part that accounts for their self-awareness, free choice, and moral conscience. It is the supernatural part that will live forever in union with God, or perhaps haunt the natural world after death. Therefore, the soul is not the same as the physical body, or even the brain.

On reflection, the idea of a soul raises some baffling questions. Is the soul a substance, a process, or what? How is it connected with the body? Yet it is no less difficult to understand the alternative, that humans have no soul. For example, there seem to be some things going on "inside" us that defy explanation in purely physical terms. Consider the simple occurrence of seeing a red apple. By studying the eye, we know that a complex series of causes leads up to this experience. The apple has certain surface properties that absorb some frequencies of light waves and reflect others. Light waves enter your eye and get translated into nerve impulses that travel up your optic nerve to the vision centers of your brain. But then something quite extraordinary happens. There is an *experience of the redness* of the apple. Something or someone has a sense of what redness is like.

Philosophers call this sensed quality of a conscious state—like the "redness" of the apple—its **qualitative content**. It seems that in the causal sequence involved in seeing the apple, the final step is of a totally different variety from those that went before. It seems there is a world of difference between the mechanical interaction of light waves and nerve cells and the conscious experience with qualitative content. It is baffling how you could be capable of having such experiences if there is nothing more to you than flesh and blood, body and brain.

Corresponding to our conflicting reflections on the soul, there is a historical competition between different views of human psychology. According to one major competitor, called **dualism**, human beings have physical bodies and minds or souls that are constituted by nonphysical entities or processes. According to **physicalism**, the mind itself is constituted by physical entities or processes. In light of the general humanist flight from things supernatural, we can identify as humanist the physicalist conception of mind, as listed in chapter 1:

2. We are physical systems with minds, but devoid of immaterial souls.

Most philosophers and scientists are now convinced that dualism and the belief in supernatural souls is incorrect. However, they disagree among themselves about which form of physicalism is correct. In no small part this is because the science of the mind is still developing. But even at this stage it is possible to show that some versions of physicalism are implausible. As a consequence, some interpretations of the humanist theme are implausible.

To begin, we examine the philosophical and religious roots of dualism and show why it is now widely rejected as a theory of the mind. We then consider competing versions of physicalism and arrive at the most plausible version. Finally, we observe that there is no necessary link between a religious worldview and a dualistic view of human nature.

MIND-BODY DUALISM AND THE SOUL

In the late eighteenth century, an unlikely celebrity began appearing before European audiences to play chess. What drew the crowds was that "the Turk," as he came to be known, seemed to be nothing more than a machine or "automaton"—an articulated mannequin done up in a dark beard and turban and apparently animated by a complex array of gears and springs that could be displayed by opening up the cabinet at which he sat. Observers were astounded as the Turk's mechanical chess moves bested almost all opponents. What they did not know what that the puppet was operated by a human chess player hidden inside the cabinet.[9]

Skeptics were not surprised when they discovered that the Turk's feats were accomplished with someone else's intelligence. They knew better than to think that crude springs and gears could generate the cognitive powers necessary to play chess. Indeed, many agreed with Descartes, who in the previous century had argued influentially that no machine could ever be intelligent. Descartes stated one of his main reasons as follows: "[A]lthough machines can perform certain things as well as or perhaps better than any of us can do, they infallibly fall short in others, by which means we may discover that they did not act from knowledge, but only from the disposition of their organs. For while reason is a universal instrument which can serve for all contingencies, these organs have need of some special adaptation for every particular action." From this he concluded: "[I]t is . . . impossible that there should be sufficient diversity in any machine to allow it to act in all the events of life in the same way as our reason causes us to act." A machine might be able to go through the motions of some of our behaviors, but it will always be critically limited because it has no genuine *knowledge* or *understanding* of what is going on.

Descartes's position had an unavoidable consequence: If no mere machine can do what we do, then we can be no mere machines. Our bodies may behave mechanically, but our minds must be different. Descartes proposed that what makes our minds different is that they are composed of an entirely different substance. They are composed of an *immaterial substance,* a substance that lacks weight, divisibility, extension in space, and all other physical properties. It has the properties of sensing and thinking alone. A human being is, like the Turk, a conglomerate of two very different entities: an unthinking mechanical body and an invisible thinking thing that directs its behavior from somewhere hidden within. Descartes's theory of the mind is now called **substance dualism**, for it asserts that the world contains two fundamentally distinct substances: material substance and mental or spiritual substance. (A weaker form of dualism, *property dualism,* holds that human beings are physical substances who possess some nonphysical properties—namely, mental properties.)

In developing his dualist theory, Descartes articulated a view about human nature already well established in Western civilization. Christian doctrine had drawn on an earlier dualism put forward by Plato, who claimed that everything in the material world is an imperfect replica of an ideal Form. The Forms—such as mathematical, geometric, and philosophical concepts and ideals of virtue and beauty—do not exist in the same way as material objects do. They are nonmaterial, eternal, and unchanging. By associating the realm of the mental and spiritual with the realm of Platonic Forms, theologians created a Christian mind-body dualism. Meanwhile, Christian folklore adopted a less esoteric conception, depicting the soul as a homunculus, a tiny manlike creature nested in the body like a chess player in a cabinet.

Some form of dualist understanding of the soul is assumed in most major religions. In Vedic and Hindu traditions, the thinking thing is typically spatially unmeasurable and independent of the body. (However, Advaita Vedanta, one of the three major philosophical systems in Hindu, is not dualistic. It claims there is only one kind of substance in the world: *Brahman,* the transcendent "Absolute" that is the ground of all existing things.) Some traditional African and Native American religions posited multiple souls in each individual body. Anthropologists have pointed out that certain mundane experiences had by people everywhere might naturally lead them to the idea of the soul.[10] Viewing your reflection in water presents a model of how a ghostly, ephemeral object could nevertheless be you; the phenomenon of dreaming gives the impression that you can separate from your body and travel to distant locations without it.

Dualism has been woven deeply into religious systems for a number of reasons. First, many theistic religions have depicted deities as invisible forces not confined to a physical body. If gods are made of spiritual substance, then dualism must be true. In an anthropocentric vein, gods are often linked with humans through a shared "divine spark," our soul. Second, the soul has been seen as the thing that enables the special capacities necessary for a religious life or a meaningful relationship with the divine, such as self-awareness, a moral conscience, free will, rationality, or comprehension. How could a mere machine love or worship its maker?

Most experts now agree that dualism has two fatal flaws. First, scientific and technological limitations of their day led early dualists to underestimate the power of the physical brain to think and the potential of machines to "reason." Second, dualism failed to show how the soul could possibly interact with the body so as to cause its behavior.

First of all, the early dualists underestimated machines. They did not foresee the invention of the computer, or experiments in artificial intelligence. Having only devices like the Turk as a model, it was entirely reasonable for them to doubt that a machine would ever be able to actually play and beat a person at chess. However, today's model is Deep Blue, a supercomputer developed over ten years by a team of IBM scientists, capable of calculating two hundred million chess positions in a single second. In May 1997 Deep Blue defeated world chess champion Garry Kasparov, regarded by many as the greatest player of all time. The tremendous power and complexity of contemporary information-processing machines has significantly increased the plausibility of the physicalist claim that a machine could have a mind.

The early dualists also underestimated the brain. This is something that the French philosophe Julien Offroy de La Mettrie grasped in 1748. Against the dualists of his day he declared, "Let us then conclude boldly that man is a machine." The only obstacle to a satisfactory physicalist theory, he thought, was that "Man is so complicated a machine." In the era of the early dualists, brain sciences were still in their infancy. Now, as advances in the cognitive and neurological sciences reveal just how extraordinarily complex the brain is (with its many billions of neuronal connections), the Cartesian claim that physical processes cannot account for thought has less and less appeal. La Mettrie appears to have been correct: While undoubtedly there is a vast difference in *quantity* or organization between the enormously complex human body and simple contraptions like the Turk, there is no difference in *quality* or substance.

In addition, increased knowledge of the brain has revealed numerous highly specific correlations between mental states and brain states that we would not have expected given dualism. For example, particular cognitive abilities such as language use and spatial reasoning appear to be localized in particular areas of the brain. Certain sorts of brain injuries cause very distinctive changes in perception, cognition, and personality. The manipulation of chemicals in the brain by medication can alter one's mood. Finally, some diseases affecting the mind such as Down syndrome and schizophrenia have been shown to have a genetic component.

Second of all, dualism's fundamental philosophical flaw was pointed out even in Descartes's day: its failure to show how an immaterial mind and a physical body could interact. For interaction to be possible, each entity must have some means of causing changes in the other. In the case of the Turk, we can see the points of causal contact: the operator's hands manipulate mechanical controls to exert force on the body of the puppet. But the Turk's body, the controls, and the operator's hands are all material objects. What could be the point of causal contact between a material body and an *immaterial operator*? How could an immaterial substance—lacking mass, electrical charge, or even location in space—operate a machine with these material properties and nothing more? In the philosophical literature this problem is called the **mind-body problem**. To the extent that dualism insists on the absolute metaphysical distinctness of mind and body, it is incapable of explaining how mind and body could possibly interact. It is therefore inadequate as a theory of the mind.

Now, according to some versions of classical theism, God is a thinking substance. If God is a thinking substance, then dualism is at least in part vindicated. Should theism be included in the total evidence for dualism as a theory of mind? That is a question addressed by the discussion in chapter 7.

THREE TYPES OF PHYSICALISM

Suppose the mind is not an immaterial, indivisible, thinking substance. Mental states such as beliefs and desires are not states of the soul. But then what exactly are they? In the various answers to this question we find some of the main interpretations and difficulties of physicalism, and thus of humanism as well.

There have been many cases in intellectual history in which people came to realize that common or accepted ways of thinking on a particular subject were at odds with the facts as revealed by science or philosophical reflection. People in the West once believed that demons and spirits caused various diseases. But with the rise of the germ theory of disease and the success of modern medicine, it became unclear what role demons and spirits could have in explaining illness. In cases such as these, there is an apparent conflict between two different modes of conceiving and talking of something, or between discourses. The discourses conflict because they present apparently competing **ontologies**, views about which entities the world really contains. As we discuss next, there are various ways one might try to resolve a conflict between discourses with competing ontologies.

One straightforward way to resolve the perceived conflict is to eliminate the problematic ontology. This is what became of demons and spirits in the history of medicine. It eventually became apparent that we could best explain and counteract disease by appealing to natural entities such as germs, viruses, and immune systems. Because they no longer fit into our understanding of disease and no longer had any explanatory value, demons and spirits were discarded and replaced by natural entities.

Sometimes, however, it is possible to retain the problematic ontology by identifying it or "reducing it" to the other ontology. Arguably this happened in the field of genetics. Even before the development of modern genetics, the units of biological heredity were called "genes." It was later discovered that the deoxyribonucleic acid molecules in the nucleus of the cell, commonly known as "DNA," are the units of heredity. But this discovery did not eliminate the concept of a gene in favor of DNA. Rather, people reasoned that because DNA molecules do more or less what genes were supposed to all along, genes *are* DNA molecules. Thus, genes are reduced to DNA. A third alternative is to argue that the apparent conflict between the discourses is only apparent. With some additional assumptions, the ontologies can be understood as irreducibly different, yet consistent.

Corresponding to these three options—elimination, reduction, and nonreductive integration—there are three broad sorts of physicalism, depending on how one characterizes the relationship between the mental ontology and the physical ontology of brain and body states: eliminative physicalism, reductive physicalism, and nonreductive physicalism.

DIFFICULTIES WITH PHYSICALISM

The theory of **eliminative physicalism** says that our discourse about minds is like our discourse about demons. It belongs to a "folk theory" of psychology, which we use in everyday life when we explain people's behavior by attributing beliefs and desires to them. Defenders of eliminative physicalism claim that as scientific psychology progresses, we will find there is nothing at the neurobiological level that remotely corresponds to the mental concepts of the folk theory. Just as a mature science of disease has no place for demons, a mature science of the brain has no place for beliefs and desires. Therefore, we have no reason to think that there are such things. Strictly speaking, we have no beliefs, desires, or intentions, and so, strictly speaking, we have no minds!

This result flies in the face of common sense, yet eliminative physicalism cannot be refuted on that ground alone. Perhaps common sense is misleading in this instance. It wouldn't be the first time. However, the theory faces two powerful objections. First, it is not at all clear that the folk theory of the mind is a failed theory. Unlike the postulation of demons to explain disease, the postulation of beliefs and desires to explain everyday behavior works quite well. If you desire a sandwich, and you believe that a sandwich lies in the refrigerator, then, all else being equal, we can predict that you will go to the refrigerator to get it. Furthermore, eliminative physicalism fails to address the felt aspect of consciousness, what we earlier called its qualitative content. An important part of our discourse about minds concerns experiencing qualities such as the color red or the feeling of pain. But how could anyone possibly deny that we all have such experiences?

Due to the weakness of its case against folk psychology and its denial of qualitative experience, most philosophers find eliminative physicalism to be an unacceptable theory of the mind. Rather than eliminating mental states, many philosophers argue that mental states are identical with or reducible to states of the body or brain. Defenders of **reductive physicalism**, or "the identity theory," claim that a mature psychological science will show that, for example, the belief that it is raining is *the same thing as* a physical brain state of a certain type. Reductive physicalism does not seek to eliminate the mind. Rather it hopes to show how minds can be real. Just as the discovery of DNA helped establish what genes really are, neuroscience will help establish what minds really are.

The problem with reductive physicalism is that the same mental state can be produced by different physical states, and therefore mental states cannot be identical with physical states. This phenomenon is sometimes called "variable realization."

To see that thoughts and intentions are capable of variable realization, we need look no further than the fact of biochemical diversity among humans. The body is made of at least ten thousand different kinds of enzymes and other proteins, and each of us differs from all of the unrelated people around us by at least one, probably several, rare enzymes. Taking into consideration the additional diversity in blood groups and other chemical structures, it is undeniable that except for identical twins, every individual's body is biochemically unique.[11]

If reductive physicalism were true and mental states were identical with physical states, then no two people (non-twins) could have the same type of mental state, given the fact of biochemical diversity. Yet this is clearly not the case. When two different people believe that it is raining, they are in the same type of mental state. The reduction of minds to bodies fails because minds are variably realizable. (In fact, some would say genes cannot be reduced to DNA for much the same reason!)

Today the dominant view in the philosophy and science of the mind is a theory that attempts to retain a noneliminative form of physicalism while taking into account the variable realization of mental states. This general view is called **nonreductive physicalism**. Reductive physicalism erred by claiming that a particular *type* of mental state, such as the desire that it stop raining, can be reduced to a particular type of physical state. This type-to-type reduction ran afoul of variable realization because there was no neat match between types. However, one can instead make the more modest claim that individual instances or "tokens" of mental states are identical with individual tokens of physical states. For instance, although there are many different ways to physically realize the desire that it stop raining, any particular instance of that desire will be identical with *some* physical state or another. This is what nonreductive physicalism claims.

Therein lies its weakness, antiphysicalists argue. Physicalism, reductive or not, cannot account for the qualitative aspects of consciousness. It appears that all physical properties are knowable from a third-person, objective point of view. For example, the size and mass of an apple are in principle open to inspection by anyone. But, as we noted earlier, qualitative content is not like that at all. Even if we opened up your brain and examined it while you were experiencing a color or a sensation of flavor, we would not thereby know what the experience is like for you. Only you can have your experiences. Since consciousness fails to be knowable from a third-person, objective point of view, it cannot be identical with any physical property. Because physical properties are necessarily objective properties, conscious properties cannot be physical properties.

Considerations such as these have led some to embrace a more modest form of dualism, **property dualism**, in which minds are considered to be physical systems that have some nonphysical properties—namely, their mental properties. Arguably, this form of dualism is compatible with the humanist idea since it affirms that minds are physical systems and denies that there is an immaterial soul (at least, one that could exist independently of the physical body).

Philosopher John Searle contends that people's insistence—in the face of the facts—that consciousness could not be physically caused only reflects the deep imprint of dualism on Western thought.[12] Our concept of the physical is still a substance dualist concept, which holds that by definition, no mere matter—no machine—could have a mind. It is this dualistic way of thinking that we are still struggling to overcome.

Issues such as these continue to be hotly debated in the philosophy of mind and the cognitive sciences. Yet nonreductive physicalism (in one form or another) has emerged as the most attractive view of the mind. It also captures an interpretation of a basic humanist theme: We are physical systems with minds, but devoid of immaterial souls. Meanwhile, dualism is widely rejected even as the religious worldviews that have historically depended on it continue to thrive.

WORLDVIEWS WITHOUT A SOUL

It is important to realize that not all major religious traditions have posited a soul or embraced substance dualism. Aquinas and later scholastic philosophers defended hylomorphism, the doctrine that everything is a combination of matter and form. The worldview found in the Bible is nondualist. The Hebrew words generally translated as "soul" refer to breath, or the animation of a living body. The biblical, physicalist understanding of humanity was muted by the synthesis of Christianity with dualistic Greek philosophy, but it has continued to hold influence in mainstream Judaism. Talmudic rabbis neither conceived of the soul's immortality as separate from that of the body nor imagined the transmigration of the soul from one body to another. Body and soul were understood to be separate only in origin, with the body deriving from the human parents and the soul originating with God. Only in kabbalistic mysticism has the doctrine of the transmigration of souls been central.

No doubt a physicalist theory of human nature raises some puzzling questions when combined with the belief in an eternal afterlife. (Bodies are located in space. If we are resurrected as bodies, then the afterlife will have a location in space—but where could it be?) The following section will examine some of these puzzles. Suffice it to say a religious worldview does not necessarily commit one to a dualistic view of humanity. It is entirely possible to embrace a form of physicalism, which, as we have seen, has the advantage of being the most philosophically and scientifically promising theory of the mind presently available.

CONCLUSION

In its skepticism of the supernatural, humanism has historically rejected dualism and embraced physicalism. The tenability of substance dualistic views of the mind has been undermined by advances in computing and the brain sciences. But some forms of physicalism are implausible. Noneliminative, nonreductive physicalism and property dualism seem to hold the most promise. Both of these views capture the basic humanist idea of the mind and soul.

SECTION 2.3

You Only Live Once: Life and Beyond

George Eliot (Mary Ann Evans) drew criticism in her day not just for her atheism but also for her fascination with depicting the ordinary lives of rural working people, warts and all.

In the middle of her novel *Adam Bede* (1859), she directs a comment to her critics, explaining her "realist" aesthetic by citing the example of Dutch paintings and their "faithful pictures of a monotonous homely existence":

> I turn without shrinking from cloud-borne angels, from prophets, sibyls, and heroic warriors, to an old woman bending over her flower-pot, or eating her solitary dinner, while the noonday light, softened perhaps by a screen of leaves, falls on her mob-cap, and just touches the rim of her spinning-wheel, and her stone jug, and all those cheap common things which are the precious necessaries of life to her. . . . There are few prophets in the world; few sublimely beautiful women; few heroes. I can't afford to give all my love and reverence to such rarities: I want a great deal of those feelings for my everyday fellow-men, especially for the few in the foreground of the great multitude, whose faces I know, whose hands I touch, for whom I have to make way with kindly courtesy.[13]

Eliot's expression of affection and reverence for things profane and earthly echoes a world-affirming theme of philosophical humanism, which can be put as follows:

> 3. This earthly life is the only one we can hope for and the only one we need.

As a matter of the cultural history of the West, this sort of positive attention to earthly things is linked to the Renaissance humanists' revival of classical learning and ethos. Renaissance worldliness represented a revolt against one powerful strain of Christianity, the strain of asceticism and renunciation of the world. With the emergence of the monastic tradition in the third and fourth centuries, the spiritual models became those who cast off earthly and bodily imperatives to embrace religious devotion and imitation of Christ. The subject of the Christian narrative was the undying, redeemable spirit temporarily caged in and then freed from a decaying and corrupting body.

Theological developments within the evolution of Christianity also played a part in turning the culture earthward. The philosopher and intellectual historian Charles Taylor has identified what he calls "the affirmation of everyday life" as one of the great cultural legacies of the Protestant Reformation.

> Thus by the same movement through which the Protestant churches rejected a special order of priesthood in favor of the doctrine of the priesthood of all believers, they also rejected the special vocation to the monastic life and affirmed the spiritual value of lay life. By denying any special form of life as a privileged locus of the sacred, they were denying the very distinction between sacred and profane and hence affirming their interpenetration. The denial of a special status to the monk was also an affirmation of ordinary life as more than profane, as itself hallowed and in no way second class. The institution of the monastic life was seen as a slur on the spiritual standing of productive labor and family life, their stigmatization as zones of spiritual underdevelopment. The repudiation of monasticism was a reaffirmation of lay life as central locus for the fulfillment of God's purpose. Luther marks their break in his own life by ceasing to be such a monk and by marrying a former nun.[14]

The Protestant reaffirmation of lay life elevates earthly existence, but by linking its value to one's spiritual calling. Later, with the rise of deism and theological skepticism in the eighteenth and nineteenth centuries, the orientation toward the this-worldly was increasingly coupled with an incredulity about the afterworldly. Interestingly, many philosophers clung to the reality of the afterlife even more tightly than the belief in the God of classical theism because they saw it as the key to religious morality. Aside from the motivation provided by the threat of everlasting punishment or the enticement of everlasting reward, the promise of heaven was the promise that in the end justice will be done, the wrongs righted, and the broken made whole.

It may be difficult for ordinary people in today's developed countries to imagine doing other than affirming the worth of worldly things, absorbed as we are by cultivating romantic love, earning money, consuming luxury goods, and being entertained. But it is worth asking whether the everyday is enough. The belief that this life is only a prelude to another more perfect and everlasting life continues to pervade humanity. What reasons can be given to sustain this hope, and what would be lost in giving it up?

PERSONAL SURVIVAL

When facing the prospect of no afterlife, people often emphasize other forms of "immortality" that are within our reach. Some thinkers interpret religious talk of surviving death as metaphorical descriptions of a spiritual state that is to be sought in the present life, such as overcoming sin or selfishness. It is said that we can "live on" by being remembered, bearing children, making an impact on culture or history, or giving something of ourselves to others. Certainly those things may be worth caring about (although not as such—dictators and serial killers make more of a memorable impact than most ordinary decent people, for example). We also care about *what happens to us* when we die. There can be great value in living a life whose significance survives well beyond the death of the body. But that is still no substitute for being the thing that survives. (Of course, another challenge to the notion of "living on through others" is that every one of those others will eventually perish too, along with all living things—if certain plausible scientific scenarios about the ultimate fate of the universe are correct.)

It is this latter form of immortality, personal survival, that we examine next. The question of personal survival turns out to be intimately connected to the classical philosophical problem of **personal identity**, the problem of stating what would make it the case that you are a person (as opposed to a bunch of thoughts, biological drives, and so on), and what would make it the case that you remain the same person over time and through changes. If the afterworldly existence of some entity is to count as *your* survival, then that entity must satisfy the conditions of personal identity.

DUALIST SURVIVAL

If we are to survive the death of our bodies, what sort of existence must we have? According to dualist theories of the mind and self, we are essentially a nonphysical substance or soul that interacts with the body but exists independently of it. There is no reason to think that such a substance must perish when the vital organs and brain stop working. Thus, substance dualism appears congenial to survival. (Although dualism does not *guarantee* survival, either. The soul may be independent of the body, and yet constituted so as to cease to exist at the same time that the body dies or disintegrates.)

Heaven in a Chip: Can Science Conquer Death?

The rapid advances in science, genetics, and technology have led some to speculate that people may someday relatively soon cheat death through scientific means such as genetic modification, cryogenic life extension, and nanotechnology (for example, by deploying millions of atomic-scale machines into the body to repair damaged cells). Communities of "transhumanists" and "extropians" have sprung up in the expectation of techno-transcendence in their lifetimes. According to Bart Kosko, a popular author and electrical engineer at the University of Southern California, death is a technical problem that can be solved by transferring the mind to more efficient and durable "hardware."

> I think engineering will supply our demand for a "spiritual" life after meat death. The immediate problem with our meat brains is that they have no back-up. We can lose the most precious information we have from one bump on the head or stroke. You want a mind system with back-up that can access other databases. I think that it's a matter of time. Chip capacity doubles about every 18 months. When will we reach the required raw, computer-processing level—in 2020 or 2040? That's anyone's guess. But at some point in the not-too-distant future computers will greatly outstrip the processing power of the human brain. At some point after that, the human-chip interface will first allow implants and then outright chip replacement. . . .
>
> The ultimate parts replacement is to replace the whole brain with a chip. One quick consequence of a chip brain would be that our subjective sense of time would change. Right now, the burning of a match takes place on an interesting time scale. In a nanochip, that event could seem like years. And if you were able to think, reason and fantasize at ultra-fast speeds, have access to vast databases, create things simply by willing them, and do so for thousands of years (until the chip ran out of energy), you would have a de facto working approximation of heaven—heaven in a chip. Concepts of religion may now be goals of science and engineering. With cryonics as a form of resurrection, we complete the rivalry of science with religion. Instead of religious law, we have scientific laws. Instead of the immortal soul, we now have the 1-0 bit-stream patterns of information on a chip.*

* Interview with Bart Kosko, conducted by *NetWorker*, www.usc.edu/isd/publications/networker/97-98/Jan_Feb_98/innerview-kosko.html. See also Bart Kosko, *The Fuzzy Future: From Society to Heaven in a Chip* (New York: Harmony Books, 1999).

The previous section surveyed some of the objections to substance dualism that have led most contemporary thinkers to reject it. Property dualism (human beings are physical substances who possess nonphysical mental properties) avoids some of the disadvantages of substance dualism, but by making the mind and self dependent on the body, it gives up the distinctive advantage of substance dualism in arguing for the possibility of immortality.

However, even if a tenable formulation of substance dualism could be found, there would be serious obstacles to a substance dualist account of survival. One obstacle results from the fact that a dualist soul is supposed to be the *subject* of our thoughts and experiences, but not *constituted* by them. The philosopher L. Nathan Oaklander explains,

> [T]he soul is not the human body . . . , and the soul is not (composed of) the thoughts or experiences that it is connected to and is the subject of. It would seem, however, that once you

> separate the thoughts, memories, experiences, and all psychological characteristics from the person, and once you separate the body from the person, then the person is nothing more than a bare particular, that is, nothing at all. (Admittedly, the Cartesian substance has a nature, i.e., it is a thinking substance, but certainly that is a nature that we all possess and so cannot alone form the basis of our *personal* identity.)[15]

Substance dualism may be able to provide for the survival of my soul, but it would not thereby provide for the survival of *me*. A more general objection is that an immaterial soul cannot be the bearer of personal identity because some aspects of personal identity are necessarily *bodily*.

> The characteristics of being handsome or grotesque, being athletic or being sedentary, having a characteristic gait, manner of speech, being kind, being loving, being thoughtful, and other defining characteristics may very well go into characterizing what it is to be me. However, such a unique set of universals cannot be separated from a particular bodily appearance and behavior.[16]

Difficulties such as these, as well as the more general failures of dualism as a theory of mind (failing to account for the systematic and sensitive correlations between changes in cognition and feeling and changes in the physical brain, and failing to suggest how mental and physical substance could possibly causally interact) have forced many thinkers to abandon dualist theories of personal survival.

PHYSICALIST SURVIVAL

As noted in the preceding section, dualism is not inextricably linked with Western religions, including Christianity. Although the narrative of the immaterial soul being borne "up" to heaven in death is very much a part of the commonsense or folk theology of some forms of Christianity, it has much less credence with theologians and other scholars. The Bible says that Jesus will return to earth and physically raise all those who have died, giving them back the bodies they lost at the end of their earthly lives. These will be the same bodies people had before. The bodies of the righteous will be transformed into a glorified state, freed from suffering and pain, and enabled to perform many of the amazing things Jesus did with his glorified body. The apostle Paul speaks in 1 Corinthians 15:35–42 of a "celestial body":

> But some man will say, How are the dead raised up? and with what body do they come? Thou fool, that which thou sowest is not quickened, except it die: And that which thou sowest, thou sowest not that body that shall be, but bare grain, it may chance of wheat, or of some other grain: But God giveth it a body as it hath pleased him, and to every seed his own body. All flesh is not the same flesh: but there is one kind of flesh of men, another flesh of beasts, another of fishes, and another of birds. There are also celestial bodies, and bodies terrestrial: but the glory of the celestial is one, and the glory of the terrestrial is another. . . . It is sown in corruption; it is raised in incorruption.

The difficulties with dualism have prompted many thinkers to turn afresh to the nondualist heritage of Western religions, and to develop theories of resurrection and immortality based on physical survival. What are the prospects for such theories?

Physicalist survival has been fleshed out in several different ways. One scenario is *re-creation:* at some point after death, God re-creates one's physical body and restores its consciousness. The re-creationist scenario faces several objections. First, there is the question of what the re-created resurrection body is made out of. We normally think that for an object O at t_1 to be the same object at a later time t_2, there must be some kind of continuity in the material stuff of which O is composed at t_1 and t_2. Presumably the material of the resurrection body is not immediately "recycled" from the corpse, since we know that corpses decay where they are left. But if the resurrection body is created only much later, then the particles of which it is composed will have dispersed, and may have been destroyed or incorporated into other objects or other person's bodies. Another problem with re-creationism is captured in John Locke's observation that "one thing cannot have two beginnings of existence."[17] The temporal gap in between the dissolution of the earthly body and the creation anew of a resurrection body seems to violate Locke's condition.

An ingenious alternative scenario has been defended by Christian philosopher Peter van Inwagen:

> It is of course true that men apparently cease to exist, those who are cremated, for example. But it contradicts nothing in the creeds to suppose that this is not what really happens, and that God preserves our corpses contrary to all appearance. . . . Perhaps at the moment of each man's death, God removes his corpse and replaces it with a simulacrum which is what is burned or rots. Or perhaps God is not quite so wholesale as this: perhaps He removes for "safekeeping" only the "core person"—the brain and central nervous system—or even some special part of it. These are details.[18]

Although it is logically coherent, van Inwagen's proposal is hard to swallow for those who would expect God to be above "body snatching."

A related proposal has God engaged in *body splitting* rather than body snatching. At the very last instant of life, each simple particle of a dying person's body divides into two different simple particles. One forms part of the corpse and the other forms part of the resurrection body.[19] Crucially, the new body is not merely a *replica*; it is the *same body* as the old body. As with re-creationism, the question arises whether there is sufficient continuity between the material of the resurrection body and the material of the body at death. Defenders of the body-splitting scenario argue that this continuity is not necessary so long as "the right causal connection" is obtained between them. What this causal connection might be, however, is not entirely clear. A recent survey of various physicalist survival theories concludes that "if you are a physicalist who wants to affirm survival, van Inwagen's body-switching scenario is still the only game in town."[20]

It is also important to note that for the most part, discussions of scenarios such as the above have been concerned with whether it is *possible* that God (understood as omnipotent) brings about bodily survival through the processes imagined. They have not presented any compelling reasons to believe that these processes *actually occur.* Beyond the questions of survival, there are also questions about where persons' continued existence occurs and what goes on there. Popular notions of Heaven and Hell suppose that persons surviving death exist in an otherworldly place (perhaps unconnected with our space-time or "outside" space-time altogether). Others believe that the afterlife will be located here but in another time. Given either vision of paradise, skeptics may be left wondering:

> How old will children be? Will they grow up in heaven? Will anyone age in heaven? Will cripples be made whole? Will the blind see and the deaf hear? Will the insane become sane? Will the aged become young? Will some or all of earth's animals be there? What about the material things that we occasionally love: a house, a ship, a city? The fields you roamed as a child?[21]

WORLDLY GOODS

Suppose that there is no reason for hope in "the life of the world to come." What then about the life of this world? What is the point to learning, working, struggling, loving, and growing old if your consciousness will be completely extinguished in a few short years? Shakespeare's *Macbeth* gives famous expression to the feeling that the finite life is absurd and futile:

> To-morrow, and to-morrow, and to-morrow,
> Creeps in this petty pace from day to day,
> To the last syllable of recorded time;
> And all our yesterdays have lighted fools
> The way to dusty death. Out, out, brief candle!
> Life's but a walking shadow; a poor player,
> That struts and frets his hour upon the stage,
> And then is heard no more: it is a tale
> Told by an idiot, full of sound and fury,
> Signifying nothing.[22]

Is this despairing attitude an appropriate response to the fact (if it is a fact) of mortality? More precisely, is earthly life of no value if it is not part of an eternal life (or at least is it of intolerably less value than it would be if it were part of an eternal life)?

One way to approach this question is to consider what goods a mortal life might lack in comparison to an everlasting afterlife. At the very least, a conception of personal survival supposes that in the afterlife we are self-aware, we think and know certain things, and we relate to other persons. If these activities have been made part of the world to come, then presumably they are not without intrinsic worth. Yet we also engage in these activities in our earthly existence. If love, friendship, and knowledge are goods in the heavens, why would they not also be goods on earth? No doubt, worldly goods can be experienced only temporarily. But why would something be less valuable *just because it comes to an end*? As Bertrand Russell observed, "Happiness is nonetheless true happiness because it must come to an end, nor do thought and love lose their value because they are not everlasting."[23]

One argument against this conclusion draws on an analogy to works of music, drama, or literature. The significance of any given event within such works is determined by the larger context of the piece as a whole, including how it begins and, especially, how it ends. Perhaps the same is true of a biological life, such that the significance of the goods within it depends on how things turn out in the end. However, even if one accepted this premise, one would be begging the question to insist that eternal communal with God is the only resolution that could preserve the value of what has gone before. After all, all the best works of music, drama, and literature stop well short of eternity. So, the argument stands in need of development.[24]

The humanist need not deny that the lives of countless millions of people have been so lacking in worldly goods, and so filled with deprivation, fear, loneliness, pain, grief, and failure that they would not choose to live them again, were they presented with the opportunity to do so. In this respect, the hope for a better world takes on tremendous power. But is not clear that afterworldly schemes have the advantage in addressing the crushing reality of awful lives. Leave to one side the fact that in many religious traditions, what awaits us can be far, far worse than any hell on earth. Still, some serious philosophical difficulties attend the notion that suffering in the here-and-now could be outweighed or "made whole" by bliss in the beyond. The following sort of example is suggestive: If I desecrate and blow up the tombstone of your grandfather, but then apologize genuinely and replace it with an exact replica, have I "made up for" the grievous wrong you suffered?[25]

Neither must the humanist deny that everlasting goods, were they available to us, might be *preferable* to temporary goods. If we can find satisfaction and significance in a life of finite goods, then perhaps we would find *infinitely more* satisfaction and significance were that life never to come to an end. (It is sometimes protested that an everlasting life would be "dull." But surely that depends on what kind of life it is. After all, a very short life of the wrong sort can be dull. Some theologians have argued that a life could be worth living forever if it were characterized by continual progress that asymptotically approaches its goals over an eternity.[26]) Additionally, there may be qualitatively special goods that can only be enjoyed in the afterlife (just as there may be special goods that could only be enjoyed in a mortal, bodily existence, as discussed above).

In this sense, a naturalistic humanist view provides cold comfort, for the affirmation of worldly goods only sharpens the sting of death, which irrevocably removes one from the possibility of experiencing them. Indeed, rationalist and humanist thinkers themselves don't shy away from contemplating this tragic conclusion, often taking pride in what they regard as their courage to fully countenance the finality of death. The following passage from Russell's *Why I Am Not a Christian* is well known:

> That man is the product of causes which had no prevision of the end they were achieving; that his origin, his growth, his hopes and fears, his loves and his beliefs, are but the outcome of accidental collocations of atoms; that no fire, no heroism, no intensity of thought and feeling, can preserve an individual life beyond the grave; that all the labors of the ages, all the devotion, all the inspiration, all the noonday brightness of human genius, are destined to extinction in the vast death of the solar system, and that the whole temple of man's achievement must inevitably be buried beneath the debris of a universe in ruins—all these things, if not quite beyond dispute, are yet so nearly certain that no philosophy which rejects them can hope to stand.[27]

So, the humanist affirmation of everyday life is not necessarily the claim that an infinite life is *no better than* a finite life; it can be the more modest claim that a finite life is *good enough*. That is, the value of life's goods is not diminished by the mere fact that they are transitory, and there are many mortal lives worth living.

CONCLUSION

In light of the difficulties for dualist and physicalist accounts of personal survival, the humanist stance on life after death is extremely plausible. It is difficult to avoid affirming the worth of (at least some) the things of this world, even if one believes in an afterworld.

SECTION 2.4

Bad to the Bone? The Moral Status of Humanity

For most people throughout most of human history, being born was dangerous enough, given the high rates of infant mortality. Remarkably, each of the major religious traditions has claimed that even apart from the ravages of disease and malnutrition, another kind of danger faces every newborn. We naturally suffer from spiritual defects or deficiencies from which we must be saved if we are to gain freedom, or self-knowledge, or escape from torment. The major religions have been *salvationist*, albeit in very different ways. Furthermore, Christianity and other theistic religious traditions have held that ultimately we cannot help ourselves or each other. Our savior can only be divine.

A humanist understanding of human nature rejects all of this. It maintains that if humanity needs rescuing, it is not from any inherent moral failure. Nor must humanity look outside itself for rescue. In sum:

4. Humanity is not fallen by nature and is capable of moral self-improvement.

To the modern ear, something about the humanist idea sounds correct. And yet, daily experience and history make apparent that human life is full of indifference, pride, malice, greed, cruelty, hatred, rape, torture, apartheid, ethnic cleansing, terrorism, slavery, war, and genocide. Given all that we now know, which makes more sense: humanism or salvationism?

To address this question, we first survey and assess the plausibility of religious views on corruption and salvation, paying particular attention to certain readings of the Christian doctrine of the Fall, which historically have been most insistent on our basic wretchedness. We will then critically evaluate the humanist idea and consider its affinity with certain religious views. As we will see, the humanist idea has taken different forms in different times and places, and some are much less tenable than others.

HUMANITY AND EVIL IN RELIGIOUS TRADITION

Historically, Christianity is exceptional for the severity of its views on human corruption. The story of the Fall—the primal sin of Adam and Eve and their expulsion from Paradise and the resulting human condition of wickedness, toil, suffering, and mortality—opens the Hebrew bible. The apostle Paul's reflections on the story of the Fall linked the event with the entry of sin into the world. St. Augustine (354–430) fleshed out Paul's narrative by developing the doctrine of Original Sin, the idea that the sinful tendencies as well as the stain of guilt resulting from the Fall are passed by hereditary transmission from generation to generation (the term "original sin" was coined by second-century theologian Tertullian). The resulting view that eventually came to prevail in Christendom for over a millennium, which we will call the "doctrine of the Fall," can be summed up in the following claims:

1. We inherit a condition of sinfulness.
2. We are by our nature morally blameworthy for our condition.

Competing Christian Understandings of the Fall

Although the Augustinian doctrine of the Fall of Man enjoyed a long period of orthodoxy, a variety of alternative accounts have coexisted with it throughout the history of Christianity. Theologians such as Pelagius (fourth–fifth centuries, C.E.) and Julian of Eclanum (fifth century, C.E.) resisted the idea. Pelagius argued that the effects of original sin do not prevent individuals from freely choosing good over evil and attaining salvation through their efforts. Although Pelagianism was condemned at the Council of Ephesus in 431, its influence continued in a moderated movement now known as "semi-Pelagianism," which in turn was condemned in 529. Nevertheless, a strong Augustinian stance was never adopted in the East.

In the Middle Ages, St. Thomas Aquinas defended a view of human nature that was slightly more favorable than Augustine's. Aquinas held that the Fall had deprived Adam of the supernatural gifts he initially possessed, leaving to his descendants only their natural faculties and appetites. This view was affirmed at the Council of Trent, in opposition to the ideas of Luther and Calvin.

Once the doctrine is plainly spelled out, it becomes clear that there is a fundamental conflict between these two points. The doctrine asserts that our sinfulness is in some way inevitable and at the same time asserts that we are accountable for it. But it seems that in any sensible moral system, people cannot be held morally accountable for things that they could not have avoided. Even one of the doctrine's most loyal defenders, postliberal theologian Reinhold Niebuhr, points out the apparent paradox.

> The Christian doctrine of sin in its classical form offends both rationalists and moralists by maintaining the seemingly absurd position that man sins inevitably and by a fateful necessity but that he is nevertheless to be held responsible for actions which are prompted by an ineluctable fate.[28]

In the traditional version, our wickedness is inevitable because it is an unavoidable consequence of something that has already occurred: Adam and Eve's disobedience to God. Yet it is clearly unjust to blame us for deeds that were not our own. What could we have done about it? The issue would perhaps be more complicated if we had *knowingly benefited* from the original parents' wrongdoing. But apparently we did not benefit. The wrongdoing of Adam and Eve only brought on a life that is short and full of toil and suffering. Even if the children of Eve had been benefited by her wrongdoing, it is not the case that each of them necessarily is aware of it. So, it could not be maintained that they are all somehow complicit in the sin.

Furthermore, it is not at all clear that Adam and Eve did wrong in the first place, even in the scriptural account's own terms. At least on any straightforward reading, they had been created so as to lack knowledge of good and evil. Hence, they lacked the competence to act and make judgments on the basis of considerations of good and bad, right and wrong. In short, Adam and Eve were not moral agents. But only agents are morally accountable. When your cat makes a mess, you might punish it in hopes of changing its future behavior, but you would not hold it morally blameworthy. It knows not what it does, morally speaking. Similarly, it is unclear how God could sensibly blame Adam and Eve, let alone their distant progeny.

The philosopher Scott MacDonald has discussed a similar difficulty with the notion of "primal sin," also found in Augustine's writings.[29] Because the instance of primal sin is the moment at which evil enters a wholly good creation, there could be nothing about the primal sinner himself that prepares the deed. The question therefore arises how the primal sin could really be *his* sin, for which he should be punished. MacDonald answers that primal sin results when the agent carelessly neglects the reasons he has that would lead him to avoid sin, but acts on some other reasons instead. The problem with this answer is that it violates the condition that the primal sin is not prepared by a prior evil feature of the sinner. Reasons relevant to avoiding sin are the weightiest of moral reasons, and presumably a disposition making one insensitive to the force of one's weightiest moral reasons is an evil disposition.

Troubled by difficulties like these, some modern Christians have abandoned the doctrine of the Fall. Others have sought alternative interpretations. Contemporary theologians such as Karl Barth, Paul Tillich, and Niebuhr have rejected Augustine's idea that sin is transmitted by procreation. Instead they claim that it is transmitted through an already corrupt *society.* But the paradox remains. If sin is inevitably transmitted—socially or not—how could we be accountable for it?

A popular reinterpretation of the scriptural story attempts to avoid the problem by claiming that the real lesson of the biblical tale is that sin is *freely chosen* and we must be held morally accountable for our choices. But if we choose to sin freely, then we must be capable of refraining from sin. In that case, we are not strictly bound and condemned to sinfulness. Why should the mere capacity to do wrong make one "fallen"? This attempt to preserve the doctrine of the Fall would save blameworthiness, but at the expense of inherent sinfulness.

In fact, rather than pointing to our depravity, this reinterpretation affirms what some would call our dignity and worth, for it implies that we are self-directed beings whose choices have moral significance. The revised understanding of humanity's relationship to sin and God makes sense precisely because it does not regard humanity as essentially corrupt.

Monotheism and Human Dignity

A saying attributed to Rabbi Burim points out how there are two sides to the understanding of human nature common to Christianity, Judaism, and Islam. People should have two pockets in their coats. One should contain the Talmudic saying, "For my sake was the world created." The other should contain the verse (from the book of Genesis), "I am but dust and ashes."

It seems that the doctrine of the Fall cannot escape the dilemma. Either sin is inevitable and so we are not accountable for it, or we are accountable for sin, in which case it is not inevitable. To accept either option is abandon an essential element of the doctrine of the Fall, and so to reject the doctrine altogether.

Although other religious traditions do not embrace the Christian doctrine of the Fall, most do teach that humans are in some way fundamentally defective by nature. In Hindu religions, for example, our defect is our ignorance of the true nature of reality. We falsely believe in the everyday world of appearances and sense perceptions, when in fact only the real thing is the transcendent and unitary "Absolute." The underlying dynamic is the cycle of karma and rebirth. Karma is the strict law of consequence with regard to action, according to which every good and bad action will have a corresponding good or bad consequence that will surface either in the present life or in a future life. Karma drives the cycle of rebirth, in which the individual self or soul (*atman*) occupies a series of beings and lives (including animals, humans, spirits) before reaching *nirvana,* where worldly desires and attachments are extinguished and the *atman* unites with the divine.

The Indian religions share with the Christian religion the view that in this life we are suffering from the consequences of some previous actions. But in this case, they are not the actions of the original parents. We suffer because of the actions of our own selves or souls, taken in previous lives. This view avoids the dilemma faced by the doctrine of the Fall. However, it runs into deep metaphysical problems of its own, for it is hard to understand what creates the required continuity between lives. What could link a now-deceased goat with me in such a way that we could say that I *used to be* that goat?

The traditional answer is that the goat had the same soul as me, where a soul is understood as a special substance that is unlike normal physical substances and yet occupies and interacts with bodies. That is a version of substance dualism, the theory of the mind that we found philosophically and scientifically lacking in a previous section. Buddhism also posits a karmically controlled continuity between lives but, unlike Hinduism, it denies any coherent soul or self that exists across incarnations. As such, it escapes the problems of dualism. At the same time, Buddhism leaves it totally obscure how there could be any connection between successive lives. If there is no shared substance or self underlying my experiences or the goat's experiences, what do they have in common? Thus, the Indian religions fail to provide a plausible account of our supposedly essential metaphysical ailment.

EVOLUTION AND HUMAN NATURE

Historically, many of those in the West who rejected the doctrine of the Fall reached a quite opposite conclusion about human nature. In chapter 1 we mentioned the broad humanist theme of the value, dignity, and rights of individual persons. For many humanists, especially the eighteenth-century Enlightenment humanists, this has meant that by nature we are essentially good and rational. Our problems are the product of contingent circumstances external to our nature such as poverty, tyranny, superstition, and error. Insofar as these circumstances can be removed by the correct application of reason and science to the human condition, evil and irrationality can be eliminated.

The Enlightenment thinkers embraced this optimistic view of humanity not only because it energized their humanitarian campaign to combat religious and political oppression and to improve the deplorable conditions of manual labor, education, welfare, health care, and prisons in their day. It is also made sense given their theories of our origins. The Enlightenment critics were mostly deists who attacked the traditional Christian notion of a personal, loving, creator God but believed that we had been perfectly constructed either by a rational, watchmaker deity or by a benevolent Nature. Adam Smith believed that everything in nature is "calculated to promote the same great end, the order of the world, and the perfection and happiness of human nature."[30] While human society can introduce mistakes into the system, Nature's products are optimally designed.

Stephen Jay Gould and geneticist Richard Lewontin have called this attitude toward nature "panglossian," after Dr. Pangloss, the satirical character in Voltaire's novel *Candide* who always insists that "all that is, is for the best." The panglossian believes that we are optimally designed. Unfortunately for the Enlightenment deists, the panglossian understanding of human nature has not survived the progress of biological and psychological science.

The problem is that our nature is a product of evolution. As a design procedure, evolution is far from optimal. First, it is a nonrational, nonteleological process that can only engineer new models by tinkering with previous models. Second, the ultimate design criterion under natural selection is beating everyone else at reproducing oneself—by any means necessary. So even when a trait is a success from an evolutionary point of view, we should hardly expect it to be a success from a moral point of view.

Although natural selection acting over time is the principal explanation of the nature of living things, biologists recognize a number of additional, nonselective processes that also have been at work. To take just one example, sometimes a trait becomes part of a species because it is a byproduct of a trait favored by selection. In a phenomenon known as pleiotropy, a single gene may have more than one effect. Selection for one effect also saddles the species with another, which can be adaptively neutral or even harmful. The same gene that causes the blood disease sickle-cell anemia can also cause increased resistance to malaria. Inheriting both of the sickle-cell alleles can be fatal, but inheriting only one can be beneficial. As long as the average benefits are significant enough, natural selection can favor traits with harmful byproducts, even those that doom countless unlucky individuals.

Because it results from a process influenced by such nonselective mechanisms, human nature includes numerous arbitrary, redundant, nonfunctional, and even dysfunctional features. Furthermore, as we discuss shortly, even features that have been well crafted by natural selection are often for that very reason suboptimal in other, more disturbing, ways.

Before moving on, it is worth observing two other important ways that evolutionary theory has forced us to rethink older views of human nature. First, pre-Darwinian theories of human nature were typically essentialist. **Essentialism** (about a creature's nature) is the view that every individual creature is an instance of a general type, which can be defined in terms of certain essential properties. Just as bread knives have essential properties—a handle and a sharp blade—so do living things. To explain a being's nature, then, is to explain its essence. Most famously, many have believed that the essence of human nature is our rationality. On this view of human biology, an insane or

The Human Eye: Wonder or Blunder?

It is often said that our eyes are marvels of biological engineering. And indeed, even reading the words on this page is no small feat for a clump of cells. Nevertheless, as acclaimed biologist George Williams points out at length in his book *The Pony Fish's Glow,*

> not all features of the human eye make functional sense. Some are arbitrary. To begin at the grossest level, is there a good functional reason for having two eyes? Why not one or three or some other number? Yes, there is a reason: two is better than one because they permit stereoscopic vision and the gathering of three-dimensional information about the environment. But three would be better still. We could have our stereoscopic view of what lies ahead plus another eye to warn us of what might be sneaking up behind. . . . When we examine each eye from behind, we find that there are six tiny muscles that move it so that it can point in different directions. Why six? Properly spaced and coordinated, three would suffice, just as three is an adequate number of legs for a photographer's tripod. The paucity of eyes and excess of their muscles seem to have no functional explanation.
>
> And some eye features are not merely arbitrary but clearly dysfunctional. The nerve fibers from the retinal rods and cones extend not inward toward the brain but outward toward the chamber of the eye and source of light. They have to gather into a bundle, the optic nerve, inside the eye, and exit via a hole in the retina. Even though the obstructing layer is microscopically thin, some light is lost from having to pass through the layer of nerve fibers and ganglia and especially the blood vessels that serve them. The eye is blind where the optic nerve exits through its hole. The loose application of the retina to the underlying sclera makes the eye vulnerable to the serious medical problem of detached retina. It would not be if the nerve fibers passed through the sclera and formed the optic nerve behind the eye. This functionally sensible arrangement is in fact what is found in the eye of a squid and other mollusks . . . , but our eyes, and those of all other vertebrates, have the functionally stupid upside-down orientation of the retina.*

* George C. Williams, *The Pony Fish's Glow and Other Clues to Plan and Purpose in Nature* (New York: Basic Books, 1997), 9–10.

mentally handicapped person is like a dull knife: a knife, but somehow not quite as much of a knife as it could be.

Darwinian biology utterly undermined essentialism because it showed that what is real and important in the generation of life are not the so-called types of organisms, but the individual organisms themselves. If one looks at any actual species, including our own, one finds an enormous bell curve of genetic, structural, and behavioral diversity. There is absolutely no justification for singling out one point on the curve as the "essence" of the species, thereby labeling the rest as deviations from a norm. In evolution, deviation *is* the norm. And it is this actual endless variation among individuals that fuels natural selective change. The notion of a species essence is an attempt to force the overwhelming diversity of nature into a convenient box. Post-Darwinians know better. Once again, evolution is no panglossian.

So if we don't have an essence, what do we have? Some philosophers argue that we should throw away the very concept of human nature along with the notion of a species essence. But most biologists refurbish the notion of a nature by equating it with "species-typical traits," or "traits that have been fixed in the population." In this way, they might say that having two eyes is a trait that is part of our nature, without denying the real interpersonal variation in chemical composition, color, shape, position, and function, or implying that someone born without two eyes is somehow not a "real" human.

Another ancient theme in theories of human nature identifies our nature with what is "innate," "instinctual," or "inborn," in contrast to the "acquired," "conditioned," or "learned." The dichotomy is now called "nature versus nurture." The truth is that in the case of a great many animals (ourselves especially), nature *is* nurture. Because primates specialize in an ultrasocial way of life, our patterns of learning and socialization—like language acquisition and imitation of parents and siblings—are as much a part of our nature as blink reflexes and digestive enzymes. The contemporary biological understanding of human beings does not answer the question, "Which is more important, nature or nurture?" It rejects the question as being based on a false dichotomy. So, when biologically informed thinkers comment on human nature, they are not just talking about what is genetic and "fixed." They are also talking about what is cultural and malleable.

HUMAN, ALL TOO HUMAN?

The latest attempt to construct a biologically informed theory of human nature comes from the emerging field of evolutionary psychology. Evolutionary psychology is a research program that attempts to combine the tools of evolutionary theory with the tools of cognitive psychology, a field that focuses on mental "information-processing" devices. Evolutionary psychologists claim that the mind, like other organs, has been shaped by natural selection in response to cognitive tasks—such as recognizing facial expressions or outsmarting adversaries—that were adaptively important to our distant evolutionary ancestors.

The portrait of human psychology emerging from such research gives important new roles to sociality, coalition-building, and genuinely altruistic behaviors. But it also includes numerous features that are much less welcome from a moral point of view. Our evolutionary history appears to have been characterized by intense competition among small groups. This environment has probably endowed us with a xenophobic, "in-group, out-group" psychology. For example, in social psychology experiments that divide people into arbitrarily chosen groups to complete some collective task, they almost effortlessly identify strongly with their side and feel rivalry and unwarranted antagonism toward the other.

On the other hand, highly elaborate status hierarchies have characterized life within human groups. Constructed out of cues as subtle as bodily comportment or voice modulation in conversation, perceptions of "social dominance" have gone a long way to determining one's basic prospects in life. Today people everywhere are extremely sensitive to status perceptions, and anxiety, anguish, rage, and violence can often result. The single greatest factor in homicide worldwide is altercations between strangers or acquaintances (mostly men) stemming from otherwise trivial inconveniences or insults that caused someone social humiliation.

Given an evolutionary history in which coping with intergroup antagonism and negotiating social hierarchies were as important to survival and reproduction as shelter and food, we would expect natural selection to have molded our psychology in ways that now lead to xenophobia and status-driven aggression. If so, then our nature leaves much to be desired, morally speaking.

This conclusion should not be surprising, given the nature of the process that produced us. Selection favored individuals and groups who were for or against each other when and wherever their reproductive interests demanded. T. H. Huxley, a humanist and early champion of Darwinism, noted:

> [T]he practice of that which is ethically best—what we call goodness or virtue—involves a course of conduct which, in all respects, is opposed to that which leads to success in the cosmic struggle for existence. In place of ruthless self-assertion it demands self-restraint; in place of thrusting aside, or treading down, all competitors, it requires that the individual shall not merely respect, but shall help his fellows; its influence is directed, not so much to the survival of the fittest, as to the fitting of as many as possible to survive.[31]

Huxley's point is that the evolutionary dynamic of competition for reproductive supremacy by any means necessary is fundamentally opposed to some of our most central moral values and social norms.

Recent research has also shown that evolution has not equipped us with optimally rational minds either. For one thing, without fairly intensive training, we are awful at even basic reasoning about probability and evidence.

The lesson of evidence such as this is that we are neither perfectly put together, nor perfectly morally good and rational by nature. As Darwin himself exclaimed, "What a book a Devil's Chaplain might write on the clumsy, wasteful, blundering low and horridly cruel works of nature!" On this point, contemporary humanism parts company with Enlightenment humanism, rejecting its theory of human nature as empirically untenable. But then isn't contemporary humanism in agreement with the doctrine of the Fall after all?[32] Not if we are careful to observe two crucial distinctions.

First, the Fall says that we are heir to an inherently moral condition: sin. We are not just defective. We are damned. There is nothing in principle that we alone can do about that because we are incapable of altering the moral order itself. On the naturalist account of evil, however, we exhibit certain species-typical psychological conditions, which are at root causal (not spiritual or supernatural) conditions. And there is every reason to think that we can alter and change the causal order. This is even clearer once we set aside the phony nature-nurture dichotomy and realize that much of our nature is open to—indeed, is made up of—socialization. Biology is not destiny. Just ask the millions of women and men who have lived fulfilling and meaningful lives without ever procreating. Thus, unlike the doctrine of the Fall, the naturalist account holds out some reasonable hope that many of our defects can be improved by human effort.

Second, recall that the crux of the doctrine of the Fall is that we are morally blameworthy for our inherited faults. On a humanist view, there are aspects of our nature that are imperfect and even morally bad, which we ought to and perhaps can counteract. They are morally bad in the specific sense that the world would be morally better were we to not have them. That is not to say that we are *morally blameworthy* for having them. Humanism acknowledges that we are imperfect by nature, but denies that we are culpable for it. We are born in need of work, not redemption.

Among religious traditions, the humanist understanding comes closest to Judaism and Confucianism. In the mainstream Jewish reading, the Fall of Adam does not result from a fundamental fault, and emphasis is placed on the knowledge and opportunity thereby gained by humanity. Jewish thinkers have long claimed that human nature is characterized by two contradictory dispositions: "evil inclination" and "good inclination." Evil inclinations are connected to our natural impulses. As such, they cannot be totally eliminated without also eliminating essential human functions such as marriage and raising children. Instead, the evil inclinations must be channeled and kept in check by proper study and observance of the Torah. We inherit inclinations to do wrong. But unlike in the doctrine of the Fall, we do not inherit blameworthiness for a primal sin.

The Confucian tradition is divided on the essential goodness or badness of humanity. But the most influential interpretation comes from Mencius, a fourth-century B.C.E. writer who argued that the seeds of virtue reside originally in every human heart. By carefully cultivating these seeds, everyone is capable of attaining moral excellence.

CONCLUSION

Many salvationist religions claim that humanity needs rescuing from an essentially fallen or defective state. It was argued that some of these salvationist claims involve problematic views on moral agency, responsibility, the soul, and the person. The humanist idea denies the reality of the Fall and the necessity for external salvation. Humanists have historically differed about our natural imperfection, however. A post-Darwinian interpretation belies Enlightenment optimism about human nature. Even still, it suggests that our suboptimal nature is not beyond our control and that we are capable of self-improvement. Most importantly, we are not born into blame. On this view, we may be tangled, but we are not fallen.

SUMMARY

Humanist ideas about human nature include the anthropocentric notion that we are superior to the rest of nature in our value, powers, and place in the world; the physicalist or property dualist notion that we are physical systems lacking immaterial souls; the notion that this earthly life is all there is and not without value; and the notion that we are not fallen by nature but are capable of moral self-improvement. Recent intellectual and scientific developments have undermined the credibility of the anthropocentric notion, while increasing the credibility of the others.

STUDY QUESTIONS

1. Describe cosmological anthropocentrism and one objection to it.
2. Describe biological anthropocentrism and one objection to it
3. Describe psychological anthropocentrism and one objection to it.
4. What is teleology?
5. In what ways is the humanist tradition anthropocentric?
6. In the philosophy of mind, what is qualitative content? Cite some examples.

7. Describe substance dualism (and contrast it with property dualism). Summarize the scientific evidence against substance dualism. Summarize the mind-body problem in connection with dualism.
8. Describe eliminative physicalism and one objection to it.
9. Describe reductive physicalism and explain the objection from variable realization.
10. Describe nonreductive physicalism (distinguishing type-reduction and token-reduction) and one objection to it.
11. Distinguish personal survival from other sorts of "immortality."
12. What is the philosophical problem of personal identity?
13. Explain a substance dualist theory of personal survival and one objection to that theory.
14. Explain a physicalist theory of personal survival and one objection to that theory.
15. Contrast the dualist and physicalist elements of Christianity.
16. State the traditional doctrine of the Fall and some alternative interpretations of it.
17. State in your own words the paradox of inherent sinfulness, as articulated by Reinhold Niebuhr.
18. What is panglossianism in Gould and Lewontin's sense?
19. How was Enlightenment humanism panglossian? How is contemporary evolutionary theory nonpanglossian?
20. Contrast an evolutionary biological perspective on human failings with a salvationist perspective.

DISCUSSION QUESTIONS

1. Does evolutionary theory state that living things are produced "by chance"? Defend your answer.
2. Suppose we discover a species of primate with all of the important human capacities such as language use, abstract conceptual thought, reasoning, and so on, but in a more highly developed state than in humans. How should this discovery change the way we think about natural history and humanity's place in it, if at all?
3. Could self-awareness have emerged *gradually* in the course of human evolution? Are there *degrees* of self-awareness?
4. Is humanism necessarily speciesist?
5. Are there versions of theism that do not imply anthropocentrism?
6. Formulate some hypotheses about why substance dualism is so common crossculturally.
7. If some form of physicalism were true, would people be less valuable or worthy of respect, morally speaking? Can you owe moral obligations to something with no soul?
8. Is it possible that everyone besides you is a *zombie*—a person who has no qualitative consciousness but behaves indistinguishably from those who do? How could you determine whether or not another person is a zombie?
9. Does a chess program understand what it is doing? What about the robots in the *Star Wars* films? Is this the right question to ask?

10. Is God an immaterial mind? Does theism entail the truth of substance dualism?
11. Think of five activities you find highly worthwhile or enjoyable. Would their value to you change if you could only do them once a month? Once a year? Once in your entire life? Explain.
12. Describe who you are by listing ten characteristics. To what extent could you possess these characteristics if you were a disembodied spirit?
13. Do you think God could be a body snatcher in the way that Peter van Inwagen supposes? Why might God use this method of preserving our bodies after death rather than another?
14. Suppose I borrow a pair of your shoes and accidentally ruin them. If I buy you an identical replacement pair, have I made things right? Now imagine that you are brutally killed by a burglar in your home. If I miraculously restore your life and sufficiently punish your killer, would that make things right? Is this the way "divine justice" would operate? Why or why not?
15. Is the belief in an afterlife a necessary part of religion?
16. If someone is guilty of being separated from God, how serious is this offense? Does it deserve punishment, and if so, of what severity?
17. The "insanity defense" is familiar in law. Under what circumstances does one's psychological makeup morally exempt one from blameworthiness?
18. Try to construct a theory that coherently integrates a naturalistic account of evil with the theological doctrine of the Fall.
19. Can one love and respect other people if one believes the doctrine of the Fall? What if one believes in a naturalistic account of evil?
20. Could there be a person who is wholly free yet never commits a morally evil act? Could a human being be such a person?

FIELD PROBLEM

Identify examples of narratives in popular culture (novels, songs, movies, television programs) that contain a substance dualist model of the person.

SUGGESTIONS FOR FURTHER READING

Barkow, Jerome H., Leda Cosmides, and John Tooby, eds. *The Adapted Mind: Evolutionary Psychology and the Generation of Culture*. New York: Oxford University Press, 1992.

Blackmore, Susan. *Dying to Live*. Amherst, N.Y.: Prometheus Books, 1993.

Churchland, Paul. *The Engine of Reason, the Seat of the Soul*. Cambridge, Mass.: MIT Press, 1989.

Davies, Paul, ed. *The New Physics*. Cambridge: Cambridge University Press, 1989.

Dennett, Daniel C. *Darwin's Dangerous Idea: Evolution and the Meanings of Life*. New York: Simon & Schuster, 1995.

Edwards, Paul, ed. *Immortality*. New York: Macmillan, 1992.

Feenstra, Ronald, and Cornelius Plantinga, Jr., eds. *Trinity, Incarnation, and Atontement*. Notre Dame, Ind.: University of Notre Dame Press, 1990.

Gould, Stephen Jay. *Wonderful Life: The Burgess Shale and the Nature of History*. New York: Norton, 1989.
Guttenplan, Samuel, ed. *A Companion to the Philosophy of Mind*. Oxford: Basil Blackwell, 1994.
Hart, W. D. *The Engines of the Soul*. Cambridge: Cambridge University Press, 1988.
Hick, John. *Death and Eternal Life*. New York: Harper and Row, 1976.
Kim, Jaegwon. *Supervenience and Mind: Selected Philosophical Essays*. Cambridge: Cambridge University Press, 1993.
Kitcher, Philip. *Vaulting Ambition: Sociobiology and the Quest for Human Nature.* Cambridge, Mass.: MIT Press, 1985.
Lewontin, R. C. *Biology as Ideology.* New York: HarperCollins, 1991.
Matthews, Gareth B., ed. *The Augustinian Tradition*. Berkeley: University of California Press, 1998.
Noonan, Harold. *Personal Identity.* London: Routledge & Kegan Paul, 1989.
Pagels, Elaine. *Adam, Eve, and the Serpent*. New York: Random House, 1988.
Perry, John. *Personal Identity and Immortality*. Indianapolis: Hackett, 1979.
Quinn, Philip L. "Sin and Original Sin." In *A Companion to Philosophy of Religion,* ed. Philip L. Quinn and Charles Taliaferro. Oxford: Basil Blackwell, 1997.
Searle, John. *The Rediscovery of the Mind*. Cambridge, Mass.: MIT Press, 1992.
Sober, Elliott, ed. *Conceptual Issues in Evolutionary Biology*. 2d ed. Cambridge, Mass.: MIT Press, 1995.
Stich, Stephen. *From Folk Psychology to Cognitive Science: The Case against Belief.* Cambridge, Mass.: MIT Press.
Williams, George C. "Huxley's *Evolution and Ethics* in Sociobiological Perspective." *Zygon* 23 (1988): 383–438.
Williams, George C. *Natural Selection: Domains, Levels, and Challenges.* New York: Oxford University Press, 1992.
Williams, N. P. *The Ideas of the Fall and of Original Sin.* London: Longmans, Green, 1927.

NOTES

1. Thomas Hobbes, *Leviathan,* ed. Edwin Curley (Indianapolis: Hackett, 1994), 3.
2. John T. McNeill, ed., *Calvin: Institutes of the Christian Religion* (Philadelphia: Westminster Press, 1960), 186.
3. Carl Sagan, *The Dragons of Eden: Speculations on the Evolution of Human Intelligence* (New York: Random House, 1977).
4. From an interview with Stephen Jay Gould, conducted by David Gergen, and aired on PBS's "The NewsHour with Jim Lehrer," 26 November 1996.
5. David Gergen, in an interview with Stephen Jay Gould.
6. Chondrichthyes is the biological classification that includes cartilaginous fish such as sharks and rays.
7. Paul Taylor, "The Ethics of Respect for Nature," *Environmental Ethics* 3 (Fall 1981): 197–218.
8. David Schmidtz, "Are All Species Created Equal?" *Journal of Applied Philosophy* 15, no. 1 (1998): 57–68.
9. See Gerald M. Levitt, *The Turk, Chess Automaton* (Jefferson, N.C.: McFarland, 2000).
10. See Dan Sperber, *Explaining Culture: A Naturalistic Approach* (Cambridge, Mass: Blackwell, 1996).

11. Richard Lewontin, *Human Diversity* (New York: Scientific American Books, 1984), 42.
12. See John Searle, *The Rediscovery of the Mind* (Cambridge, Mass.: MIT Press, 1992).
13. George Eliot (Mary Ann Evans), *Adam Bede* (New York: Random House, 2002), 177.
14. Charles Taylor, *Sources of the Self: The Making of the Modern Identity* (Cambridge, Mass.: Harvard University Press, 1989), 217.
15. L. Nathan Oaklander, "Personal Identity, Immortality, and the Soul," *Philo* 4, 2 (Fall/Winter 2001), 188.
16. Oaklander, "Personal Identity, Immortality, and the Soul," 191–92.
17. Quoted in William Hasker, *The Emergent Self* (Ithaca, N.Y.: Cornell University Press, 1999), 217.
18. Peter van Inwagen, "Possibility of Resurrection," in *Immortality*, ed. Paul Edwards (New York: Macmillan, 1992), 245–46.
19. Dean Zimmerman, "Compatibility of Physicalism and Survival: The 'Jumping Elevator' Model," *Faith and Philosophy* 16, 2 (1999). According to the author, there may be other ways that the bodily "fission" could take place.
20. Hasker, *The Emergent Self*, 231.
21. Martin Gardner, *The Whys of a Philosophical Scrivener* (New York: Quill, 1983), 298.
22. Act 5, Scene 5.
23. Bertrand Russell, *What I Believe: 3 Complete Essays on Religion* (1925).
24. Patrick Sherry, "Redeeming the Past," *Religious Studies* 34 (1998).
25. See Marilyn McCord Adams, *Horrendous Evils and the Goodness of God* (Ithaca, N.Y.: Cornell University Press, 1999).
26. One such theologian is Richard Swinburne. For discussion, see Jerry L. Walls, *Heaven: The Logic of Eternal Joy* (New York: Oxford University Press, 2002), 93–97.
27. Bertrand Russell, *Why I Am Not a Christian* (New York: Simon & Schuster, 1957), 107.
28. Quoted in Edward T. Oakes, "Original Sin: A Disputation," *First Things* 87 (November 1998).
29. Scott MacDonald, "Primal Sin," in *The Augustinian Tradition*, ed. Gareth B. Matthews (Berkeley: University of California Press, 1998).
30. Adam Smith, *The Theory of Moral Sentiments*, ed. D. D. Raphael and A. L. Macfie (Indianapolis, Ind.: Liberty Fund, 1984), 168.
31. T. H. Huxley, "Evolution and Ethics."
32. Philosopher Patricia A. Williams argues for such a conclusion in "Christianity and Evolutionary Ethics: Sketch Towards a Reconciliation," *Zygon* 31, 2 (June 1996).

3

Freedom and Destiny

Lewis Vaughn

Picture yourself waking up on a normal day and doing normal things in your normal way. You brush your teeth, eat breakfast, look out at the sky, grab your umbrella, and walk out the door as you always do. Throughout the day, as usual, you do a thousand other important and trivial things, making countless other decisions big and small, hardly conscious of many of these actions and very much aware of others. You act, you choose, you decide—freely, as always.

On the next day the story is much the same, except for one thing: Just under your skin at the base of your skull a tiny computer chip is humming away. You're completely unaware of the chip—and that a crazed, genius computer hacker secretly inserted it into your neck the night before to test whether the chip, his latest invention, could completely control the mind and actions of a human being. All of your actions and thoughts seem completely normal to you, and your friends believe that you are your regular self. But the hacker has succeeded in programming a set of thoughts and behaviors into your brain that he thinks you ought to have. You seem normal, but you are not.

Is there an important difference between your situation on the first day and the second day? After all, neither you nor your friends can detect any difference in you. Life goes on with hardly a ripple. However you felt on day one—contented, depressed, upbeat, distracted—is much the same way you felt on day two. Most of the things you did on day one you did on day two. What's the difference? Does it matter?

Most people would not hesitate to say that the difference is enormous and that it matters immensely. They would probably believe that the very idea of someone secretly taking over someone else's consciousness is, well, creepy. But beyond the creepiness lies a more serious issue. We all want to believe that we can make conscious choices, that these choices are *ours*, that they are somehow *up to us,* and that the choices are *real*—that we could have chosen otherwise. We want to believe, in other words, that we are free persons or—to use the philosopher's term—that we have free will. This kind of freedom is missing on day two of our scenario, and to most of us it makes all of the difference in the world.

But even more hangs on the issue of free will. The idea of moral responsibility is also at stake. Persons can be held morally responsible for what they do only if they are free in some meaningful way. That is, they can be blamed or praised only for acts over which they have control. It would make no sense, for example, to blame or praise someone whose mind had been taken over by, say, a mad scientist, a demon, or a genius computer-hacker. Their actions would not be the result of free choices but of events that are out of their hands, events that just happen to them. More down to earth, in law and in everyday life we usually distinguish between acts performed freely and those not performed freely by people who are insane, mentally impaired, or under the influence of drugs or alcohol. We would think it inappropriate, for example, to blame someone for committing violent acts after being forcefully injected with a drug that causes temporary insanity and violent behavior.

Upon such ideas about freedom and moral responsibility rest many social institutions. Our penal system, for example, is built on the principle that people are generally free to choose to abide by the law or break it. If they choose freely to commit illegal acts, they deserve to be punished. They are responsible for their actions and should be held accountable for them. This principle is at the root of current controversies about the state-sanctioned execution of the mentally handicapped.

Generally, humanists have argued for the idea that humans are free to choose what they will, though they have often disagreed on the nature of this freedom. Likewise, Christian thinkers have traditionally insisted on the existence of free will, though a few have rejected it. Most great philosophers have accepted that persons, in one way or another, can sometimes act freely. Aristotle, Thomas Aquinas, John Locke, William James, and many others have tried to find a place for free action in their concepts of persons.

But the idea that people can sometimes act freely has also been vigorously disputed by a diversity of critics on several grounds. Some claim that one fact about the universe makes free will impossible: **causal determinism**. This is the idea that every event has a cause or is *determined*. Everything that happens has a preceding cause, including your actions, so that the chain of causes stretches back into the indefinite past—out of your control. Each of your actions then is the result of causes that are not up to you. Free will evaporates. The religious version of causal determinism is **predestination**, the view that everything that happens, including human actions, is caused by God. In the West, this idea is found mainly in Christian, Judaic, and Islamic thought.

Others hold to **fatalism**, the ancient (but still popular) idea that future events happen *regardless of what we do*. Fiction is full of eerie, fatalistic tales, usually about people who try hard to prevent a dire prophecy about them from coming true—but end up right where the prophecy says they will. Oedipus was fated to kill his father and marry his mother—which he did, even though he went to great lengths to try to prevent such a tragedy.

A related notion is **logical determinism**, the view that your actions are determined by the constraints of logic. For centuries philosophers and theologians have pointed out that knowing the future (as God is said to do) seems to entail that the future is fixed. If it is fixed, then we cannot change it—it *must* happen. We must perform actions determined for us, and we cannot possibly refrain from performing them. If a being knows the future, free will is just a fantasy.

We deal with all of these challenges to free will in sections 3.1 and 3.2. In one way or another down through the centuries, humanism (as well as many other worldviews) has embraced ideas of personal freedom and autonomy. Let's see if there is any justification for this stance.

SECTION 3.1

Who Is Free? Determinism, Chance, and Freedom

There are many alleged ways that people could be unfree, but we can trace most of them to just three sources: (1) nature (the way the physical world is), (2) God (as a consequence of his power or omniscience), and (3) logic (the fundamental principles that make thought possible). If any of these freedom-robbing factors is shown to be actual, we would be forced to reject some key humanist principles, including this one:

> 5. We are not determined beings in a determined universe but are in some sense free to choose our own paths.

NATURE: DETERMINISM AND CHANCE

Science and common sense have led most people to a seemingly obvious conclusion: Every event has a cause. In other words, we believe in causal determinism. We would think it very odd if someone said that her clock had stopped working but that the event happened without a cause. We may not always know what the causes are for the events we observe, but we are nonetheless sure that there are causes. But if everything has a cause, our actions—everything we do, say, and choose—have causes, too. If every action we perform is preceded by a cause, and *that* cause (event) is preceded by a cause, and so on—the chain of causes and effects continues indefinitely. Our actions then are caused by factors out of our control that stretch back in time to before we even existed. We seem to be the way we are, and to do what we do—and have no say in any of it.

The great philosopher and psychologist William James (1842–1910) sums up causal determinism like this:

> It professes that those parts of the universe already laid down absolutely appoint and decree what the other parts shall be. The future has no ambiguous possibilities hidden in its womb: the part we call the present is compatible with only one totality. Any other future complement than the one fixed from eternity is impossible. The whole is in each and every part, and welds it with the rest into an absolute unity, an iron block, in which there can be no equivocation or shadow of turning.[1]

The famous French astronomer Pierre-Simon Laplace (1749–1827) asserts that causal determinism makes the world a great, predictable mechanism. He says that if a supermind knew all the laws of nature and all the properties of everything that exists, he or she could predict every future event—and retrodict every event that already happened. Whether you wind the mechanism forward to the future or backward to the past, every event in every moment is fixed in its proper order and can happen only one, changeless way—and our lives are just cogs in this massive apparatus.

Hard Determinism

A belief in causal determinism has led many to argue for the conclusion that free will does not exist. Those who do are called **hard determinists** because they believe that causal determinism completely rules out free will. They would assert that proposition 5 is false because we are indeed at the mercy of a determined universe.

Traditionally most hard determinists have been materialists. **Materialism** is the view that everything is made of matter. This idea can be traced back to the ancient Greeks—specifically to the cofounders of atomic theory, the philosophers Democritus (c. 460–370 B.C.E.) and Leucippus (fifth century B.C.E.). They proposed that the world is composed of tiny particles called "atoms" and that everything that happens—including human behavior—is a result of collisions between atoms. Materialism eventually became the prevailing view among seventeenth- and eighteenth-century scientists and is still attractive today to many scientifically minded people. Modern science, however, has veered away from classic materialism because of developments in physics: the discovery that matter and energy are interchangeable; the realization that some subatomic particles are not material; and the understanding that some very real things (like fields and space) are not made of matter at all. In any case, to some people it has always seemed a short step from the belief that everything is material to hard determinism.

Hard determinism, however, runs counter to some of our most deeply held beliefs based on commonsense experience. For example, we believe that people sometimes deserve our respect, praise, gratitude, disdain, resentment, blame, and the like. But if all our actions are determined—if they are caused by forces beyond our control—these attitudes would make no sense. Blaming or praising people for doing something beyond their control would make about as much sense as blaming or praising the weather.

Skinner's Determinism

Some people argue that our environment controls our behavior. The most famous determinist to take this view was the psychologist B. F. Skinner (1904–1994). He argued that our behavior is conditioned by many factors in our environment. Our actions are constantly reinforced by our surroundings so that we learn to perform certain behaviors and avoid others. Thus, according to Skinner, free will is an illusion, and if it is an illusion, we need to make some radical changes in society. For example, we should stop punishing and blaming people for bad behavior and instead manipulate the environment to reinforce appropriate behaviors and reduce unwanted behaviors. This view would take away people's responsibility for their actions. As Skinner put it:

> By questioning the control exercised by autonomous man and demonstrating the control of the environment, a science of behavior also seems to question [human] dignity and worth. [The traditional view is that a] person is responsible for his behavior, not only in the sense that he may be justly punished when he behaves badly, but also in the sense that he is to be given credit and admired for his achievements. A scientific analysis shifts the credit as well as the blame to the environment, and traditional practices can then no longer be justified.*

* B. F. Skinner, *Beyond Freedom and Dignity* (New York: Bantam, 1972), 17, 19.

This conflict between hard determinism and our commonsense beliefs raises doubts about the theory. We need to somehow resolve this conflict. Until we do, we are not justified in believing either hard determinism or free will.

Let's start by examining the hard determinist's argument:

1. Every event has a cause (causal determinism).
2. If every event has a cause, there are no free actions.
3. Therefore, there are no free actions.

This is a logically valid argument; the conclusion follows from the premises. To be a sound argument, however, the premises must also be true.

Let's examine the truth of premise 1.The most impressive reason given to back up premise 1 is that both science and common sense show that it is true. For centuries science has been uncovering the causes of countless physical phenomena, revealing that everything from comets to cells behave according to unchanging laws of nature. Thus science is said to confirm that everything has a cause. Likewise, common sense is supposed to support the same conclusion. Even after careful reflection on our commonsense experience, we still must conclude that everything has a cause. Some people have argued that unless we believe that everything has a cause, we could not make sense of the world. If we are to understand the world, we must presuppose causal determinism.

These arguments fail, however. Contrary to what many believe, science has *not* shown that every event has a cause. In fact, modern physics shows that not everything has a cause. At the level of subatomic particles (the so-called micro level), some events are known to have no cause at all. Some particles pop into existence uncaused, then pop out again. Subatomic particles are not governed by deterministic laws, but by statistical laws. In addition, there are no well-confirmed theories in any field of science that prove that *all* human actions are caused. Even genetics and neurophysiology cannot make this boast.

We are justified in believing the deliverances of common sense only if we have no reason to doubt them. (Common sense has been wrong in the past, so we need to be careful.) But on this score, we have reason to doubt common sense: science's discovery that some events are uncaused. No scientist has detected such indeterminacy beyond the subatomic level (the micro level)—that is, at the level of human action (the macro level). Nevertheless, indeterminacy, even on the macro level, is physically possible. For example, random subatomic events could be linked to, say, a television set via a device (like a Geiger counter) used to detect such subatomic events. The device detects a random micro event, the detection is signaled by a tone on the device, and the tone triggers the TV to turn on. Maybe this kind of indeterminacy comes into play at crucial junctures in our decision-making. Maybe it kicks in when our choices seem evenly balanced among conflicting alternatives.

Do we need to assume causal determinism in order to make sense of the world? Perhaps. But even if we can understand the world only by assuming causal determinism, it doesn't follow that causal determinism is actual.

So neither science nor common sense justifies acceptance of causal determinism. Premise 1 of the hard determinist's argument seems to be false, and the hard determinist's case is unproved.

Indeterminism

The weakness of premise 1 is bad news for the hard determinist, but is it good news for those who want to find a place for free will in the world? Some have thought so. The doctrine that some events are uncaused is called **causal indeterminism**. Some have reasoned that if the world is not entirely determined—if causal indeterminism is true—then uncaused actions are possible, and uncaused actions are free actions. Free will could find a niche in an otherwise determined universe. The view that free actions are uncaused is known as **indeterminism**.

The ancient atomists Democritus and Leucippus left no room in their deterministic system for free action—every event, even human choices, was reducible to a causal chain of atoms. Later atomists, the Epicureans, realized the full implications of their atomistic view and modified it to allow for human freedom. They postulated random "swerves" in the motions of atoms, leaving open the possibility of uncaused, and therefore free, actions. William James took this tack, also maintaining that free actions are uncaused:

> Indeterminism thus denies the world to be one unbending unit of fact. . . . Do not all the motives that assail us, all the futures that offer themselves to our choice, spring equally from the soil of the past; and would not either one of them, whether realized through chance or through necessity, the moment it was realized, seem to us to fit that past. . . ?[2]

Inspired by the indeterminacy on the subatomic level, some modern physicists have also endorsed indeterminism.[3]

Indeterminism fits well with the findings of both science and common sense, but it conflicts with our notions of moral responsibility. We are responsible for an action only if we did it. But if the action is uncaused, we didn't do it. If our legs move uncaused, randomly bending and thrusting this way and that, then we do not cause these motions—they just happen to us. They occur by chance. We cannot be held responsible for our leg movements if we do not cause them. Such random, or chance, actions are not free actions because they are not actions at all. Actions are things that we intend to happen. But we cannot have anything to do with uncaused events. Causal indeterminism, therefore, is no help to people who want to show that free will exists.

NATURE: FREEDOM AND NECESSITY

We seem to have made some progress here, though we have not yet solved the mystery of free will and determinism. We have found that hard determinism is not a satisfactory theory of free will. A key premise in the argument for hard determinism is dubious. But indeterminism seems unsatisfactory too. Uncaused events would rob us of free will, for uncaused events are ones that we cannot control.

So our key concern persists: How can we be free? Most people who have thought carefully about free will and determinism have concluded that we can act freely in some sense, and they have rejected hard determinism and indeterminism on the same grounds mentioned earlier. But they have differed on how free action is possible. The two most influential approaches are **compatibilism** and **libertarianism**. Most contemporary philosophers fall into one of these camps. Let's examine each one in turn.

Compatibilism

Compatibilism is the view that determined actions can still be free actions. Compatibilists accept causal determinism as a fact about nature but assert that it does not preclude freedom. Even if every event has a cause, you can still be free. So compatibilists accept the first premise in the hard determinist's argument (every event has a cause), but they reject the second premise (if every event has a cause, there are no free actions). Compatibilists then are determinists, but not hard determinists. They are sometimes called **soft determinists**, and their view, *soft determinism*.

How can we be free yet determined? Traditional compatibilists offer an analysis of freedom that accommodates both of these properties. Free actions are not uncaused, they say. On the contrary, free actions *must* have a cause; they must be caused by the will. But they also must be unfettered. That is, they must not be externally constrained. An action is externally unconstrained if the person performing the action could have done otherwise. A person could have done otherwise if, had she chosen to do otherwise, nothing would have stopped her from doing otherwise. So the compatibilist's view is that for an action to be free, it must be (1) caused by the will and (2) not externally constrained.

Philosopher Thomas Hobbes (1588–1679) was the first to set forth the compatibilist position. He says: "[H]e is free to do a thing, that may do it if he have the will to do it, and may forbear if he have the will to forbear."[4] So according to this notion of free will—what philosophers call freedom of *voluntariness*—persons can act freely even if causal determinism is true. Even if everything is determined, our actions can still be free as long as they are caused by our will and we could have done otherwise.

Hierarchical Compatibilism

Philosopher Harry Frankfurt (1929–) advocates an interesting kind of compatibilism. He makes a distinction between what he calls first-order desires and second-order desires. First-order desires are those directed at objects or states of affairs, such as food and health. Second-order desires are those directed on first-order desires. For example, you have a first-order desire to eat chocolate cake, but you also have a second-order desire to not overeat—that is, to not give in to the first-order desire. In other words, you have a desire about a desire. Presumably animals have only first-order desires, but humans have both first-order and second-order desires. Frankfurt suggests that if you never have second-order desires or if you do not act on the second-order desires you do have, your actions are not free. So for Frankfurt, free actions are those caused by second-order desires (or to be more precise, second-order desires that you decisively identify with).

Hierarchical compatibilism then, like traditional compatibilism, maintains that actions can be free even if they are ultimately determined. This view, though, is criticized for introducing the same kind of problem that traditional compatibilism has: Ultimately the agent has no control over second-order desires.

The classic example of a lack of free will in this sense is an unknowing prisoner. A man is carried into a jail cell while asleep. He awakes the next day to find himself locked in a cell with a friend he wants to talk to. He enjoys the company of this friend so much that he decides to stay in the cell. So staying in the cell is a voluntary action; it's caused by his will. But it is not a free action because the man could not do otherwise; he is externally constrained. Even if he wanted to leave the cell, he couldn't.

Compatibilists believe that people can be held responsible for their actions even if causal determinism is true. All that is required is that the actions be caused by the will. Traditional compatibilism seems to be a better theory than either hard determinism or indeterminism. Unlike hard determinism, it accommodates freedom in human actions and, unlike indeterminism, does so without positing a notion of freedom that is incoherent.

Many critics, however, think that traditional compatibilism is inadequate because it conflicts with our commonsense understanding of free actions. They point to scenarios in which someone fulfills both compatibilist criteria for free action but, nevertheless, is not free. Let's say that all of your actions are in accordance with your volitions, just as they are supposed to be, and they are unconstrained. But, without your knowing it, someone implants a device in your brain that causes all of your volitions. With this device he ensures that all of the volitions you have are the ones he gives you. He gives you the volition to assault your best friend, and you—being without any external constraints—proceed to commit the assault. So here is a case in which both conditions of traditional compatibilism are met—your actions are caused by your will, and they are not externally constrained. If you had chosen to do otherwise, you would have done otherwise. Under these circumstances, can you plausibly be said to be free?

Not at all. If you had chosen to do otherwise, you would have done otherwise—but you *cannot* choose to do otherwise because someone else is manipulating your choices. So the traditional compatibilist's notion of free action seems mistaken.

Philosopher Richard Taylor provides a more down-to-earth scenario that makes the same point:

> One can, for instance, be given a compulsive desire for certain drugs, simply by having them administered to him over a course of time. Suppose, then, that I do, with neither my knowledge nor consent, thus become a victim of such a desire and act upon it. Do I act freely, merely by virtue of the fact that I am unimpeded in my quest for drugs? In a sense I do, surely, but I am hardly free with respect to whether or not I shall use drugs. I never chose to have the desire for them inflicted upon me.[5]

A hard-core drug addict—say, one addicted to cocaine or heroin—can act on his desire for drugs and thus meet both compatibilist conditions for free actions: The addict's use of drugs is caused by his own will, and it is not externally constrained, so his actions are supposed to be free. But that doesn't seem right. Hard-core addicts are not free. They are determined by their addiction.

These examples suggest that the traditional compatibilist's concept of free action is mistaken. Your actions may be caused by your will and not be externally constrained—and still not be free. If your will is not your own, if it is not under your control, your actions are not free.

Libertarianism

Compatibilists try to show that causal determinism and free will are not at odds with one another, that they are, well, compatible. But as we have seen, the notion of freedom implied by traditional compatibilism seems implausible. Other forms of compatibilism have the same defect (see the box "Hierarchical Compatibilism"). This failure suggests that causal determinism and free will are not compatible after all, a view known as **incompatibilism**.

Given this incompatibility, do we have any reason to believe that the free-will side of the equation is any stronger than the causal determinism side proved to be? What evidence is there to show that we sometimes act freely?

Many philosophers have suggested that the best evidence is our own commonsense experience. We all frequently have the impression that we can freely choose and that the choices we make are up to us. In countless situations, we have the impression that there are alternatives open to us and that nothing prevents us from choosing any one of them. Philosopher Carl Ginet says, "My impression at each moment is that I at the moment, and nothing prior to that moment, determine which of several open alternatives is the next sort of bodily exertion I voluntarily make."[6]

Because our experience suggests that our actions are sometimes free, we have good reason to believe they are free. As long as we have no good reason to doubt what this experience suggests, we have good reason to believe that we do have free will.

In fact, it is virtually impossible for any of us to assume that we do *not* have free will in our daily lives. A major reason why we do believe it—even after reflecting on our belief—is that we all *deliberate*. We all occasionally decide which of several actions to perform. We can deliberate about doing something only if we believe that it is in our power to do it or not do it. If you believe that it is now no longer possible to meet your friend at an appointed time, you cannot seriously deliberate whether or not to meet her. Since you believe that you cannot meet her—that you have no choice about it—you cannot seriously engage in deciding whether to meet her. So when we deliberate, we must believe that we act freely. The belief that we can sometimes act freely is thus a belief of reflective common sense—which means that we are entitled to accept it unless we have good reason to doubt it.

But what if we are deceived? What if our experience or belief of freedom is misleading? Some people have suggested that we may feel free because we simply are ignorant of all the ways in which we are determined. Therefore, they reject the argument from commonsense experience. But this tack is a mistake. From the fact that we *can* be mistaken it does not follow that we *are* mistaken. As the philosopher René Descartes (1596–1650) showed, it is possible that we are all dreaming right now, but this possibility does not prove that we *are* dreaming. The important principle is that we are justified in believing what our experience reveals until it is shown to be illusory. Therefore, we are justified in believing that sometimes we do act freely until we discover good reason to believe otherwise. So far, neither the hard determinist nor anyone else has given us good reason to believe otherwise.

From the existence of free will, some have argued to the conclusion that causal determinism is false. They are incompatibilists, just as hard determinists are, but they turn the hard determinist's argument on its head:

1. If every event has a cause (causal determinism), then there is no free will (incompatibilism).

2. There is free will.
3. Therefore, it is not the case that every event has a cause (causal determinism is false).

This argument suggests that we are free from causal determinism, but it also exposes a mystery. If causal determinism is false, then causal indeterminism must be true. But causal indeterminism is not a satisfactory theory of free will. Free action cannot be based on chance. So if causal indeterminism is true but a poor foundation for free will, how can we explain the existence of free will, something that our commonsense experience supports?

Libertarians (incompatibilists who believe in free will) offer an interesting solution to the mystery. They want to avoid indeterminism for the very reasons mentioned above, so they suggest that free actions are indeed caused—but not in the same way that, say, a falling domino causes another domino to fall. Libertarians believe that there are two types of causation—**agent-causation**, in which an agent or person brings about an event, and **event-causation**, in which one event brings about another event, as in falling dominoes. Libertarians claim that free actions are indeed caused, but not by events but by agents (persons, selves)—agents who are not caused to act by something else. This solution to the free will problem is known as libertarianism. This view posits a very different idea of freedom than that of the compatibilists. Libertarian freedom is not the freedom of voluntariness, but the freedom of *origination* because free actions originate with, and are caused by, the agent.

Libertarianism, or something very much like it, has been advocated by several notable philosophers, including Carneades (c. 214–129 B.C.E.), a head of Plato's Academy; Thomas Reid (1710–1796); and Immanuel Kant (1724–1804). Carneades thought that persons act freely when they are the source of their own actions and when forces outside the persons do not cause the actions. Persons are not free when they are caused to act by some external force.

Thomas Reid was a tough critic of compatibilism. Being able to do otherwise if you were to choose otherwise, he says, does not constitute free will. The reason is that you may not be able to choose otherwise in the first place. Free will means being able to choose otherwise; the choice must be up to the agent. As Reid puts it,

> If, in any action, he had power to will what he did, or not to will it, in that action he is free. But if, in every voluntary action, the determination of his will be the necessary consequence of something involuntary in the state of his mind, or of something in his external circumstances, he is not free; he has not what I call the liberty of a moral agent, but is subject to necessity.[7]

What is the evidence for this view of free action? As we have seen, our commonsense experience tells us that we sometimes have the power to choose otherwise. Common sense also suggests that actions by an agent are possible and, often, actual. We know, for example, that statements such as "I raised my arm" and "Jill picked up the pail" are sometimes true. If they are true, they suggest that an agent brought about an action or caused something to happen.

To show that agent-causation does not exist (and that everything that happens is a result of event-causation), a determinist would have to demonstrate that all statements attributing an action to an agent are reducible to statements about event-causation. But so far, determinists have not been able to do this.

Libertarians can also point out another difficulty that determinists must overcome in rejecting agent-causation. We normally think that our actions have intentionality—that they are accompanied by states of mind directed at aspects of the situation. Our thoughts are *about* the goal of our action. But intentionality is not the kind of thing that can be reduced to physical properties. It therefore seems doubtful that our actions can be reduced to physical properties that are subject to event-causation. Agent-causation does not seem to be the sort of thing that could ever be reduced to event-causation.

Despite such considerations, libertarians have been accused of positing one mystery (agent-causation) to explain another mystery (free will), which explains nothing. Usually the gist of the criticism is that there is nothing mysterious about event-causation, about one physical event causing another physical event—but what on earth is agent-causation? What kind of causation could arise from an agent, affect certain events, yet not be part of the usual causal chains in which one event brings about another?

There is indeed a mystery here. Libertarians respond to the charge of mystery-making by asserting that agent-causation is no more mysterious than event-causation. Libertarians have not been able to provide a complete analysis of the difference between agent-causation and event-causation, between one event causing another and an agent causing an event. But neither have determinists been able to give a complete analysis of the difference between one event happening right after another event and one event causing another.

Actually, some philosophers have recently made progress in taking some of the mystery out of agent-causation. They have put forth several proposals to explain how a choice can be up to us and yet not be random.[8] One suggestion, for example, is that there is nothing incoherent in the idea that an agent can be undetermined and still freely act in light of relevant reasons. Critics have claimed that there always must be some further reasons (beyond the immediate reason that motivates an agent) that cause an agent to act, and behind

Richard Taylor on Agent-Causation

Philosopher Richard Taylor (1919–) is a strong advocate of agent causation. Here's how he describes this idea:

> The only conception of action that accords with our data is one according to which people—and perhaps some other things as well—are sometimes, but of course not always, self-determining beings; that is, beings that are sometimes the cause of their own behavior. In the case of an action that is free, it must be such that it is caused by the agent who performs it, but such that no antecedent conditions were sufficient for his performing just that action. . . . Now, this conception fits what people take themselves to be; namely, beings who act, or who are agents, rather than things that are merely acted upon, and whose behavior is simply the causal consequence of conditions that they have not wrought.*

* Richard Taylor, *Metaphysics*, 4th ed. (Englewood Cliffs, N.J.: Prentice-Hall, 1992), 45–53.

these reasons must be still more reasons, and so on in an infinite regress. There is no free action in such a causal chain. The problem seems to be in thinking that the reasons must produce the actions. But, some philosophers ask, why couldn't a self-determining agent (who is free to decide otherwise) simply decide in light of reasons available at the time? The reasons would explain the action even though they do not cause it. The action would be the agent's own (because it came from the agent), and the relevant reasons would be motivating factors that help explain the agent's choice.[9]

Libertarianism seems to fit well with our commonsense experience of free actions and agency, so it is a better theory than hard determinism, which belies our experience without providing good reason to doubt it. Libertarianism is superior to indeterminism because it does not entail the dubious phenomena of uncaused actions, which cannot be free. It offers a better explanation of free action than compatibilism because it captures the notion that free actions and choices must ultimately be up to the agent, not just an externally unconstrained product of the agent's will. If this analysis is correct, libertarianism is the best theory of free will and the best response to denials of proposition 5: We sometimes do act freely.

Some people, mostly compatibilists, may still reject this analysis on the grounds that freedom of origination (the kind embraced by libertarians) is just not their idea of freedom, preferring instead the freedom of voluntariness. If free will simply amounts to being able to do as we choose, or will, to do, then almost everyone has free will—and again proposition 5 is sustained. So the truth of either libertarianism or compatibilism would support the humanist's claim of freedom.

SECTION 3.2

Beyond Our Control: Fate, God, and Logic

For many people determinism does not seem much of a threat to personal freedom. A bigger worry for them is fate or God. The ancient Greeks were big believers in fate—and so are many people today. Likewise, the concern that God's omnipotence or omniscience could somehow prevent free action goes back thousands of years, though it seemed to loom largest among the medieval Scholastics—and still haunts thoughtful people. Both views conflict with a humanist notion of free will:

6. Humans are not controlled by fate or divine power but are sometimes free to do otherwise.

FATE: NO WAY OUT

Are you fated to read this entire book? If so, then you will read it no matter what you do to avoid reading it, such as throwing the book in the trash. This notion of the inevitability of events is known as **fatalism**. It is the view that all future events will happen no matter what anyone does. The future is fixed and will be a certain way regardless of our deliberations and actions. In modern times, fatalism seems to be an enormously popular idea. Soldiers have been known to say something like "If there's a bullet with my name on it, I'll get it. If there's no bullet with my name on it, I won't get it. Either way, I can't change it, so worrying is a waste of time." Some people express fatalistic sentiments with the old cliché, "Que sera, sera—whatever will be will be." However it's expressed, fatalism rules out free will. If what you do cannot affect future events, you have no control over them. You are locked into a specific course, and there can be no deviations from it.

Fatalism, however, is not the same thing as causal determinism. Causal determinism says that future events happen as a result of preceding events. These preceding events include things that we do, so many future events happen because of what we do. Fatalism says that future events happen *regardless of what we do*. Causal determinists reject fatalism because they believe that people's actions play a role in events that are determined. A causal determinist would say that it was determined that Neil Armstrong would walk on the Moon in July 1969. A fatalist would say that Armstrong was fated to walk on the Moon in July 1969—and he would have walked on the Moon in July 1969 even if he had tried to sabotage the entire American space program in 1960.

Strangely enough, the idea of fatalism is attractive and comforting to some people, while causal determinism seems to lack the same appeal. For some, fatalism implies order in a chaotic world, an unchanging pattern laid down at the beginning of time. Belief in fate can engender a feeling of resignation and peace in the face of imminent death, just as soldiers in war find solace in the idea that their destiny has already been decided. Fatalism also has a reputation as the world's best excuse for people who choose to not do anything to make their lot better: If I am meant to get a job, fate will give me a job.

Fate is a popular plot device in books, movies, and television dramas. Fatalistic stories usually end up inducing some strange, eerie feelings in the audience, as the tale of Oedipus does. A Hebrew folktale manages this nicely:

> King Solomon's servant came rushing into the court. He begged the king for his fastest horse so he could be in a town ten miles south by nightfall. When King Solomon asked for an explanation, he said, "I just met Death in the Garden! He looked me in the face. I know that I am to be taken, and I don't want to be here when Death comes to claim me." The king replied, "My fastest horse has hooves like wings. Take him." So the servant left, and the king walked into the garden, where he saw Death with a puzzled look on his face. "What's the matter," King Solomon asked. Death replied, "Tonight I'm supposed to claim the life of your servant, the one I just saw in your garden. But I'm supposed to claim him in a town ten miles south of here. Unless he has a horse with hooves like wings, I don't see how he could get there by nightfall."

The question at hand, however, is whether there are any reasons for accepting fatalism. As it turns out, there are no good arguments in its favor. More to the point, fatalism flies in the face of commonsense experience. Our everyday experience suggests that it is just not the case that our actions do not affect future events. It is obvious that what we do *does* affect subsequent events. Human action may or may not be determined, but it certainly is effectual. In fact, our commonsense experience seems to discourage anyone from being a consistent fatalist—someone who always refuses to lift a finger to help himself because everything is fated anyway. The notion of fatalism then is no threat to proposition 6.

GOD AND LOGIC: FIXED FUTURES

In Western philosophy, God has been thought to alternately make human freedom possible and take human freedom away. God's threat to free will is supposed to come mainly from two sources—his omnipotence and his omniscience. In either case, an attribute of the divine seems to throw people back into what William James calls the "iron block" of determinism.

The notion that God's power rules out free will has been around for centuries. Augustine, for example, saw that people need free will if they are to be held accountable by God, but he ultimately came to believe that human beings, without the power and grace of God, can do nothing but sin. People cannot save themselves; God must select them. They, therefore, are predestined to make the choices they make. Augustine admits that even though he "tried hard to maintain the free decision of the human will, the grace of God was victorious."[10]

Protestant reformers Martin Luther (1483–1546) and John Calvin (1509–1564) held similar views. They thought that to suppose that people have any autonomous freedom or power of their own was to detract from the power of God. The human will, determined by God, is predestined to be damned or saved. Luther declared free will an illusion; Calvin asserted that all actions are necessitated by God's grace.

Nevertheless, the doctrine of predestination is open to the same basic argument that undoes hard determinism. That is, there is no evidence to support this form of hard determinism, but there is good reason to believe that we act freely—namely, our commonsense experience of free action.

The restrictions on freedom related to God's omniscience may be more serious. The central problem is this: If God knows everything, he then knows that X will happen to you tomorrow. If he knows that X will happen to you tomorrow, then it is true that X will happen to you tomorrow. (It is impossible, after all, to know something that is false.) If it is true that X will happen to you tomorrow, then it *must* happen—there is no way that it could not happen. So if X will happen no matter what, you are not free to avoid X's happening tomorrow.

If God knows that you will break your leg on Tuesday, then it is true that you will break your leg on Tuesday. Therefore, you *must* break your leg on Tuesday, and you can do nothing to prevent this mishap. In this way, God's foreknowledge seems to destroy free will. This is the most worrisome form of logical determinism.

Perhaps the most pointed statement of the consequences of God's foreknowledge comes from the Roman philosopher and theologian Boethius (c. 480–524):

> Therefore, there can be no freedom in human decisions and actions, since the divine mind, foreseeing everything without possibility of error, determines and forces the outcome of everything that is to happen. Once this is granted, it is clear that the structure of all human affairs must collapse.[11]

For many thinkers, the biggest sticking point is that logical determinism seems to rob not only ordinary mortals of their freedom, but God as well. If God is all-knowing, then he knows his own future, which is therefore determined. If his future is determined, there are things that he cannot do. He cannot then be omnipotent. God, it seems, cannot be both omniscient and omnipotent.

Over the centuries, many Christian scholars have wrestled with the conflict between their belief in free will and the idea that God knows everything that happens—past, present, and future. Augustine, Aquinas, and Carneades recognized this tension and tried to reach some kind of accommodation between foreknowledge and free will. Martin Luther and the American philosopher and theologian Jonathan Edwards (1703–1758), however, bit the bullet and argued that God's omniscience does indeed render human actions unavoidable and determined, just as God's omnipotence does.

Traditionally, the main argument for the coexistence of free will and God's omniscience has been this: God may know what you will do at any given time, but this does not mean that he *causes* you to do what you do. Augustine, Aquinas, and Carneades all argued that God can somehow see what will happen without *making* it happen. Augustine thought that God's foreknowledge was like ordinary memory. Just as a person remembers an event without causing it to occur, so God foresees events without bringing them about. God can foresee without causing because he somehow exists outside of time. Our usual notions about the past, present, and future of time simply do not pertain to God. As Boethius says,

> [I]f we may aptly compare God's present vision with man's, He sees all things in his eternal present as you see some things in your temporal present. Therefore, this divine foreknowledge does not change the nature and properties of things; it simply sees things present before it as they will later turn out to be in what we regard as the future.[12]

Maybe Boethius is right. Perhaps God's omniscience itself does not cause or preordain human actions. But the logic of foreknowledge remains: If God knows what you will do tomorrow, then you will do it, and you cannot *not* do it. Free will slips away.

Remember that our main issue here is whether God's foreknowledge, as a possible impediment to free will, constitutes evidence against proposition 6. Our conclusion above is that *if* God is omniscient (knows everything, including the future), then free will is ruled out. So there are no free actions—and proposition 6 is undermined—*if* God's omniscience is actual. But is God's omniscience actual? We take up the existence and attributes of God in chapter 7, so we will withhold judgment until then. For now we can point out that the argument for God's omniscience must be a very strong one to undermine our best reason for claiming to have free will—our commonsense experience.

SUMMARY

The problem of free will is a conflict between two beliefs that seem to be highly plausible: causal determinism and the freedom to do otherwise. Those who think that causal determinism rules out free will are called hard determinists. It appears, though, that causal determinism is false (because some events on the quantum level are uncaused). The doctrine that some events are uncaused is known as causal indeterminism; the view that free actions are uncaused is called indeterminism. The idea that free actions are uncaused, however, is implausible because an action that has no cause is a random action, which cannot be free.

The two most influential approaches to the problem of free will are compatibilism and libertarianism. Compatibilism is the view that determined actions can still be free. This kind of freedom is the freedom to do as one desires. In this view if (1) your actions are caused by your will and (2) they are not externally constrained, they are free actions. But it is possible for actions to fulfill both these requirements and still not be free (e.g., when you have no power to choose what to choose).

Libertarianism is the doctrine that free actions are caused—but not by other events. Free actions are caused by an agent (or person). The evidence for this view is our commonsense experience of causing certain actions and making real choices unconstrained. Because our experience suggests that our actions are sometimes free, we have good reason to believe that they really are free.

STUDY QUESTIONS

1. What is causal determinism? How does it differ from fatalism?
2. What is hard determinism? How well does it fit with our commonsense experience?
3. What is indeterminism?
4. What is compatibilism? How do compatibilists explain the phenomenon of someone being both free and causally determined?
5. What is libertarianism? How does it differ from compatibilism?
6. What is logical determinism?

DISCUSSION QUESTIONS

1. Compatibilists and libertarians have radically different ideas about freedom. What are these differences and why do they matter?
2. Which kind of freedom would you rather have—the kind advocated by compatibilists, by libertarians, or by a William James type of indeterminism? Why?
3. If God knows everything he will do in the future, is he free to do anything he wants? If God knows everything that you will do, are you free to do otherwise?
4. If the actions of humans are determined, can we be held responsible for crimes or sins that we commit?
5. Let's say that someone deliberately and intentionally commits a crime and then declares that he could not help himself because he had an awful childhood. Should his excuse get him off the hook?

FIELD PROBLEM

Consider a society that assumes that people's actions are determined by previous causes so that no one is free to do otherwise. What are some possible implications of this view for social institutions? For example, how would the penal system change? How would the legal system change? How would the educational system change?

SUGGESTIONS FOR FURTHER READING

Dennett, Daniel. *Elbow Room: The Varieties of Free Will Worth Wanting*. Cambridge, Mass.: MIT Press, 1984.

Dworkin, Gerald. *Determinism, Free Will, and Moral Responsibility*. Englewood Cliffs, N.J.: Prentice-Hall, 1970.

NOTES

1. William James, "The Dilemma of Determinism," *The Will to Believe and Other Essays in Popular Philosophy* (Cambridge, Mass.: Harvard University Press, 1979), 117–18.

2. James, "The Dilemma," 118.

3. Arthur Eddington, *New Pathways in Science* (New York: Macmillan, 1935).

4. Thomas Hobbes, "Questions Concerning Liberty, Necessity, and Chance," in *The English Works of Thomas Hobbes,* ed. William Molesworth (Aalen: Scientia Verlag, 1966).

5. Richard Taylor, *Metaphysics*, 2nd ed. (Englewood Cliffs, N.J.: Prentice-Hall, 1992), 49–50.

6. Carl Ginet, *On Action* (Cambridge: Cambridge University Press, 1990), 90.

7. Thomas Reid, *Essays on the Active Powers of Man IV,* in *The Works of Thomas Reid*, ed. Sir William Hamilton (Hildesheim, Germany: Georg Olms Verlag, 1983), 599.

8. See *Agents, Causes, and Events*, ed. Timothy O'Connor (Oxford: Oxford University Press, 1995).

9. O'Connor, ed., "Agent Causation," *Agents, Causes, and Events,* 188–89.

10. Augustine, *Retractationes*, vol. I.2, in *The Works of Saint Augustine: A Translation for the Twenty-First Century* (Hyde Park, N.Y.: New City Press, 1990.)

11. Boethius, *The Consolation of Philosophy*, trans. Richard Green (New York: Bobbs-Merrill, 1962).

12. Boethius, *The Consolation of Philosophy*, in *The Consolation of Philosophy: An English Translation,* trans. W. V. Cooper (London: Dent, 1902).

4

The Moral Life

Lewis Vaughn

In the beginning there was **morality**—that is, ideas of right and wrong, good and bad, just and unjust. Probably as soon as homo sapiens began making deliberative choices, morality became a fact of life, no less than the wind, rain, and the quest for food. Human beings have been preoccupied with moral issues ever since.

No wonder: Moral concerns are nearly impossible to avoid. We all spend an enormous amount of time thinking about them, reacting to them, and making decisions because of them. We behave like amateur ethicists (those who spend a lot of time thinking about moral issues) because we *are* amateur ethicists. In fact, we all have what philosophers call a **moral theory**—a view of what morality is and is not, what actions are right or wrong, and what things are good or bad. Even if you think that there is no such thing as right and wrong, *that* is a theory of morality. If you believe that all moral theories and moral theorizing are bogus, *that* is also a theory of morality. If you are sure that all religious moral theories are superior to secular ones (or the other way around), you are leaning on a specific view of morality. Whether you think that moral judgments are objective, subjective, universal, relative, or meaningless, you have some definite ideas about what morality is all about.

You may even have a general idea about how to answer one of the biggest moral questions of all: *What is the basis of morality*? That is, what makes an action right? To put this question another way, if you have a moral theory, and you make moral decisions, *what is your justification for taking your theory and your decisions seriously*? Do you think, for example, that your moral theory—whatever it is—comes from God via holy scriptures or the Ten Commandments or some inner sacred voice? Do you believe, on the other hand, that the source of morality is entirely secular—that your moral theory is based on standards of behavior derived from human nature, from conscience, from cultural conventions, from a sense of altruism or devotion to human welfare, from some logical or cognitive intuition?

This question about the foundation of morality marks some of the major fault lines among moral theories. Some people argue that the ultimate ground of any moral ideas must be *religious*, some would say *secular*, and some, *humanist*. Religious moral theories depend substantially on ideas about theistic or supernatural states of affairs. They may focus on compassion, love, punishment, or aspects of philosophical humanism, but the distinguishing property is in some sense otherworldly or transcendent. Secular moral theories leave out the transcendent ideas. Humanist moral theories are also secular but emphasize a rational basis for morality and a respect or concern for the welfare and the rights of human individuals. The differences between religious and secular (or humanist) theories can be stark and often show up vividly in debates about abortion, euthanasia, capital punishment, women's rights, gay rights, teen violence, cloning humans, and more. In some cases, though, the differences are minimal, with references to the supernatural almost the only contrasting element.

For a variety of reasons, questions regarding the underpinning of moral theories, whether religious or secular, seem to be especially vexing to people. After all, when you probe a moral theory, you are often striking at important assumptions that people have maintained for years, perhaps since childhood. For those who are brave enough to examine their moral theory, however, there are tools available that can make the job easier, tools that have already been honed in the field of **ethics**. Ethics, or moral philosophy, is *the philosophical study of morality—of the nature and validity of moral value judgments.* In large part it is the philosophical investigation of *how we should live our lives*. Its core activity is the creation and evaluation of moral theories—tasks that philosophers have been able to illuminate far more than most people realize. Moral philosophy makes fair examination of moral theories possible, for it proceeds without assuming that any particular path—religious, secular, or humanist—is best. Ethics, then, can help us assess humanist ideas about morality as well as competing notions from all quarters.

This kind of analysis is the focus of the following sections. Before jumping into them, though, let's try to get a bird's-eye view of the conceptual terrain.

When people try to think of a theory of morality, they often come up with a moral code, or set of rules. Take the Ten Commandments, for example. This view assumes that the ten rules set down in the Old Testament can constitute a complete theory of morality. (Some people think that morality *is* the Ten Commandments, while many others, including some religious people, would reject this presumption as ethically naive and simplistic.) This theory—what we will call the **Ten Commandments theory** of morality—says that right actions are those that conform to the ten Old Testament rules. The rules are absolute, allowing no exceptions, no "wiggle room" for transgressors, and the consequences of people's actions are irrelevant. As some advocates of the theory would say, "The Ten Commandments are not the ten *suggestions,* but the ten *laws.*"

Now, if people want to cite a secular or humanist theory of morality, there is a good chance they will think of **act-utilitarianism**, the view that right actions are those that maximize happiness, everyone considered. That is, an action is right if it results in more happiness than any other action, taking everyone into account. In act-utilitarianism, being moral is a matter of making sure that your actions maximize the common good. Absolutist rules do not matter; the consequences of your actions for sentient beings are everything.

The differences between these two systems are clear enough. But they also share some common ground. Both theories assume that moral knowledge is possible, that moral principles can be applied universally, and that there are important reasons for acting morally. Both theories also assume that moral knowledge (such as whether an action is right, or whether a person is good) is *objective*—that it does not depend on any one person's state of mind. The Ten Commandments theory is thought to make objective moral judgments possible, and utilitarianism is an objective theory because determining the consequences of actions is a matter of objective observation. These common elements run through many other theories of morality, both religious and secular.

The Ten Commandments Theory

Some people say that their moral theory consists of the Ten Commandments, or Decalogue, which they view as a self-contained moral code (set of rules or commands) needing no additional theoretical underpinnings. (There are many other people who say that the Ten Commandments are just guidelines that help them fill out a larger moral theory.) This view—what we will call the Ten Commandments theory—says that right actions are those that conform to the ten Old Testament rules. The Decalogue certainly gets a lot of respect from both religious and nonreligious people, but does it make a good moral theory?

The Ten Commandments theory is a type of divine command theory, so it has the same flaws as any other divine command theory. But it also has some defects that are common to absolutist moral codes, secular or religious.

A major problem is that the Ten Commandments theory, like all moral codes, is *unworkable*—that is, it provides little or no help in making moral choices. Moral codes have sets of rules that are inherently vague. They therefore cannot offer much help to people who need specific answers to specific cases. The Commandments say "honor thy father and thy mother." But does this mean that children should honor their parents even if their parents abuse them? What if the father or mother is criminally insane? Does the rule apply to stepfathers? foster mothers? the parents of test-tube babies? The Commandments are just not clear.

In addition, the theory is unworkable on another score. Plausible moral theories are supposed to help us resolve moral dilemmas, but the Ten Commandments theory (like other moral codes) cannot do this. When two commandments or rules conflict, there is no way to remove the conflict without appealing to a moral theory that is *outside the scope* of the Commandments. We are commanded not to kill and not to steal, but what if the only way to avoid killing someone is to steal? Or what if the only way to avoid killing a hundred people is to kill just one? We are told not to bear false witness, but what if by bearing false witness we can save the lives of a thousand innocent people? The Commandments give rise to many conflicts like this—but can't resolve them. Resolving them requires interpretation of the theory, but interpreting the theory requires adding a different theory of morality.

Perhaps the most troubling problem with the theory is that it conflicts with our considered moral judgments. The Commandments are categorical—they allow no exceptions. In the Ten Commandments theory a rule is a rule, and the impact that following the rules might have on people's well-being cannot be taken into account. But say a terrorist steals a nuclear device and threatens to blow up a major city, killing millions of people. The only way to stop this catastrophe is for you to break the Commandment against killing and murder the bomber. According to the theory, killing the terrorist—*even as a means to save the city*—would be wrong because the Ten Commandments forbids such actions. But this cannot be right. Our considered moral judgments suggest that there are times when the consequences of our actions do matter and should be taken into account. These failings make the Ten Commandments theory a poor theory of morality.

All of the preceding points may have tipped you off to a key fact that will become even clearer as we proceed: Generalizations about the worth of all religious theories compared to that of all secular ones are likely to be very iffy. There are faulty secular theories and faulty religious theories. This means that *every moral theory must stand on its own merits,* and every moral theory must be judged on its own merits. Simply lumping a theory into a secular or sacred category won't help much.

Theories of morality are theories of right action—that is, theories about what makes an action right. Philosophers usually categorize moral theories into two major types: **consequentialist** (or **teleological**) and **formalist** (or **deontological**). Consequentialist moral theories claim that the rightness of an action depends on its consequences. Act-utilitarianism is a consequentialist theory because right actions are supposed to result in more happiness than other possible actions. To put the point crudely, the basic idea behind such theories is that the end justifies the means.

Formalist moral theories claim that the rightness of an action depends on the action's form. Here the consequences of an action don't matter (or matter very little), but the form, or nature, of the action does. Such a theory might claim, for example, that killing an innocent person is always wrong because of the nature of that action, and this would be so whether or not the killing resulted in a great deal of good such as saving the lives of a hundred people. By this definition the Ten Commandments moral code is a formalist theory.

Consequentialist theories may be either religious or nonreligious. A religious person might say that an action is right if it results in the greatest amount of respect for sacred artifacts. A nonreligious person might claim that an action is right if it results in the greatest amount of pleasure for the greatest number of people. Formalist theories can also be religious or nonreligious. Christian theories of ethics have traditionally been formalist, often maintaining that a certain kind of action is right or wrong no matter what the results. Nonreligious formalist theories are common as well. Some of them claim, for example, that an action is right if it constitutes the performance of a certain duty.

All humanist theories are nonreligious, and they too can be either consequentialist or formalist. Not all nonreligious theories, however, can be plausibly considered humanist. Humanism as a worldview has traditionally incorporated a respect or concern for the welfare and the rights of human individuals. So utilitarianism earns the label of humanist because the crux of the theory is maximizing the happiness or pleasure of other human beings. But the secular theory known as **ethical egoism**, for example, cannot plausibly be called humanist. Ethical egoism is the view that right actions are those that promote one's own self interest—a kind of moral self-absorption alien to humanist views of humanity. Ethical egoism also permits all manner of heinous acts as long as they are in the best interests of one's self, acts that humanism would not condone.

Some moral theories are **naturalistic** and some **nonnaturalistic** (or **rationalist**), an important distinction philosophers have debated for centuries. Naturalistic theories assert that morality can be reduced to, or defined in terms of, natural phenomena. That is, people can know moral facts in the same way that a scientist can know empirical facts. A naturalistic theory, for example, might maintain that ethical terms such as "morally right" can be equated with empirical phenomena such as "producing more pleasure than pain." It also might say that being moral means meeting certain common human needs. Utilitarianism is a naturalistic moral theory.

Nonnaturalistic theories reject the idea that moral truths are somehow empirical facts. Proponents of these theories claim that moral terms cannot be reduced to empirical terms. The most famous nonnaturalistic slogan is "you can't get an 'ought' from an 'is'," a point often attributed to the eighteenth-century philosopher David Hume (1711–1776). The most famous nonnaturalistic moral theory is that of Immanuel Kant (1724–1804), who asserted that people have certain absolute moral duties derived not from empirical facts but from logical considerations. Some modern-day philosophers hold the nonnaturalistic (and nonreligious) view that there are universal moral principles that are logically self-evident.

Some people use the term "naturalistic" as a synonym for nonreligious. But in ethics, most philosophers define "naturalistic" as we did above, using the term to emphasize the critical distinction between morality based on, and not based on, natural phenomena. They would therefore want to say that religious moral theories can be naturalistic (empirical facts may define morality) or nonnaturalistic (morality comes from a god) and that secular theories can also fall into either category.

Given the multiplicity of moral theories and their conflicting claims, how can we possibly weigh their merits? We can start by recognizing that theories of morality are like theories in science. Scientific theories try to explain the causes of events, such as a chemical reaction, the orbit of a planet, or the growth of a tumor. A plausible scientific theory is one that's consistent with all of the relevant data. Moral theories try to explain what makes an action right or what makes a person good. A plausible moral theory must also be consistent with all the relevant data. The data moral theories must explain are what philosophers call our "considered moral judgments"—moral judgments that we accept after thinking critically about them. Any worthy moral theory will be consistent with those judgments. If it is not—if, for example, it approves of obviously immoral acts—the theory is flawed and must be discarded. If our moral theory sanctions, say, the inflicting of undeserved and unnecessary suffering on innocent children, we must conclude that something is very wrong with our theory.

Plausible scientific theories must also be consistent with all relevant background information. A theory about the explosion of a star, for example, must not only be consistent with data regarding the explosion itself, but with facts we already know about gravity, space, heat, light, and scientific measuring instruments. Likewise, plausible moral theories must be consistent with the relevant background information—that is, with our experience of the moral life. Whatever else our moral experience entails, it certainly involves (1) making moral judgments, (2) occasionally getting into moral disagreements, and (3) sometimes acting immorally. Any theory that suggests that we do not have these fundamental experiences must be deemed suspect.

It is logically possible that our experience of the moral life is a delusion, only *seeming* to involve moral judgments, disputes, and mistakes. But unless we have good reason to dismiss our experience as delusion, we are justified in accepting it at face value. Another way of putting this is that our experience of the moral life is a matter of common sense. Common sense, of course, has been wrong about many things, including the shape of the Earth and the causes of disease. But it does not follow that because common sense is sometimes wrong, it is always wrong. The most reasonable approach is to accept common sense unless its alternative is clearly superior.

The point of having a moral theory is that it gives guidance in choosing the right actions. And the most important guidance is the kind that helps us resolve moral dilemmas—situations when moral principles or judgments are in conflict. Any moral theory that offers us no help with these problems is said to be *unworkable,* and any unworkable theory is a poor theory.

So all plausible moral theories must . . .

- Be consistent with our considered moral judgments.
- Be consistent with our experience of the moral life.
- Be workable.

In science there is a kind of tension between theory and data. The data affect the theory because the theory is supposed to explain the data. On the other hand, a good theory—one that explains the data better than any other theory does—can lead scientists to call the data into question. The goal is to ensure that the fit between data and theory is as tight as possible. Moral theories work the same way. Our moral experience or considered moral judgments affect our moral theory because any adequate theory must explain such data. And a good moral theory can cause us to accept or reject some moral data. The objective is to get a good fit between theory and data—to achieve what philosophers call "reflective equilibrium."

In section 4.1 we apply these criteria to several religious moral theories, including versions of the divine command theory and the ethics of love theory. In section 4.2 we use the same criteria to evaluate some secular and humanist theories—act- and rule-utilitarianism, Kantian ethics, moral intuitionism, and virtue ethics. Most importantly, we will see what important lessons can be gleaned from all of these theories.

SECTION 4.1

Ethics from Above: Testing Religious Moral Theories

Morality is based on or derived from religion. That, anyway, has been the view of many people from ancient times to the present. The great Christian philosopher Augustine (354–430) maintained that the ultimate authority in morality was God. In the Middle Ages the philosopher William Ockham (1285–1347) held that the rightness or wrongness of actions was willed by God. The idea of morality issuing from God is in the writings of philosophers John Locke (1632–1704) and George Berkeley (1685–1753). Even a few atheistic thinkers have thought that there can be no moral law without God. Philosopher Jean-Paul Sartre, for example, did not believe in God and declared, "If God is dead, everything is permitted." The Russian novelist Dostoyevsky (1821–1881) held the same view. More recently, some famous politicians, including former U.S. Democratic vice-presidential candidate Joseph Leiberman and former president Ronald Reagan, have asserted that religion is the source of morality. They were not saying anything new. They were echoing a common sentiment in the Western world.

Many others, however, have demurred. In the fifth century B.C.E. Greek philosophers were the first to inquire about what morality is, what makes actions right, and what purpose morality serves. They therefore invented moral philosophy. But their moral theories were mostly nonreligious and posited rational, naturalistic grounds for morality.

Protagoras (c. 490–421 B.C.E.) claimed that morality was a useful human creation relative to specific times and cultures. Thus no god was required to give force to the ideas of right and wrong. He declared his famous dictum, "Man is the measure of all things." Plato (c. 427–347 B.C.E.) rejected Protagoras's relativism, insisting that morality was not mere convention but was something objective and universal. But Plato agreed that morality did not need the divine. He argued that God and morality had to be independent of one another.

During the Enlightenment, ethical naturalism blossomed. Several noted thinkers—including Thomas Hobbes, Samuel Clarke, Ralph Cudworth, and Mary Wollstonecraft—thought that, in various ways, moral principles were inherent in human nature or in the universe as a whole. Morality didn't require a divine lawgiver, for the moral law was folded into the nature of things, waiting to open to anyone who cared to look closely. Jeremy Bentham (1748–1832) built the first classic version of utilitarianism, a theory in which morality rested not on the will of a deity, but on a single "principle of utility" that made maximizing happiness the ultimate moral test of actions. Immanuel Kant (1724–1804) veered away from both ethical naturalism and utilitarianism. He proposed instead that morality consisted of conforming one's actions to a moral law that was derived from reason. Kant believes in God, but his moral theory doesn't need the divine.

Out of this mixed legacy of ethical theorizing sprang humanist ideas about morality and the moral life. The most radical of these notions says:

7. Morality cannot be based on the supernatural or the nonrational.

Notice that this claim does not concern the social effects of morality. It does not maintain, for example, that religion-based morality is harmful to society, or that religious people are immoral, or that the world would be better off embracing a secular moral theory. Some humanists have accepted all of these assertions, just as many religious moralists have believed the opposite. But the impact that a moral theory may have on people's lives is a separate issue. The humanist idea here is that morality does not necessarily entail any religious elements.

Are the humanists right about this? To find out, we will examine the case *for* religious moral theories—theories that are in direct conflict with the humanist proposition.

THE DIVINE COMMAND THEORY

Can someone be moral without God? That is, can a person behave morally even if he or she is an atheist? Nowadays most people in the West would probably answer yes to this question. If there are moral standards of behavior, then it seems that anyone can live by them. But our concern here is not whether someone can be moral without belief in God, but whether morality itself is possible without God. The view that morality does require God is called the **divine command theory**. It says that an action is right if God commands or wills it. In other words, certain actions are right or wrong only because God says they are, for he is the author of the moral law. God's commanding an action is what makes it right; God's forbidding it is what makes it forbidden.

Those who accept the divine command theory could consistently think that they should perform actions that promote the common good, as an act-utilitarian would. Or they could believe that they should always act to serve their own interests, as an ethical egoist does. Or they could assume that their duty is to act according to a set of deontological principles. But no matter what approach they take, they would still maintain that ultimately an action is right because God commands it.

Some divine command theorists believe that God's commands are expressed legalistically—as specific rules stated clearly in scripture or made plain in nature. The Ten Commandments theory is a prime example of a legalistic divine command theory. Other divine command theorists think that God's commands are expressed not in a set of unbendable rules, but in the dynamics of each moral situation. **Christian ethics**, though it can take many forms, is usually construed as a type of divine command theory in which the commandments are those of Christ's teachings, especially of the injunction to "love thy neighbor."

To many critics of the divine command theory, the most obvious questions are: (1) Does God exist? (because the existence of God is presupposed by the theory) and (2) How do we know what God's commands are? (because knowledge of God's commands must be possible or the theory is unworkable). Both questions raise troubling issues for the divine command theory, issues that we address in chapters 5 and 7. For now, though, we will discuss difficulties of the theory that would come to fore even if God's existence and our knowledge of his will are assured.

The main problem for the theory—a problem that also afflicts some secular moral theories—is that it is not consistent with our experience of the moral life. We can ask this troubling question, as Plato did twenty-five hundred years ago: Are actions right (or wrong) because God says they are, or does God say they are because they just *are* right (or wrong)? If the divine command theory is correct, then what God says goes, for he *makes* rightness or wrongness. But what if he says that torturing innocent children is right, or that killing your neighbor is right? According to the divine command theory, if God says that these acts are right, then they are right. But this cannot be. Murdering your neighbors and torturing children is wrong whether God says they are or not. If the divine command theory says that such acts would be right if God said they were right, something is very wrong with the divine command theory. The idea of such acts being right is in direct conflict with the realities of our moral life. This absurdity suggests that the theory is unfounded and that morality must not be dependent on God. Beginning with Ralph Cudworth (1617–1680), many religious thinkers have agreed with this argument and rejected the divine command theory.

Some critics—including theists—have argued that if actions are right or wrong only because God says they are right or wrong, then God is unworthy of our praise or worship. If rightness is not independent of God's will, then God cannot do anything because it is right—because there is no rightness. Whatever he does, then, is simply what he chooses to do. In other words, whatever he does is arbitrary. If what he does is arbitrary, he is not worthy of our praise or worship. If true, the divine command theory would not demonstrate God's moral authority—but destroy it.

Now, to shore up the divine command theory against these arguments, someone could say something like this: God would never command the murder of your neighbor, the torture of children, or any other evil acts because God is all-good. But to say this is to argue in a circle and undermine—not strengthen—the divine command theory. The theory is supposed to tell us what morality is, what makes something good. But if goodness is a defining property of God, then God cannot be used to define goodness. Such a tack would result in an empty definition of the divine command theory: Good actions are those commanded by an all-good God. Contrary to appearances, this assertion actually tells us nothing about what makes something good.

Leibniz on Morality and God

Gottfried Wilhelm Leibniz (1646–1710) was an ardent theist who rejected the divine command theory. He thought that if the theory were true, God's choices would be arbitrary, rendering God unworthy of worship:

> In saying, therefore, that things are not good according to any standard of goodness, but simply by the will of God, it seems to me that one destroys, without realizing it, all the love of God and all his glory; for why praise him for what he has done, if he would be equally praiseworthy in doing the contrary? Where will be his justice and his wisdom if he has only a certain despotic power, if arbitrary will takes the place of reasonableness, and if in accord with the definition of tyrants, justice consists in that which is pleasing to the most powerful. Besides it seems that every act of willing supposes some reason for the willing and this reason, of course, must precede the act.*

* G. W. von Leibniz, "Discourse on Metaphysics," in *Leibniz Selections,* ed. Philip P. Wiener (New York: Scribner, 1951), 292.

Some people might contend that even if the divine command theory is unsupported, we still should do what God commands because he will reward us for obedience and punish us for disobedience. But this view quickly crumbles into ethical egoism, insisting that we ought to do what is in our own best interest, namely, to seek reward and avoid punishment. As we have seen, a theory of morality built on self-interest is not a very good theory.

THE ETHICS OF LOVE

These arguments against the divine command theory seem conclusive, but some people may still assert—on different grounds—that morality somehow has a divine source. Some may insist that the religious foundation of morality is simply obvious: The basis of all morality is love, and this ethics of love is based on God's teachings. In other words, they embrace a religious version of what we call the **ethics of love theory**, which says that right actions are those that are based on love toward others. All other moral principles are supposed to be derived from this one principle.

The religious ethics of love theory is summed up in the Bible in Matthew 22:37–40, which commands us to "love the Lord thy God with all thy heart" as well as "love thy neighbor as thyself." Here the imperative to love extends to God as well as to humans. This kind of ethics of love theory has been called **agapism** (from *agapē*, the Greek word for love), and it has been very influential in the Judeo-Christian tradition. (A secular formulation omits the injunction to love God and emphasizes the obligation to love humankind. The secular type can be a humanist theory of morality.)

One appealing form of agapism contains a strong element of **situationalism**, the notion that moral judgments cannot be based on rules but on the dynamics of each situation. (**Situation ethics** is the general term for moral theories based on situationalism.) The idea is that each situation is a separate and unrelated state of affairs in which we must confront the unique set of facts and ask what is the most loving action possible under the circumstances. In a situational ethics of love theory there are no legalistic mandates—just (sometimes) rules of thumb and the ideal of love.

Joseph Fletcher, the foremost proponent of situational agapism, insists that love is the only universal good: "This means . . . that in the framework of ethics, whether theological or autonomous, the terms good and love mean the same thing. Love = good. . . . The writers of the New Testament, for instance, used 'love' when they meant 'good.' As Augustine said later, 'Ethics is *ordo amoris*.'"[1]

Does agapism show that morality is a religious or theistic phenomenon? Even if love is the basis of all morality, and God's favorite theory is agapism, these facts would not demonstrate that morality has a divine source. As the failure of the divine command theory shows, morality—in whatever form it takes—is independent of God. God cannot make actions—including loving actions—right. They either *are* right or not. God may endorse agapism, but he cannot make it a good or bad moral theory.

None of this is to deny the important contribution Christianity has made to Western ethics through its emphasis on love for others and the equal moral status of humans. But the influence of the concept of Christian love is not the same thing as its justification.

An important implication here is that every moral theory must be judged on its own merits, if it is to be judged at all. God's endorsement does not guarantee that a theory will be good. Judging theories is a job we must do ourselves.

Aside from the difficulties mentioned above, is the ethics of love theory itself plausible? Let's see. Loving others certainly seems to be consistent with our considered

Joseph Fletcher on Christian Situation Ethics

The philosopher and theologian Joseph Fletcher advocated an approach to ethics that is opposed to ethical legalism—that is, morality based on adherence to a set of laws or rules. He insisted instead that there is only one rule (to love) and that its application is different in every new circumstance:

> *Christian* situation ethics has only one norm or principle or law (call it what you will) that is binding and unexceptionable, always good and right regardless of the circumstances. That is "love"—the *agapē* of the summary commandment to love God and the neighbor. Everything else without exception, all laws and rules and principles and ideals and norms, are only *contingent,* only valid *if they happen* to serve love in any situation. Christian situation ethics is not a system or program of living according to a code, but an effort to relate love to a world of relativities through a casuistry obedient to love. It is the strategy of love. This strategy denies that there are, as Sophocles thought, any unwritten immutable laws of heaven, agreeing with Bultmann that all such notions are idolatrous and a demonic pretension.*

* Joseph Fletcher, *Situation Ethics: The New Morality* (Philadelphia: Westminster Press, 1966), 17–31.

moral judgments. Some ethicists argue that we have a duty to act lovingly toward others—especially toward those who have acted lovingly toward us. But how much guidance can love give us when we are faced with moral dilemmas, when we find ourselves in situations that require us to make tough moral judgments? The answer is, unfortunately, not much.

The injunction to love is a noble sentiment, but it cannot tell us how to act or what rule to follow or what path to choose. The issue of euthanasia is a good example of the problem. Let's say your mother is terminally ill, suffering terribly—and begging you to put her out of her misery. Because you love her, you want her to be free of pain, to be free of disease, to live. But what guidance can the ethics of love give you here? Should you do what

Natural Law Theory

The basic idea of natural law theories of ethics is that there is an unchanging moral structure that is part of the natural world. This moral structure takes the form of principles of right conduct or a set of basic human goods that are discoverable by universal human reason, which is ours "by nature." The canonical formulations are due to Thomas Aquinas and the Roman lawyer Cicero, who wrote in his *Republic*:

> True law is right reason in agreement with nature; it is of universal application, unchanging and everlasting; it summons to duty by its commands, and averts from wrongdoing by its prohibitions. . . . We cannot be freed from its obligations by senate or people, and we need not look outside ourselves for an expounder or interpreter of it . . . and there will be one master and ruler, that is, God, over us all, for he is the author of this law, its promulgator, and its enforcing judge. Whoever is disobedient is fleeing from himself and denying his human nature. . . .

Today, natural law theory is often associated with Roman Catholic moralists who argue, for example, that the purported wrongness of homosexuality, masturbation, and contraception has to do with their "unnaturalness." However, natural law theory insists that moral knowledge of rights, duties, or values (and, in some cases, their foundation as well) is autonomous of religious and theological considerations, being open to rational reflection by believers and unbelievers alike. To this extent, natural law theories are consistent with the humanist idea that morality has a rational basis. Furthermore, they have exerted tremendous influence on the development of secular ethical defenses of human rights and liberal political systems, beginning in the early modern period with the work of Hugo Grotius.

Traditional natural law theory faces some serious objections, including the objection that it appears to generate a number of obviously unsound ethical judgments. If we understand naturalness in terms of biological proper functions, then many ostensibly acceptable actions would be immoral. For example, it is not the proper biological function of our legs to pedal a bicycle, but there is clearly nothing morally objectionable about doing so. We might try to avoid this problem by restricting the prohibition to actions that *frustrate* the performance of a natural function, in the way that homosexuality might be said to frustrate procreation. One difficulty with this thought is that while a lifetime of homosexuality may frustrate procreation, individual acts of homosexual sex—which the theory supposes to address—do not.

your mother asks and end her life because you love her? Should you refrain from taking her life because you love her? Should you grant her wish—or ignore her wish?

Or say that you're a doctor who must decide which person among one hundred desperate patients will receive a life-saving organ transplant. You care about every patient, but only one can get the transplant. The rest will probably die. To whom should you give the transplant—the five-year-old girl because she's the youngest, the middle-aged man because he's in the greatest pain, the thirty-something man because he's your best friend, or the medical scientist because her research could one day save many lives?

Love may indeed be part of any good moral theory, but the ethics of love theory itself is unworkable. Situation ethics theories suffer from the same problem—even those theories that replace love as the guiding ideal with something else such as humanism or virtue.

The preceding arguments show that moral principles cannot be founded on a supernatural or nonrational basis, so proposition 7 from chapter 1 seems to be justified. We should note, however, that this conclusion is not exclusively humanist. It has been endorsed by many theists who think that morality must be independent of God but may be *sanctioned* (not created) by him.

SECTION 4.2

Ethics from Below: Testing Secular Moral Theories

On April 19, 1995, Timothy McVeigh parked a truck loaded with a massive bomb in front of an office building in Oklahoma City, intending to detonate it and murder as many people as possible. The bomb went off, killing 168 people, including 19 children. Most of us, when calmly considering this event, would judge McVeigh's action to be morally wrong. But what do we understand ourselves to be doing when we make this judgment?

According to our ordinary understanding of morality, we do not think that we are only letting off steam, expressing our emotions (although expressions of emotion may accompany our judgment). We do not think, for example, that our judgment is merely a display of outrage, anger, or shock. Furthermore, we do not think that we are just expressing the majority opinion of our society, merely evaluating the action by the standards of our society, as though our judgment would be different if our society were different. We think, instead, that we are making a true statement about an objective fact: McVeigh's action was wrong regardless of our emotions, our society's standards, or any contrary opinions. A judgment is objective if its truth does not depend on anyone's state of mind, and we understand at least some of our moral judgments to be objective in this way.

Some philosophers, however, dispute the objective character of our moral experience. They have, for example, argued that moral statements only express emotions of approval or disapproval, not facts about what is right or wrong, good or bad. (See the box "Emotivism versus Moral Truth.") Others have thought that moral judgments are not objective but *relative*—entirely dependent on what persons or societies happen to believe. (See the box "Relativism: Is Morality a Matter of Taste?") But most moral philosophers have rejected these views precisely because they cannot explain our ordinary moral experience.

Emotivism versus Moral Truth

Some people claim that there are no moral facts or moral knowledge. Moral judgments or statements don't express facts; they are just not the type of thing that can be true or false. Moral statements are, instead, expressions of emotion, such as "capital punishment—boo!" "euthanasia—hooray!"

This view is known as **emotivism**, and it has some serious problems. It conflicts with common sense. If emotivism is true, then moral disagreement is impossible. But moral discourse does seem to involve disagreements. In addition, emotivism implies that nothing is good or bad, right or wrong, because terms like "good" or "wrong" do not refer to anything. This too flies in the face of our experience of the moral life.

The apparent objective quality of our moral judgments is the key feature in our moral experience. But how do we account for this property? As we have seen, those who accept the divine command theory have a ready answer: God makes objective moral facts. An action is objectively right or wrong because God wills it to be so, and we are somehow able to discern what these objective facts are. The divine command theory, however, has proved

Relativism: Is Morality a Matter of Taste?

Some people argue that what makes an action right for someone is that it is approved by that person. So moral judgments are supposed to be relative to what each person believes. Nothing is universally right or wrong. If you say that abortion is wrong, then it is wrong (for you). If someone else says that abortion is right, then it is right (for her). This view—called **ethical relativism**—can be very comforting (since you can make something right just by believing it right), but it has some weird consequences.

First, the theory implies that each person is morally infallible. If we believe that an action is right, it is right, and we cannot be mistaken. So if convicted murderer Timothy McVeigh believed that bombing a federal building and killing hundreds of innocent people was right, then he was right. Subjective relativism also makes moral disagreement nearly impossible. We disagree with others when we think they're mistaken. But according to subjective relativism, no one could be mistaken. So what is there to disagree about?

Subjective relativism implies that all moral disagreements are about what other people think. So when we disagree with someone about moral issues, what we're really disagreeing with is whether or not that person approves of it. But this is implausible. Moral disputes are not about other people's mental states. Subjective relativism is therefore completely at odds with our experience of the moral life.

to be unfounded. So without divine underpinnings, how do we explain the seeming objectivity of our moral experience?

Philosophers have investigated ways to answer this question since the dawn of secular ethics in ancient Greece. In the broadest sense, the answer has always been the same—the basis for objective morality is either *reason* or *nature*. Some philosophers have thought that objective morality has a logical structure that is somehow "beyond" or "above" nature. Moral principles are either self-evident or deduced from self-evident or fundamental precepts. This approach is the way of nonnaturalistic, or rationalist, moral theories. Others have maintained that objective morality is inherent in nature itself—in the objective properties of human beings or the natural order of the universe. Thus we can investigate moral properties in much the same way that scientists investigate physical properties. This tack is the way of naturalistic moral theories. In either view, moral principles or constraints are thought to be "out there," independent of states of mind, and rational thought is supposed to help us uncover moral realities.

Many people—religious and nonreligious—embrace both approaches. Both theists and nontheists, for example, think that morality is a naturalistic affair and a matter of logic. Likewise, some humanists are ethical naturalists and some are not. So the key humanist idea (though not exclusively humanist) is this:

8. Morality has a rationalist or naturalistic basis.

If this proposition turns out to be unjustified, then all humanist theories of morality will be suspect—and so will many other types of theories.

How can we evaluate such a statement? How can we assess whether morality springs from rational or empirical considerations? One way is to indirectly assess the truth of proposition 8 by evaluating moral theories that purport to have a rationalist or naturalistic source.

Let's begin by evaluating some naturalistic theories, then some rationalist ones, and finally the prospects for establishing either type of theory.

NATURALISTIC THEORIES

How can nature serve as a basis for morality? Aristotle thought that moral virtues are dispositions to behave in accordance with the essential nature, or function, of human beings. Moral actions are those that fulfill the functions of being human, so what humans *are* dictates what they should *do*. Many other thinkers posit that our moral judgments are based on certain feelings or sentiments inherent in humans. The philosopher David Hume (1711–1776) argues that all humans have a capacity for empathy, or "fellow-feeling," and that this natural empathy leads us to regard certain virtues (such as benevolence, courage, and fidelity) as useful or agreeable to ourselves and to others. These virtues are then the source of our moral judgments. Other thinkers assert that certain moral principles are like laws of nature. Samuel Clarke (1675–1729), for instance, reasons that we should "promote the welfare and happiness of all men," and that this rule is derived from the natural "fitnesses" of things.

Can Morality Be "Naturalized"?

The core concept in naturalistic ethical theories is that moral properties can be defined in non-moral, natural terms, or that moral properties just *are* natural properties. In other words, morality can be *naturalized.* The usual hope behind such a formulation is that moral properties can then be investigated or recognized in the same way that science investigates or recognizes any empirical, natural fact. Moral principles will be objective, quantifiable, and less mysterious. But the question is: Does it make sense to claim that morality is identical to, or defined in terms of, natural facts about the world?

There are two famous responses to this question. One of them is often attributed to the great philosopher David Hume (1711–1776). He argues that there is a clear distinction between facts and values. To put it another way, you cannot simply derive an *ought* from an *is.* For example, from the fact that an action would increase the amount of pleasure in the world you cannot infer that you *should* try to enhance pleasure in the world. At least you cannot do so without inserting some kind of moral premise into the statement of fact. As a matter of logic, you simply cannot derive a statement of value (of what you *should* do) from a statement of fact (of what *exists*). Some philosophers, however, reject the fact/value distinction, insisting that some factual claims do contain value elements. For example, they might claim that from the fact that you signed a legal contract you could infer that you *should* honor the contract. Other philosophers think that there is something fishy about such an inference—that the inference is flawed or that the factual premise really is value-laden after all.

The other famous response comes from philosopher G. E. Moore (1873–1958). He claims that no one can plausibly equate concepts like "good" or "right" with a natural property such as "happiness" or "survival value." To do so is to commit what he calls the **naturalistic fallacy**. To support this claim he offers his famous "open-question argument." The ethical naturalist, he says, may stipulate that "good" (or "right") is identical to "pleasant," but you could still legitimately ask, "But *is* 'pleasant' good?" His point is that you could substitute any natural property in this equation—and it would still be an open question as to whether that property was truly good (or right). Since this open question can arise in any naturalistic moral theory, it must be the case that natural properties cannot be identical to good or right.

Moore's open-question argument has been criticized mostly on semantic grounds. Critics point out that (1) the meaning of "good" and "right" is unclear to begin with, so it's not surprising that the open question arises, (2) "good" and "pleasant" may not be synonymous terms, but they can still refer to the same property (just as the "morning star" and "evening star" are not synonymous, but they refer to the same object), and (3) what people mean by different terms (of any kind) is sometimes hard to pin down, but this does not mean that no definition can be correct.

So where does all of this leave naturalistic ethics? Even if we dismiss the arguments of Hume and Moore, we are still confronted with the fact that naturalistic definitions of "good" or "right" seem to conflict with our moral experience. Most of the time, we tend to separate natural properties from moral properties. We think that our factual assertions do not hide some recommendation or prescription or approval or disapproval. They are neutral. But our ethical judgments are a different matter: They carry all kinds of evaluative elements. It would seem odd if we thought something was good but were completely neutral about anyone pursuing it or doing it.

Even if we accepted a naturalistic definition of moral terms, we would still be left with the task of justifying those definitions. Simply offering a definition is not enough. If "good" is identical to "happiness," we might be able to direct our actions accordingly. But what are the reasons for accepting such an equation in the first place? Such an equation amounts to a moral theory, and moral theories demand justification.

A modern take on naturalistic ethics comes from the field of evolutionary biology. Some suggest that biology implies morality because (1) some human actions are more likely to help ensure the survival of the species than others (i.e., have more survival value), (2) some moral values increase the likelihood of such survival actions, and (3) actions that increase the chances of survival and reproduction are "good." So right actions are those with the greatest survival value. (See the box "Can Morality Be 'Naturalized'?")

One of the more alluring naturalistic theories is utilitarianism. It was, for a time, probably the most influential secular theory in the Western world. It is, in its strong emphasis on human happiness and the promotion of the common good, starkly humanist. Jeremy Bentham (1748–1832) founded the theory and gave it its famous formula: Right actions are those that achieve the greatest happiness for the greatest number. By this one simple principle all actions could be judged.

John Stuart Mill (1806–1873), who later refined Bentham's theory, says that: "By happiness is intended pleasure and the absence of pain, by unhappiness, pain and the privation of pleasure. . . . [P]leasure and freedom from pain are the only things desirable as ends, and that all desirable things (which are as numerous in the utilitarian as in any other scheme) are desirable either for the pleasure inherent in themselves, or as means to the promotion of pleasure and the prevention of pain."[2]

In the nineteenth century utilitarianism seemed to be so much more rational and commonsensical than previous moral theories that demanded adherence to rigid rules whose basis was dubious. The theory inspired reformers who demanded social changes that seem obvious now but were radical then—the abolition of slavery, more respect for women's rights, the elimination of child labor, and the recognition of the rights of prisoners.

Bentham's and Mill's theory took on two major forms: act-utilitarianism and rule-utilitarianism. Let's examine them more closely.

Act-Utilitarianism

In its simplest form **act-utilitarianism** says that what makes an action right is that it maximizes overall happiness, everyone considered. As long as an action maximizes happiness in the world, it is morally correct—regardless of the motives of the people involved or how the happiness is achieved. So doing the right thing means calculating how much happiness can be gained from several possible actions and choosing the one action that achieves the greatest amount of happiness.

As a moral theory, act-utilitarianism is far superior to ethical egoism because it insists that we should try to maximize the total amount of happiness in the world—not just our own happiness. It also focuses on an aspect of our moral experience that many other theories ignore—the *consequences* of our actions.

This end-justifies-the-means approach to morality, however, conflicts with some of our considered moral judgments. One of them is that certain things should not be done to people even if doing them would produce the greatest amount of happiness. In other words, people have certain rights, and those rights should not be violated just to promote the common good. Is it right to falsely accuse, convict, and punish an innocent person if doing so would result in greater happiness for a whole town of people? If the total amount of happiness of a dozen people could be increased by torturing one of them, is it right to torture him? Our considered moral judgment says no; act-utilitarianism says yes. If violating someone's rights or committing an injustice maximizes happiness, the action is morally correct. But in many cases we are loathe to violate people's rights and commit injustices just because happiness might be enhanced.

Consider this scenario: There are two possible actions, X and Y, that are exactly equal in their potential to maximize happiness in the world. Both X and Y can produce, say, a thousand units of happiness. But X involves causing a serious injustice, or a broken promise, or a violation of someone's rights. According to act-utilitarianism, X and Y are equally right. But this verdict seems an outrageous contradiction of our considered moral judgments.

Act-utilitarianism is also in conflict with our ordinary understanding of duties. There seems to be no getting around duties that we have to other people, duties like keeping our promises, for example. Act-utilitarianism, however, says that our duty is to maximize happiness—regardless of whether we have to break promises to do it. Breaking promises is just another means to an end. But our commonsense understanding of promises suggests that they are more important than utilitarianism would have us believe. They have more moral weight than some other kinds of statements we could make, otherwise promises would cease to function as promises.

Another way to formulate and extend this criticism about duties is that utilitarianism seems to ignore *backward-looking reasons*. Sometimes we have reasons for acting that arise out of past events. We made a promise to someone yesterday, so now the obligation to keep it gives us good reason to fulfill it. A week ago we harmed someone who did not

Jeremy Bentham on the Principle of Utility

I. Nature has placed mankind under the governance of two sovereign masters, *pain* and pleasure. It is for them alone to point out what we ought to do, as well as to determine what we shall do On the one hand the standard of right and wrong, on the other the chain of causes and effects, are fastened to their throne. They govern us in all we do, in all we say, in all we think: every effort we can make to throw off our subjection, will serve but to demonstrate and confirm it. In words a man may pretend to abjure their empire: but in reality he will remain subject to it all the while. The *principle of utility* recognizes this subjection, and assumes it for the foundation of that system, the object of which is to rear the fabric of felicity by the hands of reason and of law. Systems which attempt to question it, deal in sounds instead of sense, in caprice instead of reason, in darkness instead of light.

II. The principle of utility is the foundation of the present work: it will be proper therefore at the outset to give an explicit and determined account of what is meant by it. By the principle of utility is meant that principle which approves or disapproves of every action whatsoever, according to the tendency which it appears to have to augment or diminish the happiness of the party whose interest is in question: or, what is the same thing in other words, to promote or to oppose that happiness. I say of every action whatsoever; and therefore not only of every action of a private individual, but of every measure of government.*

* Jeremy Bentham, "Of the Principle of Utility," *An Introduction to the Principles of Morals and Legislation* (Oxford: Clarendon Press, 1879).

deserve such treatment, and now we appear to have a duty to somehow make it up to that person. Five years ago someone murdered a young boy, and that fact seems like a good reason to punish the murderer today. For utilitarianism, however, these facts about the past cannot give us reason to act in the present because the only relevant factors are those about the future. The only thing that matters is how much happiness *will* be created if we take a certain action. But in our ordinary moral experience, some facts about the past do matter.

These conflicts with our considered moral judgments and moral experience are act-utilitarianism's biggest failing—and the main reason why many philosophers have abandoned the theory. Some humanists have also rejected utilitarianism on the same grounds, even though the theory is "humanist" in that it makes human welfare its focus.

There is, though, an important truth in all forms of utilitarianism: The consequences of actions do matter. Consistently following a set of absolutist rules while ignoring the consequences of doing so flies in the face of our considered moral judgments. Most of us, for example, would probably think it wrong to refuse to tell a lie even if the lie would prevent the slaughter of thousands of innocent people. If the stakes were high enough, we would think that we were justified in breaking at least some rules.

Rule-Utilitarianism

Some thinkers have contended that there is a form of utilitarianism that fits better with our moral life and judgments—**rule-utilitarianism**. It focuses not on how much happiness a certain *action* can produce, but on how much happiness a certain *rule* can produce. According to rule-utilitarianism, right actions are those in accord with an exception-free rule that—if consistently followed—would result in the greatest happiness, everyone considered. So to determine if an action is right, you must first ask what rule the action is in accord with, then ask if following the rule consistently would produce the greatest happiness. Under this theory, it may be right to consistently obey a rule like "don't steal" even if, in a particular case, not stealing may result in the least degree of happiness.

On the face of it, rule-utilitarianism does seem like an improvement over act-utilitarianism, but it too conflicts with our considered moral judgments. It is fairly easy to imagine a rule that, if consistently followed, would maximize happiness in the world—but would also violate people's rights, cause injustice, or ignore duties. It's possible, for example, that a society could allow slavery and be happier overall than a society that bans the practice. So a rule like "slavery should be allowed" would result in more happiness than a ban on slavery. But slavery is wrong. If rule-utilitarianism could sanction such a practice, there must be something wrong with rule-utilitarianism.

In fact, there seems to be something wrong with the whole idea that happiness is the ultimate goal of any adequate moral system. Both major kinds of utilitarianism assume that happiness is the only intrinsic good. But we can imagine situations in which people experience the greatest degree of happiness possible and still seem to be missing some important things that make life worth living.

Philosopher Robert Nozick illustrated this point in a thought experiment. Imagine being hooked to a machine that supplies you with ready-made sensory experiences. You think and feel that you're writing a novel, making a friend, and doing a thousand other pleasant things, but you're actually just floating in a tank while the machine does its work. You are happy and blissful, believing that you are directing your own life and choosing freely at every pass. So you stay hooked up for life.

Does this scenario really sound like the good life? Spending your life suspended in a tank doesn't seem to be utopia at all—more like a kind of hell. In other words, being happy is just not enough. Any theory, then—humanist or nonhumanist—that assumes that happiness is the *only* ultimate good seems to be inadequate. Our ordinary moral experience, though, seems to suggest that considerations of happiness must play at least some part in our moral judgments. We should note, however, that some thinkers propose moral theories that are consequentialist but not utilitarian. These theories escape the experience-tank objection.

It seems that if we want to find an empirical or naturalistic basis for morality, we cannot look to utilitarianism. This humanistic theory has failed. In fact, if it is an integral part of a humanist worldview, the worldview would be an example of what we have termed naive humanism. But in utilitarianism we can see an example of how some thinkers have tried to bring ethics down to earth and fashion a moral theory based on characteristics of humankind that are objective and even subject to scientific study.

The failure of utilitarianism has not deterred those who want to explain morality in terms of natural properties. In the twenty-first century, naturalistic moral theories—or theories that have a strong naturalistic component—are as widespread as ever. Modern ethical naturalists, for example, have taken a cue from Aristotle and made virtue the primary focus of morality. The resulting theories—called **virtue ethics**—make the core ethical question not What actions should we perform? but What kind of persons should we be?

Virtue Ethics

In no small part, the contemporary field of ethics in English-language philosophy has been dominated by theories that focus on the rights, duties, or actions of individuals, rather than on their characters. It can be argued that this focus suffers from a number of deficiencies. First, it seems to give little attention to some of the most important areas in life, such as friendship, partnership, marriage, parenting, and work. Second, we tend to think that there is more to morality than the effects or intentions of individual actions. We reserve different degrees of admiration for a jealous, vengeful, and malicious person and a magnanimous and benign person, even if both keep their promises out of a sense of moral duty, for example. Considerations such as these have led many philosophers to revive and update the ancient traditions of virtue ethics. In this way, virtue theory may serve as an important adjunct to other sorts of ethical theory.

However, it is difficult to maintain that questions of character could ever completely supplant questions of what is right or good. This is because the characterization of the virtues depends on a prior understanding of right conduct. For instance, we cannot simply say that justice is what the just person does. Presumably a person's justness has to do in part with the sorts of reasons that she takes into account when deliberating about reward, punishment, or distribution of benefits and burdens. In that case, the analysis shifts to the nature of those reasons, and thus, to nonvirtue considerations such as rights.

These approaches tend to be naturalistic in that they ground morality in facts about human nature or cultural traditions. (See the box "Virtue Ethics.")

Some philosophers reject all such attempts to "naturalize" morality. They argue that they do not succeed and that no naturalistic moral theory is likely to succeed. Most of these arguments center on the difficulty of showing that facts about nature can somehow be distilled into ideas about morality—that natural properties like "maximizes happiness" or "causes human suffering" can amount to the same thing as "is right" or "is unjust." (See the box "Can Morality Be 'Naturalized'?")

RATIONALIST THEORIES

Rationalist moral theories assume that fundamental moral truths are known primarily through reason, not through experience. We are supposed to be able to know these truths just by thinking about the concepts involved and their relationships. Through reason we know that there are no square circles (a logical impossibility) and that two plus two equals four. Likewise, by reflecting about moral concepts and how they relate we know that certain kinds of actions are right or wrong. Moral rationalists would say that empirical considerations may be relevant to specific moral judgments, but basic moral truths, or principles, are not founded on empirical fact.

Historically, rationalist approaches have taken on two main forms: the ethical theory of Immanuel Kant and moral **intuitionism**. Both of these are now getting increased attention from moral philosophers. Like utilitarianism, they seem to contain some important insights that fit well with our commonsense moral life. But are they fully adequate as total moral theories?

KANTIAN ETHICS

Kant rejects the core principle of naturalistic theories, the idea that morality is somehow based on natural properties such as human happiness, pleasure, welfare, or survival. He argues that these properties are not our highest good, for they are not intrinsically valuable (good for their own sake). The only thing that is intrinsically valuable is a "good will." A "good will" is the motivation to perform our duty for its own sake—to act out of respect for our moral duty, not out of regard for the impact that our actions will have in the world or even out of feelings of compassion or love. As Kant says, "A good will is good not because of what it effects or accomplishes, nor because of its fitness to attain some proposed end; it is good only through its willing; i.e., it is good in itself."[3] So for Kant, right actions are those performed from a sense of duty for duty's sake.

But what is our duty and how do we know it? Kant says that we come to know our duty through reason. All of our duties are derived logically from a single principle, what Kant calls the "categorical imperative." (It is an *imperative* because it commands us to do something, and it is *categorical* because the command must be obeyed under all conditions.) He maintains that we know this principle "a priori"—that is, without experience in the real world, just as we know many truths of logic, such as the logical consideration that whatever has a shape has a size.

Kant on the Categorical Imperative

Perhaps Kant's most influential formulation of the categorical imperative is the injunction to never treat someone just as a *means* but always as an *end.* It affirms that humans are not things or tools—but rational beings called persons:

> Now I say: man and generally any rational being *exists* as an end in himself, *not merely as a means* to be arbitrarily used by this or that will, but in all his actions, whether they concern himself or other rational beings must be always regarded at the same time as an end. All objects of the inclinations have only a conditional worth; for if the inclinations and the wants founded on them did not exist, then their object would be without value. But the inclinations themselves being sources of want are so far from having an absolute worth for which they should be desired, that, on the contrary, it must be the universal wish of every rational being to be wholly free from them. Thus the worth of any object which is to be *acquired* by our action is always conditional. Beings whose existence depends not on our will but on nature's, have nevertheless, if they are rational beings, only a relative value as means, and are therefore called *things;* rational beings, on the contrary, are called *persons,* because their very nature points them out as ends in themselves, that is as something which must not be used merely as means, and so far therefore restricts freedom of action (and is an object of respect). These, therefore, are not merely subjective ends whose existence has a worth *for us* as an effect of our action, but *objective ends,* that is things whose existence is an end in itself: an end moreover for which no other can be substituted, which they should subserve *merely* as means, for otherwise nothing whatever should possess *absolute worth;* but if all worth were conditional and therefore contingent, then there would be no supreme practical principle of reason whatever.
>
> If then there is a supreme practical principle or, in respect of the human will, a categorical imperative, it must be one which, being drawn from the conception of that which is necessarily an end for everyone because it is *an end in itself,* constitutes an *objective* principle of will, and can therefore serve as a universal practical law. The foundation of this principle is: *rational nature exists as an end in itself.* Man necessarily conceives his own existence as being so: so far then this is a subjective principle of human actions. But every other rational being regards its existence similarly, just on the same rational principle that holds for me: so that it is at the same time an objective principle, from which as a supreme practical law all laws of the will must be capable of being deduced. Accordingly the practical imperative will be as follows: *So act as to treat humanity, whether in thine own person or in that of an other, in every case as an end withal, never as means only.**

* Immanuel Kant, *Fundamental Principles of the Metaphysics of Morals* (London: Longmans, Green, 1909).

Kant produced two formulations of the categorical imperative. The first one says, "Act only on that maxim through which you can at the same time will that it should become a universal law."[4] That is, act only on those moral principles that you could rationally want to become a moral law that applies to everyone. According to Kant, whenever you perform an action, you are implicitly acting according to a moral principle. To determine whether an action is your duty, you must ask yourself what would happen if the principle under which you are acting became a universal law, or became *universalized,* and everyone followed it. Would the world you envision be possible? Would it really make sense to want the principle to become universal? If the answer is yes, then you should act according to the principle. If the answer is no, then the principle is not acceptable.

Let's say that you stole a car and thus the principle on which you acted is: Take other people's possessions whenever you feel like it. Would it make any sense for this principle to be universalized? Note that if it was a universal law, and everyone behaved accordingly, the idea of people owning things would cease to have any meaning. Nothing would really belong to anyone, so the principle itself would not have any meaning. It would not make sense. So you could not *rationally* want the principle to be a universal law.

By applying the categorical imperative in this way, Kant derived several *categorical* duties—duties that have no exceptions in any circumstances. These include the duty not to kill innocent people, not to lie, and not to break promises.

Kant's second formulation of the categorical imperative is, "Act in such a way that you always treat humanity . . . never simply as a means, but always at the same time as an end."[5] This famous dictum seems to capture something essential in moral theories—respect for persons. We should not treat people simply as a means to an end—we should not use them as though they are tools. We should treat them instead as ends in themselves, as things valuable in their own right. Kant's view is that people are inherently valuable because they are self-conscious, rational, and free to make their own choices. Thus it is wrong to steal money from someone because doing so treats that person merely as a means to financial gain. It is wrong to lie to people because doing so manipulates them for someone else's own purposes. It is wrong to enslave someone because doing so uses them against their will for the benefit of others.

This notion of respect for persons resonates with humanist ideas. Some might even argue that the belief that humans are intrinsically valuable is the core idea of humanist thinking. But the idea is also a basic principle in Christian morality, for each person is thought to be infinitely valuable. Kant, however, has probably done the most to show that respect for persons is crucial to morality and that the principle can rest on solid footing.

Kant's theory has some advantages over utilitarianism. The main one is that it sets strict limits on what can be done to persons. No matter how much happiness could be gained in the world, certain acts should never be committed against persons *because they are persons*. Because persons are intrinsically valuable, they have moral rights—and these rights cannot be overridden by considerations of utility or the common good. Utilitarianism, however, cannot set such restrictions on the violation of rights because, at least sometimes, happiness can be maximized by such violations.

The Kantian view, though, has its own problems. One of its strengths is its weakness: The duties derived from the categorical imperative are themselves categorical—they have no exceptions. As in the Ten Commandments theory, Kant's moral duties must be honored no matter what. On Kant's view, you should not lie—not even if the lie could save a dozen lives. You should never kill an innocent person—even if such killing could avert the deaths of a million other innocent people. But this notion of categorical duties is problematic because *there do not seem to be any such duties*. We have duties, but none seem to be categorical. We can always envision possible scenarios like those above in which honoring a categorical duty would be wrong.

Along the same lines, cases are likely in which we *should* treat persons merely as a means. Wouldn't we think it morally permissible to lie to someone—use that person as a means—to prevent, say, World War III?

At the root of these problems is the fact that Kant's theory ignores the consequences of actions. In our commonsense moral experience, the effects of our acts do seem to matter to our moral judgments. Utilitarianism may put too much weight on consequences, but Kantian ethics gives them no weight at all.

Finally, Kant's theory is unworkable. Many duties can be derived from the categorical imperative, and sometimes they conflict. It is possible, for instance, that keeping a promise could cause the death of an innocent person. It's conceivable that to keep your promise to visit a friend in the hospital you ignore the pleas of a seriously injured person you could easily save, resulting in the person's death. A good moral theory would give us guidance on how to resolve these conflicts, but Kant provides no such guidance. In fact, he seems to have thought that conflicts among duties could never occur. Kant's rationalist theory, like utilitarianism, can be the backbone of philosophical humanism—a kind of naive humanism.

Intuitionist Ethics

When we appeal to our ordinary moral experience or our considered moral judgments in assessing the truth of a moral theory, we are appealing to what philosophers call our "moral intuitions." In philosophy, "intuition" refers not to hunches or gut feelings, but to rational knowledge or insight that is not based on perception or argument. We know intuitively, for example, that two plus three equals five, or what the color blue looks like, or what the concepts "near" and "far" mean. A moral intuition is one concerning moral concepts or propositions.

The appeal to moral intuitions is pervasive and well respected in ethics. Philosophers widely agree that any adequate moral theory must take into account our moral intuitions, and that moral theories that conflict with our intuitions are suspect. They know that our moral intuitions are not infallible, but they also understand that our intuitions usually constitute strong evidence unless proven otherwise.

Not surprisingly, in the past two hundred years, philosophers have put forth several rationalist theories that explicitly depend on our moral intuitions. One of the more influential intuitionist theories is that of the Oxford philosopher W. D. Ross (1877–1971). Unlike Kant, Ross argues that we don't have just one duty (the categorical imperative) from which all others are derived—we have several distinct duties. We recognize these duties, he says, in the same way we recognize mathematical or logical truths—through our intuitions. Our intuitions, he says, reveal our duties to be self-evident. A self-evident proposition is one in which, if we understand it, we are justified in believing that it is true. As Ross puts it, "That an act *qua* fulfilling a promise, or *qua* effecting a just distribution of good . . . is *prima facie* right, is self-evident; not in the sense that it is evident from the beginning of our lives, or as soon as we attend to the proposition for the first time, but in the sense that when we have reached sufficient mental maturity and have given sufficient attention to the proposition it is evident without any need of proof, or evidence beyond itself."[6]

But if we have several discrete duties, there are bound to be conflicts among them. Ross tries to solve this problem by establishing a kind of hierarchy of duties. He distinguishes between two types of duties—**prima facie** and **actual**. Prima facie (apparent) duties are those we are obligated to perform in every situation unless special circumstances provide an exception to the rule. The special circumstances are cases in which prima facie duties conflict. For example, "Do not steal" is a prima facie duty, and so is "Don't harm others." These duties would conflict, for example, if the only way you could keep from seriously harming several people would be to steal something. An actual duty is one we should perform in a particular case after we take into account any conflicting prima facie duties—that is, after we decide which prima facie duty is most important in the situation. An actual duty is our final duty.

Ross recognizes several categories of prima facie duties. These include:

1. *Duties of fidelity*—keep your promises, honor your contracts, tell the truth.
2. *Duties of justice*—deal fairly with people.
3. *Duties of beneficence*—benefit others.
4. *Duties of gratitude*—compensate others for acts of kindness.

Ross's theory seems to accord well with our moral intuitions about duties, including our sense that some duties must override considerations of the consequences of actions or of the common good. In fact, his view has been criticized because it seems to do *nothing but* reflect our intuitions—to be a kind of report on the contents of our ordinary moral experience. But as it stands, his theory is unworkable—it provides little guidance for resolving conflicts among duties. The distinction between prima facie and actual duties is some help, but it is not enough to show us how to rank prima facie duties in importance.

Ross's notion of moral intuitions has probably drawn more criticism than any other aspect of his theory. Critics have taken Ross to hold (1) that we have a mysterious faculty of mind that delivers up the Rossian moral intuitions and (2) that our moral intuitions yield "certain knowledge" of moral principles. In light of what is known about epistemology and the philosophy of mind, both of these assumptions seem implausible. Contemporary intuitionists, though, agree that these two points are questionable and maintain that there are far more plausible forms of moral intuitionism.[7] They argue that our moral intuitions need not be any more mysterious or implausible than the moral intuitions we ordinarily appeal to. A more credible view of moral intuitions is that they can be self-evident without being infallible; that they can avoid arbitrariness because they involve reflection and can be tested against the demands of a moral theory; and that they are not mysterious because they arise in the same way that other kinds of rational intuitions do—from an understanding of the concepts and properties involved.

While arguing for such an understanding of moral intuitions, some philosophers have tried to improve on Ross-type theories by providing ways to resolve conflicts among duties. One suggestion is using Kant's categorical imperative as a formula for weighing competing duties.[8] For example, if a duty to tell the truth conflicts with a duty to not harm others (as when a madman intent on murdering your friend asks you where your friend is), the deciding factor may be whether your choice could be universalized.

Another proposal is to use our moral intuitions—specifically, our duties to promote good consequences, respect persons, and care for those who care for us—as criteria for judging the correctness of our actions.[9] Scientists use certain criteria to judge the adequacy of scientific theories (criteria such as how simple a theory is or how many phenomena it explains). Likewise, we could use our core set of obligations as standards for judging actions. This view rightfully assumes that these criteria cannot be ranked in order of importance. But they can render a choice between actions as objective because the criteria do not depend on anyone's mental states.

Such intuitionist views (with some way of resolving conflicts among duties) have several advantages over all the other theories we have examined. They accord well with our considered moral judgments and moral experience and give appropriate emphasis to moral intuitions. They are not hampered by a utilitarian blindness to duties or the rights of persons. They avoid the problems of Kantian-type categorical duties. And they can accommodate considerations of the consequences of actions.

NATURALIST OR RATIONALIST

Where has this journey into ethics taken us? We have arrived at a vantage point where we can better appreciate what moral theories must do and how they might do it. Along the way we have identified some elements that any good moral theory should encompass—our considered moral judgments, our commonsense moral experience, the consequences of actions, respect for persons, and the resolution of conflicts among duties.

Robert Audi on Modern Intuitionism

Contemporary moral intuitionists are quick to point out that intuitionism need not posit that moral intuitions are infallible or that the mind has some mysterious faculty that "perceives" moral intuitions. Robert Audi explains modern intuitionism's more modest claims:

> Ethical reflectionism is not as such a form of ethical intuitionism, but its truth provides the best explanation of what the most credible forms of ethical intuitionism are committed to. In these forms, I suggest, ethical intuitionism is, in outline, the view that we can have, in the light of appropriate reflection on the content of moral judgments and moral principles, intuitive (hence non-inferential) justification for holding them. Most of the plausible versions of intuitionism also endorse a plurality of moral principles (though Moore is notable for holding an overarching, ideal utilitarian principle of right action), and most versions are also rationalist, holding that there are a priori moral principles. But an intuitionist could be an empiricist, taking intuition to be capable of providing an experiential ground for moral judgments or principles. Intuitionists typically hold that moral knowledge as well as moral justification can be intuitive, but the major ones are not committed to the view that this justification or knowledge is indefeasible, and then tend to deny that it is.
>
> If the arguments of this essay indicate how intuitionism as just broadly characterized can be plausible, they also show how an overall rationalistic intuitionists theory like Ross's can be strengthened. Moreover, if what is said earlier in support of reflectionism indicates how an intuitionist view in moral epistemology is compatible with empiricism—even if it also brings out why it is natural for intuitionists to be rationalists—it also shows how a rationalist moral epistemology can be freed of the apparent dogmatism and associated arbitrariness, the implausible philosophy of mind, and the immoderate epistemic principles often attributed to it.*

* Robert Audi, *Moral Knowledge and Ethical Character* (New York: Oxford University Press, 1997), 54–55.

Social Contract Theory

The social contract tradition has important precedents in the ancient world, but began in earnest with the attempts by early modern thinkers to establish the legitimacy of government and the political obligations of citizens without appealing to a natural or divine order that places some people—such as kings—in positions of authority over others. The idea was that political norms exist because of an agreement among people designed to regulate their social interactions, and that people are obligated to abide by these norms because they have agreed to them. This classical social contract theory was fatally flawed. As David Hume pointed out, it is apparent that no real human societies are founded on an actual agreement of their members. And if, on the other hand, the contract is supposed to represent what people *would* agree to, it then lacks normative force, for one is not obligated to keep one's hypothetical promises.

In the latter half of the twentieth century, the social contract tradition returned in the form of a family of ethical theories. They centered on the idea that moral obligations are conventions that arise from the social interactions of morally equal individuals that serve to protect their interests. In these theories, agreement is not an actual or hypothetical event, but a conceptual device that helps to identify mutually advantageous conventional norms. Broadly speaking, there are two strands of ethical contractarianism, one deriving from Thomas Hobbes and another deriving from Immanuel Kant. Hobbesian contractarianism attempts to ground morality in "enlightened self-interest," to show that it is ultimately rational for self-interested agents to adopt certain constraints on the pursuit of their interests. Kantian contractarianism aims to articulate the moral principles that would be selected by an agent who accords impartial consideration to every party involved.

Although both views continue to attract defenders, they face recurrent difficulties. Hobbesian theories are said to lead to unacceptable results because there is often no self-interested reason for agents to accept conventions that would protect or benefit those with relatively little power, such as the young, the old, the sick, and disabled. Kantian theories attempt to safeguard the interests of the weak by incorporating moral judgments about impartiality and fairness into the contract. Consequently, they invite the charge of assuming the very moral standards they should be justifying.

We have also seen how rationalists and naturalists try to account for most or all of these elements. An ethical rationalist might say that our commonsense understanding of moral facts is based on our self-evident moral intuitions, that we can systematize these intuitions by providing a rational explanation of how they are connected, and that we can use this explanation—this theory—to assess the validity of our intuitions. An ethical naturalist might maintain that a moral theory must accord with our commonsense understanding of the moral facts, that our ordinary understanding of moral facts is based on our empirical sense of what kinds of natural properties are morally relevant (because they do or do not cause human suffering, for example) or on our assumption that a certain natural property (like pain) is inherently bad, that we can systematize our moral judgments by providing an explanation of what the relevant natural properties are, and that this explanation, or theory, can help us assess the moral facts.

None of the major theories we have examined is entirely adequate, but new variations on at least some of them—namely, the revised intuitionist theories—seem both plausible and promising.[10] If an intuitionist theory (or any other kind of theory) does offer the best explanation for our moral judgments and experience, then we have excellent reasons for believing it to be true. And if it is true, morality must have a rationalistic basis, and proposition 8 must be correct. (Recall that proposition 8 would be true if morality had *either* a rationalistic or naturalistic basis.)

Even if we have not yet established a plausible rationalist or naturalist theory, we may still conclude that proposition 8 is true. After all, if morality cannot be based on a supernatural source (as our critique of the divine command theory shows), the alternative must be either naturalist or rationalist—for these two approaches seem to exhaust the possibilities.

SUMMARY

Ethics is the philosophical study of morality—of the nature and validity of moral judgments. There are two main types of moral theories: consequentialist and formalist. Consequentialist theories claim the rightness of an action depends on its consequences. Formalist theories claim the rightness of an action depends on its form or nature. All plausible moral theories must be workable (they must help us solve moral problems) and consistent with our considered moral judgments and our experience of the moral life.

The divine command theory says that morality requires God. But the theory conflicts with experience of the moral life. The problem is that if God's will makes an action right, then he can make any action right, even actions that are clearly wrong. In the ethics of love theory, an action is right if it accords with the dictum to do everything that love demands. But the theory is unworkable because it gives no guidance in how someone determines what love demands.

There are also many secular moral theories, which can be either naturalistic or rationalistic. Act- and rule-utilitarianism are naturalistic theories that are strongly consequentialist. All forms of utilitarianism, however, are inadequate because they are inconsistent with our considered moral judgments—especially those dealing with issues of justice, rights, and duties. Rationalistic theories include Kantian ethics and intuitionist ethics. Kantian ethics contains valuable insights into our moral experience but ultimately is unworkable. Intuitionist ethics appeals to our moral intuitions (rational knowledge or insight that is not based on perception or argument). Rossian intuitionist theories are unworkable. Modern intuitionism, however, does not seem to suffer from the same kind of flaws and therefore appears to be an adequate moral theory.

STUDY QUESTIONS

1. What is a moral theory? What is ethics?
2. What is the Ten Commandments moral theory and is it plausible?
3. What are consequentialist moral theories? What are formalist moral theories?
4. What is the divine command theory? Is it a plausible theory?

5. What is emotivism? What is moral relativism?
6. What is act-utilitarianism? What does it mean for an action to be judged by its utility?
7. What is intuitionist ethics?

DISCUSSION QUESTIONS

1. Can morality be naturalized? Why or why not?
2. What would society be like if everyone was an ethical egoist?
3. The Golden Rule ("do unto others as you would have them do unto you") can be made to serve as a simple moral theory. Would the Golden Rule moral theory be plausible?
4. Could Kant's categorical imperative (the version about means and ends) serve as the basis for a moral theory? How?
5. Suppose someone proposed a moral theory based on emotion; that is, it would say that an action is right if it coincides with our feelings at the time of the action. If you performed an action out of anger or love, it would be right because it coincided with your emotions. Is this a plausible moral theory? Why or why not?

FIELD PROBLEM

Some people subscribe to this principle: We should be free to perform any action as long as it does not harm others. We might call this the live-and-let-live theory of morality. Is it a plausible theory? Use the criteria for theory assessment to evaluate the worth of this theory.

SUGGESTIONS FOR FURTHER READING

Feldman, Fred. *The Moral Point of View*. Ithaca, N.Y.: Cornell University Press, 1958.
Frankena, William. *Ethics*. Englewood Cliffs, N.J.: Prentice-Hall, 1973.
Nielsen, Kai. *Ethics without God*. Amherst, N.Y.: Prometheus Books, 1973.

NOTES

1. Joseph Fletcher, "Naturalism, Situation Ethics, and Value Theory," *Normative Ethics and Objective Reason*, ed. George F. McLean (Washington, D.C.: Council for Research in Values and Philosophy, 1995).
2. John Stuart Mill, "What Utilitarianism Is," *Utilitarianism* (Amherst, N.Y:. Prometheus Books, 1987).
3. Immanuel Kant, *Grounding of the Metaphysics of Morals*, trans. James E. Ellington (Indianapolis: Hackett, 1981).
4. Immanuel Kant, *Groundwork of the Metaphysics of Morals*, trans. H. J. Paton (New York: Harper and Row, 1964), 88.
5. Kant, *Groundwork of the Metaphysics of Morals*, 96.
6. W. D. Ross, *The Right and the Good* (Oxford: Oxford University Press, 1930), 29–30.

7. Robert Audi, *Moral Knowledge and Ethical Character* (New York: Oxford University Press, 1997).

8. Audi, 279–86.

9. Theodore Schick, Jr., and Lewis Vaughn, *Doing Philosophy* (Mountain View, Calif.: Mayfield, 1999), 311–12.

10. Jonathan Dancy, "Intuitionism," in *A Companion to Ethics* (Oxford: Blackwell, 1993), 411–20.

5

Knowledge, Truth, and Faith

Lewis Vaughn

Here is a serious question most people do not take seriously: *Do we know anything?* That is, do we have knowledge about the world? Is it possible that we think we know things but in fact know very little or nothing at all?

Now, why would anyone think that such questions are anything but a little inane? After all, don't we know a great many things—that we are alive, that our hair is a certain color, that there is a tree on the lawn, that the Earth is not flat, that rabbits cannot fly? Yet from ancient times to the present day many brilliant thinkers have entertained such doubts—even though they are perfectly aware of the countless circumstances in which we seem to obviously have knowledge. Most philosophers have taken these doubts seriously and have explored how to answer the arguments put forth by the doubters.

The belief that we know much less than we think we do is known as **skepticism**, and thinkers who raise doubts about how much we know are known as **skeptics**.

Here's an example of how skepticism can arise. A very plausible view of knowledge is that knowledge requires certainty. To know something, we must be certain of it. If we are not certain—if there is reason to doubt—then we do not really know. Let's say that you go for a drive in the countryside, and you come to a beautiful pasture with several cows grazing. You count the cows—you count exactly fifty. You are careful when you count, so you declare that there are exactly fifty cows in the pasture—and that you *know* that there are fifty cows in the pasture.

But wait. Isn't it possible that you miscounted? You are not infallible, so of course it is possible. If it is possible that you miscounted, then you cannot be certain of the number of cows. You therefore do not really know that there are fifty cows.

You count them again—fifty-one. So you are taking no chances this time—you count all of the cows ten times: fifty-one. Now can you be said to know there are fifty-one cows? No, because it is at least possible that you miscounted—that you, say, mistook a sheep dog for a cow. Or maybe the summer heat made you hallucinate. Or perhaps some clever farmer wants people to think that his herd is larger than it is, so he places several ceramic cows with the living cows, throwing off your count. A skeptic would point out many more possibilities for error, no matter how careful you are. She would say that because it is always possible that you are mistaken, you cannot be certain, and you therefore cannot have knowledge.

Skeptical doubts, of course, can be much more compelling than this example. In fact, the skepticism of some great minds has changed the course of philosophy—and not only in epistemology (the study of knowledge). Skepticism has had its greatest impact in prompting philosophers to try to answer the skeptic.

The roots of skepticism go way back into history. The Greek philosopher Protagoras (c. 490–421 B.C.E.) said "man is the measure of all things." Plato (c. 427–347 B.C.E.) took this to mean that there is no objective knowledge or truth—that knowledge or truth is whatever individuals say it is—and argued against this view.

In ancient times there were two main schools of skepticism. The **Pyrrhonists**, named after Pyrrho of Elis (c. 365–275 B.C.E.), did not maintain that nothing could be known, but they sought to suspend judgment about all knowledge claims. Sextus Empiricus (who flourished about 200 C.E.) was a Pyrrhonist and the most distinguished skeptic of the ancient world. The **Academics** (third and second centuries B.C.E.) were associated with an offshoot of the Academy founded by Plato. They, unlike the Pyrrhonists, accepted an extreme form of skepticism in which nothing at all could be known.

The Academic type of skepticism has not been accepted by very many people, past or present, because it is easily shown to be unfounded. If someone claims that nothing can be known, he involves himself in a contradiction. The claim that nothing can be known is itself a knowledge claim. So if the claim is true, it cannot be known—it defeats itself.

The skepticism of Sextus Empiricus was later influential in the sixteenth century, casting doubt on ideas of religious truth and scientific knowledge. The great French essayist Michel de Montaigne (1533–1592) became a powerful voice for skepticism in France and the rest of Europe. Erasmus (c. 1466–1536) used skeptical arguments against Martin Luther's Reformation ideas. René Descartes, whose work marks the beginning of modern philosophy, was not a skeptic, but he presented probably the clearest and most famous statement of skeptical arguments that we have.

Most philosophers have not been thoroughgoing skeptics, and the same could be said of most humanists throughout history. Philosophical humanism, after all, is a set of ideas about the world and our place it, and these are consistently stated as knowledge claims. Many humanists, however, have been limited skeptics—people who deny that knowledge is possible in specific areas of inquiry. They have, for example, denied the possibility of knowledge in certain religious matters, metaphysics (the study of the nature of reality), and ethics. But very few people who have called themselves humanists have been across-the-board (or global) skeptics.

There have been—and still are—a fair share of religious people who have embraced some form of skepticism. But in general the major Western religions have assumed, or asserted, that we can know many things about the world.

As far back as Protagoras some people have also attacked the prevailing notion of truth. Knowledge, as we will soon see, is true belief supported by justification. Truth is part of the idea of knowledge; it is a relation between a statement and the world that the statement is supposed to be about. In various ways, however, some people have rejected the normal concept of truth (called "objective truth") and proposed various replacements.

So the usual ideas about knowledge and truth—which humanism has normally assumed—have been challenged from many quarters. In section 5.1 we see how well the

Is Gullibility Morally Wrong?

Some philosophers have asserted that it is morally wrong to believe a proposition without justification or evidence. One of these is the famous biologist Thomas Henry Huxley. Another is mathematician W. K. Clifford (1845–1879). This is how Clifford states his view:

> It is wrong always, everywhere, and for anyone, to believe anything upon insufficient evidence. If a man, holding a belief which he was taught in childhood or persuaded of afterwards, keeps down and pushes away any doubts which arise about it in his mind . . . and regards as impious those questions which cannot easily be asked without disturbing it—the life of that man is one long sin against mankind.*

Clifford thinks that belief without evidence is immoral because our actions are guided by our beliefs, and if our beliefs are unfounded, our actions (including morally relevant actions) are likely to be imprudent.

* W. K. Clifford, "The Ethics of Belief," in George I. Mavrodes, ed., *The Rationality of Belief in God* (Englewood Cliffs, N.J.: Prentice-Hall, 1970), 159–60.

common notion of knowledge stands up to these attacks. In section 5.2 we do the same for the idea of objective truth.

SECTION 5.1

Reason for Living: Believing, Doubting, and Knowing

How does the problem of skepticism and knowledge arise in the first place? Put another way, why would anyone think to question the possibility of knowledge when our ability to know things seems—at least sometimes—indisputable?

Skepticism gets a foothold because of this uncomfortable truth about ourselves: There is a gap between our experience of the world and the world itself. Our experience is *about* the world—it is not synonymous with the world. If this is true, then what assurance do we have that our experience gives us an accurate "view" of the world? What assurance do we have that the world is anything like how our experience suggests that it is?

Skepticism can seem like a reasonable option because the answer to this question is not obvious. If we believe that we perceive the world directly and that the world is exactly as our experience suggests—a view called **naive realism**—we provoke even more troubling questions. For example, if naive realism is true, how is it that our experience can change while things in the world do not? How are illusions possible? On the other hand, we cannot step outside ourselves to try to see the world as it "really is," So there's a gap between what *seems* and what *is*. Skepticism challenges us to show how this gap can be bridged.

Philosophical humanism, like many other worldviews, assumes that the gap can indeed be spanned. It asserts this proposition:

9. We can know many things through reason and unfettered inquiry, but skepticism and faith block understanding.

The question is whether this assumption is justified.

THE SKEPTICAL CHALLENGE

The skeptic wants to challenge our claim of knowledge. But what is knowledge? What does it mean to *know* something?

This is a question about what is called **propositional knowledge**—knowledge *that* something is the case, knowledge of a fact. It is not a question about other types of knowledge, such as knowledge of *how* to do something or knowledge of *what* something feels like. So the skeptic's doubts usually concern propositional knowledge about the empirical world.

For thousands of years the view among both philosophers and nonphilosophers alike has been that knowledge consists of three basic elements—*belief* that is both *true* and *justified*. Anything that does not have *all* of these elements cannot be knowledge. Plato was the first to suggest this account of knowledge, and from his day to ours it has proven to be very hard to dispute, at least in its most general form. It says that to know a proposition we must believe it, and it must be true—knowledge requires true belief. Certainly we cannot be said to know a proposition unless we believe it, and we cannot know it if it is false. To know a proposition is to believe that it is true.

But true belief alone is not enough for knowledge because we can have a true belief and still not have knowledge. Let's say that for no good reason you believe that at this moment your best friend is sleeping in the quad. Let's also say that, as it turns out, your best friend *is* sleeping in the quad. So here you have a true belief, but do you have knowledge?

No. Because you have no reason to believe that your best friend is sleeping in the quad, your belief is no better than a lucky guess—and a lucky guess cannot be knowledge. For your true belief to constitute knowledge, you must be justified in believing it to be true. So knowledge is justified true belief.[1] As Plato says, "True opinions are a fine thing and do all sorts of good so long as they stay in their place, but they will not stay long. They run away from a man's mind, so they are not worth much until you tether them by working out the reason. . . . Once they are tied down, they become knowledge."[2]

The skeptic generally does not dispute this definition of knowledge. Instead, her skepticism is usually directed at the justification condition of knowledge. She wants to say we do not have knowledge because we are never justified in believing we do.

Why are we never justified? We are never justified in believing something to be true, says the skeptic, because we are justified in believing something to be true only if we are certain of it—and certainty is very, very hard to come by.

This influential form of skepticism is given its greatest and clearest expression by René Descartes (1596–1650), who sought a way to answer the skeptic and not prove the skeptic right. He agreed that we can know something only if we are certain of it, but he wanted to show that certainty is achievable.

His search for certainty was inspired by mathematics. Descartes was a genius mathematician and discovered analytical, or coordinate, geometry. (The term "Cartesian coordinates" is a reminder of Descartes's accomplishment.) In mathematics he saw a beautiful system that yielded impressive certainties from which other certainties could be derived. He wondered if there might be a way to uncover similar certainties about the empirical world.

Descartes's strategy was to begin by doubting everything that could be doubted—tossing aside every piece of alleged knowledge that was not certain. If he ended up with an undoubtable proposition, he would have a certainty upon which to support claims of knowledge.

Descartes begins by asking: What about our own sense experience—isn't this a source of knowledge? But he sees immediately that our senses can deceive us. We think we see a man in the distance, but the man is actually a tree stump. In the river we see a stick bend where it enters the water, but the bent stick is actually straight. We see a patch of blue, but it turns out to be green. Our senses are deceivers. They always bring doubt with them.

To illustrate how doubt always accompanies our senses—and therefore deprives us of knowledge—Descartes offered his famous dream argument. He considers how many occasions he has sat by the fire, reading a book—only to awake and find that it was all a dream! Even worse, he says there is no procedure to prove that he is *not* dreaming: "But in thinking over this I remind myself that on many occasions I have in sleep been deceived by similar illusions, and in dwelling carefully on this reflection I see so manifestly that there are no certain indicators by which we may clearly distinguish wakefulness from sleep that I am lost in astonishment. And my astonishment is such that it is almost capable of persuading me that I now dream."[3]

Are you dreaming now? Psychologists remind us that dreams can be extremely vivid and seem entirely real. Descartes's point is that because we literally cannot make this distinction, there is no way to be certain that we are not dreaming right now. We must therefore doubt whether we are experiencing the real world or a dream. If we doubt, we cannot know.

That we are dreaming right now may seem like an outlandish possibility, but a mere possibility is all Descartes needs for his argument to go through. If it is possible—in the slightest degree—that we are dreaming now, then we cannot be sure that we are not dreaming now.

But even if we cannot be sure about whether or not we are dreaming, we can at least know that the world contains specific things, can't we? For example, because we experience heat and cold, colors, and sounds, don't we know that there are things in the world that are hot and cold, colored, and noisy? We may be wrong about this color or that, this sound or that, but how could we be mistaken about there being colored things and noisy things in the world?

Descartes proposes that we may not know even this much. It is possible that an all-powerful, malevolent being (a demon perhaps) gives us all our sensory experiences—and that these experiences have no relation to the real world at all. Everything we believe about the external world could be completely false because the demon gives us inaccurate sensory input.

Such scenarios are easily imagined, and skeptics do imagine them. A common variation on Descartes's demon is a mad scientist giving us experiences through electrodes in our brains, deceiving us into believing that we are perceiving the world truly. In another variation we are disembodied brains in a jar of chemicals, and a computer manipulates all of our sense experiences. Descartes's formulation of the skeptic's challenge, however, is the most famous and perhaps the most powerful. In a vivid way, his argument gets to the heart of the matter: If we cannot be certain about our knowledge claims—if there is even the slimmest reason to doubt—we cannot be said to know anything.

After laying waste to the great edifice of our presumed knowledge, however, Descartes tries to rebuild it, thus thwarting the skeptic by giving knowledge a foundation. He says there is something he knows after all. He knows that he thinks, and he knows that he exists. He knows that he thinks because by doubting that he is thinking—he is thinking! Doubting is a kind of thinking. So he cannot really doubt that he is thinking, and if he cannot doubt it, then he knows it. Furthermore, if he knows that he is thinking, then he exists, and this is beyond doubt. He therefore knows that he exists. As Descartes puts it in his famous phrase, "*Cogito, ergo sum*"—"I think, therefore I am."

So Descartes claims to know that he thinks and that he exists. He also knows *what* he thinks—that is, he knows what's going on inside his head. So if he seems to see a dog, then he knows that he seems to see a dog. In reality it may be a coyote, but Descartes still knows that he seems to see a dog.

With these few bricks of knowledge, Descartes can begin to build the foundation he needs. He knows how things appear to him; he just needs some guarantee that the appearances are connected to reality. His guarantee is another one of his famous principles: Whatever I clearly and distinctly perceive is true.

This principle means that if Descartes clearly and distinctly perceives a cat on the mat, then it is true that there is a cat on the mat—he thus knows that there is a cat on the mat. All Descartes needs to do is prove that the principle is true. So he reasons like this:

1. God exists and is not a deceiver.
2. If God exists and is not a deceiver, then whatever I clearly and distinctly perceive is true (because God would not be so malicious as to mislead me).
3. Therefore, whatever I clearly and distinctly perceive is true.

Descartes establishes to his own satisfaction that God exists. (He uses a type of "ontological argument," which we examine in chapter 7.) Then he infers that because God is perfect, God cannot be a deceiver. "I recognize it to be impossible that He should ever deceive me; for in all fraud and deception some imperfection is to be found . . . yet the desire to deceive without doubt testifies to malice or feebleness, and accordingly cannot be found in God."[4]

So if God is no deceiver, then he would not distort people's God-given ability to obtain knowledge (through clear and distinct perception). This ability then allows people to perceive truly, and if there are any perceptual errors, the fault is due to the frailty of humankind, not God.

Descartes's astonishingly original argument has been a touchstone for countless investigations of skepticism and knowledge. Nevertheless, the argument is problematic. For Descartes to prove his case, his argument must be valid (the conclusion must follow from the premises), and the premises must be true. The argument is indeed valid, but there is trouble in the premises.

As later discussions of the existence of God make clear, the first premise is dubious. Descartes's ontological argument for the existence of God, like all versions of this type of argument, fails. If the existence of God is in doubt (premise 1), then we cannot use his existence to prove that the principle of clarity and distinctness is true (premise 2). Thus we cannot know that the principle is true, and without the principle Descartes has no way to prove the skeptic wrong.

So the question remains: Is there any adequate reply that can given to the skeptic? Actually, Descartes's approach hints at a promising possibility. He assumes—as skeptics traditionally do—that knowledge requires certainty. He believes that if we are to know anything, we must be certain of it. Our knowledge isn't knowledge unless it is beyond any possibility of doubt. As we have seen, if knowledge does require certainty, we know very little because there are always considerations that can undermine our certainty. But does knowledge really require certainty?

Skeptics try to make their case by citing situations in which we have less than complete certainty that something is true. But it is just as easy to cite many examples in which we do seem to have knowledge—even though we do not have absolutely conclusive evidence. We usually would claim to know, for example, that it is raining, that there is a tree on the lawn, that we have two feet, that the Earth is not flat—even though we are not certain of any of these. What such counterexamples show is that Descartes's claim that knowledge

"Naturalized" Epistemology

Traditionally, epistemology (the study of the nature and extent of our knowledge) has been concerned with issues of justification, truth, reason, certainty, and skepticism. Knowledge has been thought to be about conceptual and logical relationships, about how people can properly come to have knowledge. Some philosophers, though, have insisted that this approach is hopeless or irrelevant. They prefer instead to view epistemology as an empirical or scientific study. They are concerned not with what can *justify* or constitute knowledge but with what physically *causes* epistemic activity. Epistemology, then, is thought to be a branch of science, primarily psychology, that studies a particular kind of natural phenomenon.

An example of this approach is the **casual theory of knowledge**. This is the idea that knowledge is not justified true belief (the standard theory) but is *suitably caused true belief.* "Suitably caused" means produced by the state of affairs that makes the belief true. On this view, you would have knowledge that a cat was on the mat because the cat on the mat causes you (through your perception of the cat on the mat) to believe that the cat is on the mat. You know that Spain is in Europe because that fact, through your memory, causes you to believe that Spain is in Europe. Knowledge, then, is not a matter of justification but of facts outside the mind hitting our (physical) truth-registering equipment.

Like other naturalized theories of knowledge, however, the causal theory runs into trouble. The gist of the problem is that it is possible for someone to have a suitably caused true belief and still not have knowledge. For example, suppose you are looking at barns in the countryside. The first barn you come to is a genuine barn, so you have a suitably caused belief that it is a barn. But let's say that the countryside also has numerous fake barns (mere facades that look like barns). Under these circumstances you cannot be said to *know* that you are looking at a genuine barn. Suitably caused true belief cannot constitute knowledge.*

* Alvin I. Goldman, "Discrimination and Perceptual Knowledge," *Journal of Philosophy* 73 (1976), 771–91.

requires certainty is itself doubtful. Because of these counterexamples, Descartes cannot be certain that knowledge requires certainty; he therefore cannot know that knowledge requires certainty. The skeptic's straightforward claim that no proposition can be known unless it is beyond all possible doubt is unfounded.

In fact, our reflective common sense suggests that we do know many things. We know them not because they are beyond all *possible* doubt, but because they are beyond all *reasonable* doubt. Doubt is always possible, but it is not always reasonable. It is possible that evil scientists are manipulating your brain as you read this book, but to ignore the evidence of your senses because of such a possibility would not be reasonable. Rejecting a reasonable claim to knowledge just because of the bare possibility that you may be wrong is neither reasonable nor necessary.

The upshot of all this is good news for those seeking knowledge. In proposition 9 skepticism is rejected. Now this rejection seems to be justified.

KNOWING THROUGH FAITH

If we humans possess knowledge, how do we get it? What is the source of this knowledge? There are four sources we all rely on constantly, that we assume without reflection, and that we still trust even *after* reflection: perception, introspection, memory, and reason.

Perception, or sense experience, gives us most of our information about the world. If we know the iron is hot, the sky is blue, the traffic is loud, or the tabletop is round, we know it primarily because our sense experience supplies us with the relevant data. **Introspection** gives us information about our own mental states, the contents of our minds. Through introspection we come to know our internal experience, our feelings and thoughts. **Memory** is a source of knowledge because it helps us process the data we gather from other sources. Without memory's storage and retrieval functions, information about the world would be lost. **Reason** is our ability to "see" the logical relations among concepts, propositions, and arguments. Through reason we know that seven plus five is twelve, that there are no married bachelors, that square circles are impossible, and that if John is taller than Mary and Mary is taller than Jane, then John is taller than Jane.

All these sources of knowledge, however, are fallible. We can sometimes misinterpret our sense experience, draw the wrong conclusion from introspection, have false or defective memories, and err in our reasoning. But most of the time these elementary sources serve us well. Our perception, introspection, memory, and powers of reason are generally reliable, and the mere possibility of error does not prove otherwise. We are justified in believing what these sources reveal to us—unless we have good reason to doubt it. We are entitled to claim that we have knowledge—unless we have good reason for thinking that something has gone wrong with our ordinary means of acquiring knowledge.

But what about faith? Is faith a source of knowledge? Are its credentials at least as good as those of our ordinary sources of knowledge? Religious faith, in the normal sense of the word, is belief without regard for evidence—without regard for reasons or justification for supposing the belief to be true. ("Faith" can also refer to trust or confidence in someone or something, as in "I have faith in her." This kind of belief usually does rest on some kind of justification. If your best friend has always been loyal to you, for example, you have good reason to believe that she will continue to be loyal.) For some people, this lack of justification for religious faith is a strength, not a weakness. Faith is supposed to be "knowledge that passeth understanding," a gift of God, something of an entirely different order than knowledge in the ordinary, mundane sense.

For the most part, humanists have avoided extreme skepticism about knowledge but not skepticism about faith. They have agreed with most people (including people of faith) that knowledge is possible but have insisted that faith is somehow an illegitimate or dubious way to acquire knowledge. They would generally concur with the empiricist philosopher John Locke (1632–1704) who says, "Faith is nothing but a firm assent of the mind: which if it be regulated, as is our duty, cannot be afforded to anything, but upon good reason. . . . He that believes, without having any reason for believing, may be in love with his own fancies; but neither seeks truth as he ought, nor pays the obedience due his maker, who would have him use those discerning faculties he has given him, to keep him out of mistake and error."[5]

Against such views many people have insisted that faith can indeed be a source of knowledge. Some have held that faith gives us access to truths that reason cannot plumb, and others have thought that both faith and reason can deliver up religious knowledge. Thomas Aquinas, for example, argues that the existence of God can be proved by reason while certain Church doctrines (the Trinity, for instance) can be ascertained only through faith.

Religious doctrines that can be established through reason are known as **natural theology**. Thomas Aquinas, the supreme natural theologian, thinks that the deliverances of faith can never contradict the products of reason. Others say that the truths uncovered through faith do conflict with those of reason. As the great Latin theologian Tertullian (c. 155–240) says, we accept a truth of faith "because it is absurd." In contrast, some have claimed that divine truths can be known *only* through faith, a view known as **fideism**.

Most philosophers would probably offer a very short answer to our question about the status of faith: No, faith cannot be a source of knowledge because beliefs based on faith are, by definition, unjustified—and unjustified beliefs cannot constitute knowledge.

Someone who wished to defend faith against such a claim might argue like this: It is unfair to judge beliefs based on faith by the same rational criteria used to judge ordinary claims of knowledge. Faith, after all, is an *alternative* to reason, an alternative source of knowledge that is of a radically different kind.

Maybe faith is indeed a trustworthy—but alternative—source of knowledge. But maybe it isn't. We cannot simply assume that faith is—or is not—a reliable indicator of truth. Just saying that faith is an alternative to reason does not make it so. We cannot, in other words, take the knowledge-validating power of faith on faith. Many propositions accepted on faith by millions of people have turned out to be false. Isn't it possible that faith is an unreliable path to knowledge?

So to gauge the reliability of faith, we cannot use faith itself, for that would be begging the question; we would be assuming that faith *is* reliable, which is the very idea we are trying to assess. To discover the truth about faith, we must use methods that we *already know* are reliable—our ordinary, commonsense ways of acquiring knowledge using reason and experience. The universal consensus among people of faith and those who reject faith is that these ways of acquiring knowledge can be trusted.

Kierkegaard on Faith

Søren Kierkegaard (1813–1855) was a firm advocate of the believer's leap of faith. He thought that the rational, objective approach could never yield any true insight into God. From a rational perspective Christianity itself, he said, is a paradox and entirely absurd, and people of faith believe it *because* it is absurd. As he says,

> Christianity has declared itself to be the eternal essential truth which has come into being in time. It has proclaimed itself as the *Paradox*, and it has required of the individual the inwardness of faith in relation to that which stamps itself as an offense to the Jew and a folly to the Greeks—and an absurdity to the understanding. It is impossible more strongly to express the fact that subjectivity is truth, and that the objectivity is repellent even by virtue of its absurdity. And indeed it would seem very strange that Christianity should have come into the world merely to receive an explanation; as if it had been somewhat bewildered about itself, and hence entered the world to consult that wise man, the speculative philosopher, who can come to its assistance by furnishing an explanation.*

* Søren Kierkegaard, *Concluding Unscientific Postscript*, trans. David Swenson and Walter Lowrie (Princeton: Princeton University Press, 1969), 180–99.

If the deliverances of faith and the conclusions of common sense conflict, at the very least we must admit that we do not have knowledge by faith. We know something if we have no good reason to doubt it. But if our common sense contradicts our faith, we would have plenty of reasons to doubt.

Could some form of faith ever give us knowledge? Yes. Suppose that you have believed many propositions on faith alone—and that each one of these propositions turned out to be true. (You confirmed that they were true by using reason and observation.) You then would have good reason to believe that your faith was a reliable indicator of truth. But then your beliefs would no longer be unjustified—they would be supported by good evidence—and you would no longer be acquiring knowledge by faith. Faith, as unjustified belief, would disappear. In addition, your faith would be unnecessary. This predicament shows that even an independent, rational validation of faith would not help bolster the epistemological status of faith.

All of the above suggests that the humanist's skepticism regarding faith is well founded. In addition, it shows, as proposition 9 suggests, that faith can block understanding if it is substituted for our normal knowledge-acquisition techniques.

Some would argue, though, that faith does not impair understanding because, properly employed, it does not take the place of reason and observation but gives us access to knowledge that our normal faculties cannot fathom. Reason does its job, faith does its job, and they stay out of each other's way. But, as we have seen, this response begs the question. It assumes that faith, in some way, is a source of knowledge—the very notion that is being examined.

Note, however, that if faith impairs understanding, the impairment is never total, but instead limited and selective. No sane person lives by faith alone. Most of the time we rely on our normal sources of knowledge. We would not think to use faith, for example, to do our banking or make coffee or find our way home at the end of the day. Many people—including people of faith—are quite happy to give reason, science, and common sense their due, relegating faith to a few selected spheres.

RATIONAL FAITH

By far, the most sophisticated attempt to show that belief in God does not need the support of arguments and evidence comes from philosopher Alvin Plantinga. He argues that it is perfectly acceptable for someone to believe in God's existence *even if they cannot produce evidence or argument to back up their belief.* Traditionally most philosophers insist that before we are justified in believing in God (or *any* proposition, for that matter), we must first have good reasons for doing so. We must have rational grounds for the belief—evidence or arguments that support it. Plantinga calls this requirement the *evidentialist* objection to theism. He says that the implication of this insistence on evidence is that those who believe in God without good reasons are irrational. But he rejects this label. In fact, he argues that theists are well within their intellectual rights to believe in God, even if they cannot come up with evidence or arguments to support their belief.

To make his case, Plantinga appeals to neither faith nor revelation, but to an interesting epistemological theory. The traditional theory of knowledge, known as **foundationalism**, says that to count as knowledge our beliefs must ultimately have some sort of justifying support, or foundation, to be considered knowledge. This support comes from other beliefs. Our belief that it will rain today, for example, is derived from our belief that meteorologists have predicted rain. But ultimately there are beliefs that do not receive help from other beliefs. Either they are self-supporting in that their justification does not derive from other beliefs or they are an arbitrary stopping point. Such beliefs—what philosophers call *basic beliefs*—constitute the foundation for all our other beliefs and give knowledge the underpinning it needs. Legitimate basic beliefs (called "properly basic beliefs") are thought to include those that are (1) self-evident (such as "two plus two equals four") or (2) evident to the senses or memory (as when looking at or remembering a tree shows immediately that there is or was a tree). So to be epistemologically acceptable our beliefs must be either properly basic or justified by beliefs that ultimately rest on those that are properly basic.

Plantinga accepts the main points of foundationalism, but he thinks that the list of beliefs thought to be properly basic is much too restrictive. He asserts that there is another kind of properly basic belief that has been overlooked: theistic belief. He sees no reason why belief in God could not be regarded as properly basic and, therefore, need no supporting evidence. In this way theistic belief can be just as rational as other properly basic beliefs.

To make his case Plantinga tries to show that the traditional foundationalist criteria for being properly basic are themselves without rational support. He then argues that criteria for properly basic beliefs can be derived from one's own experience by noting when a belief is, or is not, obviously properly basic. Such a procedure could show that the criteria are arrived at in a nonarbitrary way, and that belief in God can be properly basic and completely rational.

Plantinga's theory has been disputed by several critics on multiple fronts. Some, for example, have charged that because his approach permits people to formulate their own properly basic criteria from their own unique experience and perspective, almost *any* belief—no matter how bizarre—could be considered properly basic. Certainly some people might view theism as a properly basic belief, but many others might find that belief in Santa Claus and pagan gods is perfectly rational because it is properly basic. The result would be a kind of relativism in which very different (even contradictory) beliefs would have to be considered equally true and equally rational. In such a relativistic world, no religion or worldview could claim to be better than any others, no objective or neutral standards exist to evaluate beliefs, and disagreement between groups of people with different criteria could not be settled. This predicament conflicts with an important commonsense idea: Some beliefs—either our own or those of others—really are irrational.

Plantinga is aware of this criticism and tries to counter it. His critics, on the other hand, insist that his attempts to save his theory from this criticism (and others) are unsuccessful.

SECTION 5.2

The Truth and Nothing But the Truth: Subjectivism, Objectivism, and Relativism

What is *truth*? This question is not concerned with which statements are true or what truths we can know. It is about what truth *is*—what kind of thing truth happens to be. Most people never ask such a question, or if they do, they do not ask it seriously. They simply assume some idea of truth as they get on with their lives. Their lives, though, are permeated with the notion of truth. Most of us tend to think that whether a statement is *true* matters, that there is a real difference between what is *true* and what is not, that knowing what is *true* helps us succeed in whatever we do, that the goal of science and all other forms of inquiry is *truth,* and that a *true* proposition somehow grabs hold of what is real in the world. Such assumptions then affect every decision we make.

Our commonplace notion of the nature of truth is known as **objectivism**. This is the view that truth is *objective*—that there's a way things are independently of how we represent these things to ourselves, and that statements are true if they state how things are. Or, to put it another way, reality does not depend on what we think about it. An opposing view is called **relativism**. It's the notion that truth is *relative*—that the way things are *does* depend on how we represent it to ourselves, that reality does depend on what we think about it. (Ethical relativism, discussed in chapter 4, is the narrower view that moral truth is relative and depends on what people think.)

Historically, humanists stand in the objectivist camp—even though Protagoras, who gave us the first succinct expression of a humanist stance ("man is the measure of all things") also made the first classical statement of relativism. So along with most of the rest of the world, humanists have believed in objective truth. After all, humanist ideas are propositions thought to be objectively true about the world, and it is hard to see how anyone could take humanism seriously if he or she thought otherwise. Humanism then may reject divine or arbitrary authority of all kinds but respect the authority of objective truth. In other words:

10. Even in a world without God and ultimate authorities, there is such a thing as objective truth.

From the time of Protagoras to the present day, however, some have rejected the popular conviction that statements can be objectively true or false—or they have insisted that truth, if objective, is not what most people believe it is. Strangely enough, these challenges have been both accepted and rebuffed from all quarters. Humanists as well as nonhumanists—people of just about every philosophical bent—have simply assumed objective truth to be a fact of life. At the same time, a mix of humanists, religious believers, philosophers, and others have found themselves in the relativist camp. Even among objectivists, competing theories of truth try to explain what is meant by "objective truth."

RELATIVISM: TRUTH AS A MATTER OF TASTE

When we say something such as "the cat is on the mat," or "stealing is wrong," we tend to think that we are not just describing our state of mind, not just referring to things *inside* our heads that have no connection to anything *outside* our heads. We usually mean that there is a particular way that the world is—independent of our thinking—a way beyond our subjective representations of things. There really is a cat on the mat, and stealing really is wrong—regardless of what we think. We cannot make propositions true just by believing them to be true.

This notion of truth—truth as an *objective* relation—has been vigorously disputed in recent years. Relativists—mostly anthropologists, sociologists, students of language and literature, and (apparently) the majority of college freshmen—have insisted that the notion of objective truth is a myth.

Relativism is inspired, in part, by some uncomfortable facts about reality: A shocking multiplicity of opinions and perspectives exists in the world, as well as countless disagreements between individuals and cultures on every subject. Relativists would say this conceptual pluralism and fragmentation shows that objective truth is indeed a myth. If objective truth were, well, true—there would be much more uniformity of opinion. To relativists, it makes more sense to say that truth depends not on objective reality but on what people believe, or on what people's societies believe, or on a particular mindset (what philosophers call a "conceptual scheme"). That is, if someone or some society believes a proposition to be true, then it's true. Disagreement and fragmentation of views simply reflects the fact that truth is relative to individuals, cultures, or conceptual schemes. Objectivists have a ready answer to this criticism: From the true proposition that there is a great deal of disagreement about facts, it does not follow that there are no facts. Disagreement does not show that there is no way the world is.

Probably the most powerful motivation for adopting relativism is the belief that it promotes tolerance and that objectivism encourages intolerance (as well as arrogance). Relativism is supposed to promote tolerance because all viewpoints are entitled to equal respect by virtue of being equally true. Objectivism is supposed to lead to—or be synonymous with—intolerance because it is assumed to be the same thing as **absolutism**, the view that there is only one correct way to represent or interpret reality. After all, weren't the persecutions and pogroms of history carried out by people who believed they were in possession of absolute truth and couldn't tolerate others who held alternative beliefs?

Whatever the validity of objectivism, it does not necessarily entail intolerance. Objectivism, unlike absolutism, does not assert that there is only one proper way to represent reality. Objectivism says that there is a way the world is—but does not assert that there is only one correct perspective on the world. From the fact that reality exists independently of us, it does not follow that there is a single, acceptable window onto reality. Just as different types of maps can offer different perspectives on the same terrain, so there can be many different takes on reality.

There are, of course, many things about us that *are* relative—that are a certain way to us and a different way to others. Personal preferences and tastes, for example, are relative to persons. You like ice cream; someone else doesn't. Such states of affairs are obviously relative to individuals. But the relativist wants to make the more radical claim that *all truths* are relative in the sense that liking ice cream is relative. Facts are essentially matters of personal preference, of individual or cultural tastes.

Relativism is a threat to many humanist ideas because they purport to be objectively true, but relativism is at odds with more than just humanist ideas. It would undermine *all* propositions that are presumed to be making a claim about an objective world.

So is relativism right and objectivism wrong? To find out, let's examine the three main types of relativism.

Subjective Relativism

There is a notion about truth that few people can take seriously for very long. It's the view that truth is whatever one believes it to be—that one creates reality by one's beliefs. This is a kind of personal, or subjective, absolutism: If you believe a proposition, then it's true—objectively true. New Age author Shirley MacLaine seems to hold this view. She explains, "Life doesn't happen to us. We make it happen. Reality isn't separate from us. We are creating our reality every moment of the day. For me that truth is the ultimate freedom and the ultimate responsibility."[6]

Personal absolutism, however, has a serious problem. It involves a logical contradiction. According to this view, if person A believes *p* (a statement about reality), then *p* is true. If person B believes not-*p*, then *p* is not true. But one and the same state of affairs cannot both obtain and not obtain at the same time. That would be a logical impossibility. Just as we know that there can be no square circles (circles that both have and do not have the property of circularity), we know that there can be no state of affairs that both is and is not. Personal absolutism, therefore, cannot be true.

Subjective relativism, however, avoids such an absurdity. It's the view that truth is relative to what an individual believes. Truth is not absolute; it's relative. If you believe that something is true, then it is true for you. If someone else believes something else, then it is true for her. Subjective relativists can thus avoid obvious contradictions by saying, in effect: This is *my* truth, and that's *your* truth. Protagoras's relativism is subjective in this way. He says that a thing "is to me such as it appears to me, and is to you such as it appears to you."[7]

Subjective relativism, though, has some strange implications, and these implications render it implausible. For one thing, if your believing something to be true made it true, you would be *infallible*. As long as you sincerely believed a statement, you could not be wrong about it. Your mere holding the belief would guarantee its truth. You could never be mistaken about the balance in your checkbook or the cause of lower prices on eggs.

Also, if each person made his or her own truth, disagreement among persons would be pointless. You disagree with someone when you think that he is mistaken, but subjective relativism says that no one can be mistaken. Trying to persuade someone that she is wrong would be useless because she could never be wrong. It would be like disagreeing about the taste of peaches. If you say that peaches taste good to you, and your friend says that peaches taste awful to him—there is no disagreement. How something tastes is relative to each individual.

Finally, if every sincerely held belief is equally true, subjective relativism is in trouble on another score. If the doctrine is true, then the belief that it is false would be just as true as the belief that it is true. Plato points out this weird consequence of Protagoras's view: "Protagoras for his part, admitting as he does that everybody's opinion is true, must acknowledge the truth of his opponents' belief about his own belief, where they think he is wrong."[8] So if subjective relativism were true, proponents couldn't claim their theory is truer than any other. One view would be as good as the next one.

Social Relativism

Social relativism is the view that truth is relative not to the individual's beliefs, but to society's beliefs. Society constructs reality, so something can be true for Americans but false for the Chinese, true for Catholics but false for Islamic fundamentalists.

Social relativism, however, harbors some of the same problems as subjective relativism. First, according to social relativism, individuals are not infallible—societies are. Whatever your society believes to be true is true. But this notion of societal infallibility is just as implausible as individual infallibility. Is it really the case that no society can ever be mistaken about anything? Were the Nazis necessarily right about killing millions of Jews? Were medieval Europeans necessarily right about witches, the number of planets in the solar system, and the shape of the Earth? Surely, a society's belief that something is true cannot make it true.

Second, if your society really were infallible, it would be impossible for you to disagree with your society and be correct. If society determines what truth is, your claim that society is wrong about something would be false. This means social reformers could never be correct that society is in error. Reformers or social dissenters such as Martin Luther King, Jr., Susan B. Anthony, and Mohandas Gandhi could not possibly have been right when they disagreed with their society.

Third, social relativism undermines beliefs just as subjective relativism does. If truth is socially constructed, every society's belief is as true as every other's. If so, then a society's belief that p is true—and so is another society's belief that p is false. This state of affairs is implausible. It appears even more implausible when we consider its full implications. If whatever a society believes is true, no one can legitimately criticize another society. Social relativists would have to admit that if a society believes that what it is doing is right, it *is* doing the right thing—even if the "right thing" happens to be a massacre of innocent people, a brutal episode of ethnic cleansing, or the sacrifice of a million infants on a holy altar.

Fourth, social relativism implies that when individuals in a society disagree about the truth of a proposition, what they must really be disagreeing about is whether society believes it. Remember, what's true is whatever society says is true. So if we are members of the same society, when we argue about the existence of black holes or whether a drug will cure cancer, we are just disagreeing about what our society believes is the case. This implies that if we want to resolve the dispute, we must conduct a poll to find out what society really believes. In this way, if we want to determine whether God exists or pornography causes crime or dogs can give birth to kittens, we can simply ask everyone what they think, right? It should be obvious that such a truth-finding procedure is doomed from the start.

Conceptual Relativism

Conceptual relativism is the doctrine that truth is relative, not to individuals or societies, but to *conceptual schemes*. A conceptual scheme is a way of classifying things into meaningful groups. Conceptual relativists say that our conceptual scheme doesn't just enable us to "see" things in a particular way—it actually creates our world. Different conceptual schemes make different worlds, so there is no one way the world is.

According to conceptual relativism, we can sometimes be mistaken about how we classify something in our conceptual scheme, so we are not infallible. Whether a person's classification is a mistake is determined, in part, by some input from the world. But even though the world puts constraints on the truth, the world does not uniquely determine the truth. Conceptual schemes determine the truth (or "truths"). Our conceptual schemes determine the way the world is, just as a gelatin mold determines the shape of the gelatin. This is the case even though the world has some properties that aren't affected by conceptual schemes, just as the gelatin has some properties that aren't affected by the mold. Truth is relative to conceptual schemes because conceptual schemes make worlds.

A crucial notion for conceptual relativism is that the same proposition can be true in one conceptual scheme and false in another. But, of course, this is not logically possible. The same proposition cannot be both true and false. If propositions have different truth values, they are different propositions.

You can also view the problem like this. According to conceptual relativism, conceptual schemes create different worlds, and the language of each conceptual scheme refers to the unique world made by that conceptual scheme. But if the language of each conceptual scheme refers to a different world, the languages of two different conceptual schemes cannot share any meanings. The languages are about different worlds, and translation is not possible. So there can never be one sentence that means the same thing in two different conceptual schemes—much less true in one conceptual scheme and false in another.

As all of this suggests, sharing a common world is essential for communication and translation. But if we really do inhabit different worlds, how can we possibly communicate with one another—as we certainly believe we can? How can we possibly translate one language into another—as we believe we do? As philosopher Roger Trigg says,

> The result of granting that the "the world" or "reality" cannot be conceived as independent of all conceptual schemes is that there is no reason to suppose that what the peoples of very different communities see as the world is similar in any way. Unfortunately, however, this supposition is absolutely necessary before any translation or comparison between languages of different societies can take place. Without it, the situation would be like one where the inhabitants of two planets which differed fundamentally in their nature met each other and tried to communicate. So few things (if any) would be matters of common experience that their respective languages would hardly ever run parallel.[9]

Conceptual relativism, then, makes no sense. The world—and truth—must not be manufactured by conceptual schemes.

THE TERRIBLE TRUTH

The main problem with relativism in all its forms is that it is self-defeating. Relativism defeats itself because its truth implies its falsity. The relativist wants to say, "All truth is relative" (i.e., there is no objective truth). But this statement itself is supposed to be objectively true. Therefore, if "All truth is relative" is objectively true, then it is objectively false. In other words, if relativism in any of its forms is true, it's false. Relativism, then, cannot possibly be true.

The relativist, though, might try to avoid this absurdity by claiming that the statement "all truth is relative" is not objectively true but *relatively* true—that is, true relative to him, or his society, or his conceptual scheme. But this just means that the relativist thinks relativism is true, a fact that is not in contention. He provides no objective evidence for accepting relativism because he does not believe in such a thing as objective evidence. But if we are to abandon our normal understanding of truth and accept a relativistic notion of truth, the relativist must give us more than self-refuting statements or his subjective considerations.

The dilemma for the relativist is sharp. If he says that his theory of truth is objectively true, he defeats himself by giving evidence against it. If he says that his theory is only relativistically true, he defeats himself by offering no evidence for it. Either way, the relativist defeats himself, and anything that is self-defeating cannot be true.

Philosopher Harvey Siegel explains relativism's weakness like this:

> The most powerful [self-defeat argument] is that relativism precludes the possibility of determining the truth, warrant or epistemic merit of contentious claims and doctrines—including itself—since according to relativism no claim or doctrine can fail any test of epistemic adequacy or be judged unjustified, false or unwarranted. Take Protagorean relativism as an example. If "what seems true [or warranted] to anyone *is* true [or warranted] for him to whom it seems so", then no sincere claim can fail any test of epistemic adequacy or be judged unjustified or false. But if there is no possibility that a claim or doctrine can fail a test of epistemic adequacy or rightness, then the distinction between adequacy and inadequacy, rightness and wrongness is given up. If so, then the very notions of rightness, truth and warrantedness are undermined. But if this is so, then relativism itself cannot be right. In short: relativism is incoherent because, if it is right, the very notion of rightness is undermined, in which case relativism itself cannot be right. The assertion *and defense* of relativism requires one to presuppose neutral standards in accordance with which contentious claims and doctrines can be assessed; but relativism denies the possibility of evaluation in accordance with such neutral standards. Thus the doctrine of relativism cannot be coherently defended—it can be defended only by being given up. Relativism is thus impotent to defend itself, and falls to this fundamental reflexive difficulty.[10]

We are forced to conclude that *belief* may be relative to individuals, societies, or conceptual schemes—but *truth* is not. Differing beliefs do not imply relative truth. There is an external reality independent of our representations of it. *There is a way that the world is.* We can represent this world to ourselves in many different ways, but this world that we grapple with, interpret, and represent is the same for all of us.

As we have said, the notion of objective truth is the commonsense view of truth. What is so commonsensical about it? Just this: The concept of objective reality is not optional, something that we may discard as we would an outdated book. Every time we assert that something is the case, or think that something is or is not a certain way, or argue for one theory over another—we assume objective reality. As we have seen, when relativists deny objective reality, they end up refuting themselves. In the very argument over the existence of objective reality, both those who accept it and those who deny it must assume it or the argument would never get off the ground.

It seems, then, that proposition 10 is justified. But this verdict is not merely a point in favor of humanism. It is further support of a commonsense belief (objective truth) that is shared by a broad spectrum of worldviews and that is necessary for rational discourse itself.

SUMMARY

Skepticism is the view that we know much less than we think we do, and thinkers who raise doubts about how much we know are called skeptics. Skepticism is a challenge to propositional knowledge—knowledge that something is the case. René Descartes presented the most influential form of skepticism, although he used it try to show how skepticism could be overcome. His skepticism is based on the notion that knowledge requires certainty and that we can never be certain because it is always possible we are mistaken. But we often seem to have knowledge even though we do not have certainty. We, in fact, know many things—not because they are beyond all possible doubt, but because they are beyond reasonable doubt.

Faith, which is belief without evidence, is supposed to be a source of knowledge, but many philosophers would retort that belief without evidence cannot be knowledge. Faith may or may not be a source of knowledge, but we cannot take the knowledge-validating power of faith on faith. To assess the reliability of faith, we must use methods that we already know are reliable—our ordinary ways of acquiring knowledge through reason and experience.

Some people are skeptics about objective truth. They claim that truth is not objective (reflecting an objective relationship with the world), but is relative. That is, they assert that something is true relative to individuals, societies, or conceptual schemes. Something is true if an individual or a society believes it to be true. But there are many problems with this view. The most serious one is that relativism is self-defeating. Relativism defeats itself because its truth implies its falsity.

STUDY QUESTIONS

1. What is skepticism?
2. What is propositional knowledge? What are the three necessary and sufficient conditions for something to be considered knowledge?
3. Does knowledge require certainty?
4. What is the difference between propositional knowledge and faith?
5. What are the four sources of our knowledge?
6. What is subjective relativism? What is social relativism?
7. In what way is relativism self-defeating?

DISCUSSION QUESTIONS

1. Can a proposition count as knowledge if it is a true belief without justification?
2. If knowledge requires certainty, what propositions can we know?
3. What tests could we use to determine if a belief based on faith is true?
4. Can the deliverances of faith and reason conflict? If so, how can the conflict be resolved?
5. According to social relativism, truth is relative to society's beliefs. If this is the case, can we then plausibly criticize another society for, say, murdering everyone over the age of fifty?
6. Are you a social relativist? If so, how can you justify this view without at the same time undermining it?

FIELD PROBLEM

Consider this question: The same statement can be true for one person but false for another. Ask five people if they subscribe to this view. What can you then conclude about the popularity of relativism?

SUGGESTIONS FOR FURTHER READING

Audi, Robert. *Belief, Justification, and Knowledge*. Belmont, Calif.: Wadsworth, 1988.
Moser, Paul K. *Knowledge and Evidence*. Cambridge: Cambridge University Press, 1989.
Russell, Bertrand. *The Problems of Philosophy*. Oxford: Oxford University Press, 1912.

NOTES

1. Although this notion of knowledge is generally accepted, there is disagreement over what justification involves in a knowledge claim. See Theodore Schick, Jr. and Lewis Vaughn, *Doing Philosophy* (Mountain View, Calif.: Mayfield, 1999), 428–45.
2. Plato, "Meno," 98a, trans. W. K. C. Guthrie, *The Collected Works of Plato*, ed. Edith Hamilton and Huntington Cairns (Princeton: Princeton University Press, 1961), 381.
3. René Descartes, *Meditations on First Philosophy,* in *The Philosophical Works of Descartes,* ed. E. S. Haldane and G. R. T. Ross (Cambridge: Cambridge University Press, 1973), 145–46.
4. Descartes, *Meditations on First Philosophy,* 171.
5. John Locke, *An Essay Concerning Human Understanding*, ed. A. C. Fraser (Oxford: Clarendon Press, 1894), Book 4, Chapter 17, Section 24.
6. Shirley MacLaine, *Out on a Limb* (New York: Bantam Books, 1983).
7. Plato, *Theaetetus*, trans. F. M. Cornford in *The Collected Dialogues of Plato*, ed. E. Hamilton and H. Cairns (New York: Pantheon Books, 1961), 845–919.
8. Plato, *Theaetetus,* 876.
9. Roger Trigg, *Reason and Commitment* (London: Cambridge University Press, 1973), 15–16.
10. Harvey Siegel, "Relativism," in *A Companion to Epistemology* (Oxford: Blackwell, 1993), 429.

6

Science and Religion

Austin Dacey

In the 1920s, the influential American politician William Jennings Bryan spearheaded a campaign to "drive Darwinism from our schools."[1] A fundamentalist Presbyterian, Bryan opposed Darwinism because he saw it as incompatible with the Creation story presented in the Bible, which Bryan took to be accurate in every detail. During the infamous "Scopes Monkey Trial," Bryan was unexpectedly called to the stand as an expert witness to testify to the veracity of the Scripture. There he faced unrelenting questioning by the defense attorney Clarence Darrow, a famed lawyer and notorious agnostic.

> **Darrow:** Do you claim that everything in the Bible should be literally interpreted?
> **Bryan:** I believe everything in the Bible should be accepted as it is given there. Some of the Bible is given illustratively; for instance, "Ye are the salt of the earth." I would not insist that man was actually salt, or that he had flesh of salt, but it is used in the sense of salt as saving God's people. . . .
> **Darrow:** Then, when the Bible said, for instance, "and God called the firmament heaven. And the evening and the morning were the second day," that does not necessarily mean twenty-four hours? . . .
> **Bryan:** I know a great many think so.
> **Darrow:** What do you think? . . .
> **Bryan:** I do not think they were twenty-four-hour days. . . . But I think it would be just as easy for the kind of God we believe in to make the earth in six days as in six years or in six million years or in six hundred million years. I do not think it important whether we believe one or the other.[2]

At one point, a disagreement flared when one lawyer disputed the relevance of the questioning by Darrow and his team. Bryan insisted that they continue, saying, "They did not come here to try this case. They came here to try revealed religion. I am here to defend it, and they can ask me any questions they please." Bryan won the case (it was later overturned on a technicality), but he died in his sleep less than a week later. Having served as a volunteer colonel in the Spanish-American War, Bryan was buried in Arlington National Cemetery beneath the epitaph "He Kept the Faith."

Creationism as an intellectual movement has evolved considerably since Bryan's day. (The term "creationism" did not come up at the Scopes trial.) In 1968, laws explicitly banning the teaching of evolution that had been created during the 1920s were ruled unconstitutional in the landmark Supreme Court case *Epperson v. Arkansas*. In the 1980s, creationists turned to the promotion of "creation science" as a legitimate scientific discipline deserving a place in the curriculum alongside evolutionary science. But in 1987, the high court rejected this strategy as well. Since 1990 or so, creation science has given way to "intelligent design theory," or ID. The basic idea is that natural selection is unable to account for certain "irreducibly complex" biological structures, whereas the intentions of a rational designer provide a better scientific explanation. One representative of the movement claimed that by 2006, design theory will be sufficiently developed to deserve funding from the National Science Foundation.[3]

The efforts of creationist activists spurred many to come to the defense of evolutionary science. The philosopher of science Michael Ruse was called as an expert witness in a 1981 creation science legal battle in Arkansas. Contending that "creation science" is not science and therefore does not belong in science classrooms, Ruse drew a sharp contrast between science and religion: "[S]cience involves a search for order. More specifically, science looks for unbroken, blind, natural regularities (*laws*). Things in the world do not happen in just any old way. They follow set paths, and science tries to capture this fact. Bodies of science, therefore, known variously as 'theories' or 'paradigms' or 'sets of models,' are collections of laws."[4]

By contrast, says Ruse, "religion does not insist on unbroken law. Indeed, religious beliefs frequently allow or suppose events outside law or else events that violate law (miracles)." Moreover, science appeals to laws in order to explain things. "One tries to show why things are as they are—and how they fall beneath or follow from law. . . . The other side of explanation is *prediction*. The laws indicate what is going to happen: that the ball will go in a parabola, that the child will be blue-eyed."[5]

Scientific claims are *testable*: "a genuine scientific theory lays itself open to check against the real world. . . . Testability is a two-way process. The researcher looks for some positive evidence, for *confirmation*. . . . Conversely, a theory must be open to possible refutation. If the facts speak against a theory, then it must go. A body of science must be *falsifiable*."[6]

Religious claims, on the other hand, are not testable in this way. For example, "Catholic religious claims about transubstantiation (the changing of the bread and wine into the body and blood of Christ) are unfalsifiable." Relatedly, science is *tentative*. "Ultimately, a scientist must be prepared to reject his theory. . . . In this regard, the scientists differ from both the philosophers and the theologians. Nothing in the real world would make the Kantian change his mind, and the Catholic is equally dogmatic, despite empirical evidence about the stability of bread and wine. Such evidence is simply considered irrelevant."[7]

Finally, Ruse claims, good scientists have a special intellectual *integrity*: "A scientist should not cheat or falsity data or quote out of context or do any other thing that is intellectually dishonest. Science depends on honesty in the realm of ideas."[8]

Episodes such as the clash between creationism and evolution in the United States raise a number of questions about the nature and authority of science and its proper intellectual and social relationship to religion, ethics, philosophy, and the study of society and culture. For many humanists, the answer is simple: As science progresses, it inevitably displaces alternative understandings of the world—including those found in supernatural religion—with rationally superior, naturalistic knowledge. The following sections explore these questions and ask whether or in what form the humanist answers can be defended. Section 6.1 discusses the nature and authority of science and its relationship to other modes of inquiry, while section 6.2 turns specifically to the relationship between theology and the sciences.

SECTION 6.1

Check It Out: Knowledge through Science

Throughout this book, certain bodies of putative scientific knowledge (from neuroscience, evolutionary biology, and so on) have been invoked to illuminate or pass judgment on various philosophical, ethical, and religious matters. But on reflection, one might ask whether this sort of appeal to science is entirely legitimate. After all, what reason is there to think that scientific claims always trump the claims of other, quite different disciplines and discourses?

It is hard not to be impressed by the achievements of the empirical sciences over the last several centuries. Through the application of careful observation, hypothesis formation, controlled experiment, critical peer review, and replication of results, the sciences have revealed previously unknown depths and intricacies of the natural world. At the same time, they have to a large extent literally built the cultural worlds we inhabit. Humanists of many stripes have become convinced that

11. Science is a privileged source of knowledge about the world.

In the current intellectual climate, this claim is hotly contested. On each side of the debate, one finds unsophisticated, extreme views. Science's detractors allege that it does not produce knowledge at all, or produces knowledge that is no better than myth, folklore, superstition, or "pseudoscience," such as astrology. On the opposite extreme, science's boosters allege that it is the *only* source of knowledge. Meanwhile, the broad middle ground is occupied by a variety of proposals (and counterproposals) centering on **philosophical naturalism**, which in its broadest sense is the idea that all of our methods of inquiry and beliefs about the world should be brought into accord with the sciences. This section critically examines the views of science's detractors, boosters, and those in between. At the same time, it imparts some appreciation for the recent scholarship on the nature of the science itself. The overall aim is to assess the extent to which humanism is committed to an untenable notion of science and its importance.

PHILOSOPHICAL NATURALISM

In light of the extraordinary success of the sciences in their given domains of inquiry, it is worth wondering whether we can extend the scientific orientation to other areas of life. This impulse is expressed in the intellectual tradition (or rather, several related traditions) now known as "philosophical naturalism." Naturalism in its contemporary form was pioneered by the American "pragmatic naturalists" led by John Dewey, and later developed by the influential Harvard philosopher W. V. O. Quine. Its history in modern thought runs through Enlightenment skeptics like David Hume; French and German materialists such as Baron D'Holbach and Ludwig Feuerbach; the early theorists of science John Herschel, William Whewell, and John Stuart Mill; the positivism of Auguste Comte and the Darwinism of *Origin of Species* and its defenders. Today, a majority of philosophers probably consider themselves naturalists, such that one author on the subject claims, "nearly everybody nowadays wants to be a 'naturalist.'"[9] But despite this widespread appeal, there is little agreement on what precisely naturalism consists of.

Traditionally, naturalists have distinguished various commitments they wish to make: a metaphysical (or ontological, or substantive) claim and a methodological (or epistemological, or procedural) claim. Typically, the metaphysical content is expressed by saying that in any true statement about reality—be it commonsensical, philosophical, theological, ethical, sociological, or political—the entities postulated are composed of or somehow grounded in the entities postulated by the empirical sciences. Metaphysical naturalism is usually construed in a nonreductive fashion, so that higher-level entities such as social institutions and beliefs are causally determined by lower-level physical properties, without being *reduced* to them. Still, given contemporary physics, naturalism is thought to rule out many entities, including supernatural deities, Cartesian minds, and abstract objects such as mathematical sets.

The epistemological or methodological content of naturalism is typically expressed by denying the possibility of transcendent truths that are known a priori and with certainty through introspection or rational intuition. Instead, philosophical inquiry ought to pattern itself after scientific inquiry, formulating hypotheses that are evaluated on the basis of experience, broadly construed.

Critics have accused naturalism of being self-defeating. Naturalism instructs us to look to science for our beliefs and principles, but naturalism itself is not a scientific claim—it is a philosophical or metaphilosophical thesis; therefore, by its own lights, naturalism ought to be rejected.[10] Contrary to this objection, the content of naturalism need not be strictly scientific to be self-consistent, so long as it is logically implied or evidentially supported by science.[11] Another argument, due to Alvin Plantinga, contends that Darwinian accounts of the evolution of human cognitive faculties cannot assure that these faculties reliably aim at *truth*, as opposed to reproductive fitness. Consequently, if naturalism were true, then naturalists could have no rational assurance of its truth! However, it is not clear why naturalism should be identified with any particular evolutionary hypothesis.[12]

Nevertheless, there are serious obstacles to precisely characterizing naturalism's content. For example, because science is essentially fallible and subject to an ongoing process of revision, we cannot simply base our ontology on the ontology of the sciences of our day, which may turn out to be wrong or incomplete. Instead, we might look to the sciences of the future, to a time when they have reached a complete or final state (assuming that such a state can be reached). Naturalism, then, endorses an ontology that accords with the hypothetically completed scientific ontology, *whatever it turns out to be*. Unfortunately, when characterized in this way, naturalism would not be an ontological thesis at all (because as long as current science is less than complete, naturalism cannot assert or deny the existence of anything in particular). Rather, naturalism would be the claim that the methods of science can be relied upon to approximate or eventually reveal the right ontology—that is to say, an epistemological or methodological claim.

One response to this problem is to say that naturalism's metaphysical content, just like the content of science itself, is fallible and revisable. However, strictly speaking, this would mean that with every scientific advance—no matter how relatively insignificant—naturalism would be refuted and succeeded by a revised doctrine. Another response is not to think of naturalism as a philosophical doctrine at all, but instead as a research program, a historically specific body of scholarship and inquiry with a unique set of assumptions, norms, and findings.[13] In philosophy of mind and language, the naturalist program is the project of accounting for mental causation, consciousness, and intentionality within nonreductive physicalist assumptions; in social and cultural studies, the project of subjecting social phenomena to the same sort of objective, impersonal analysis as in the case of natural phenomena; in ethics, the project of showing how certain moral properties might be identical with certain natural properties; in epistemology, the project of understanding knowledge in terms that are fundamentally psychological rather than irreducibly normative; and so on. Naturalism per se will then be the aggregate of these and other more-or-less free-standing naturalistic research projects, and the case for naturalism per se will depend on their success relative to alternative, non-naturalistic projects. Such a detailed, piecemeal examination cannot be presented in this book.

However, the book has tried to survey the state of scholarship in those naturalistic projects that are directly relevant to philosophical humanism—for instance, naturalistic accounts of human nature, morality, and God.

FROM POSITIVISM TO SOCIAL CONSTRUCTIVISM

Philosophical naturalists, and the humanists among them, are often accused of embracing a naive conception of the rationality and authority of science that ignores the critiques developed by twentieth-century scholarship on science. For centuries, conceptions of science have changed along with science itself. The nineteenth-century saw the eventual division of philosophy from what is now known as science, whereas previously both had coexisted in a single discipline called "natural philosophy." Many nineteenth-century philosophers turned their attention to the science of their day, attempting to provide reasoned accounts of its foundations, structure, and logic. This enterprise is the philosophy of science, and the following sections will sample it.

The picture of science (placed in contradistinction to religion) presented above by Michael Ruse has a familiar sound. In many ways it represents a commonsense notion of science that has entered the popular consciousness. It also echoes a number of ideas that for a good part of the twentieth century were the "received views" among scholars of science.

The received views were highly influenced by the intellectual movement known as **logical positivism** or **logical empiricism**, which is associated with groups of scholars active in 1930s Vienna and Berlin, most notably Rudolph Carnap, Karl Hempel, Hans Reichenbach, and Morris Schlick.[14] During wartime, the movement was transplanted to the English-speaking world and carried on in America by A. J. Ayer and Ernest Nagel. The positivists had been influenced by Norman Campbell's 1919 book *Foundations of Science*, which suggested that axiomatizion could further science as it had mathematics, as well as

Percy Bridgman's work on "operationalizing" the meaning of scientific terms to tie them to direct observation.

Positivist philosophy of science is known for a number of distinctive theses about the nature and structure of science. Most fundamentally, positivists were convinced that the advancement of scientific knowledge was hampered by its entanglement, often unwitting, with certain "metaphysical" and religious assumptions. The hope was that by sharply distinguishing science from nonscience on the basis of the criterion of empirical verifiability, and formalizing the structure of theories in a logically transparent fashion, science could recognize and expel these troublesome metaphysical ghosts.

For positivists, scientific knowledge is structured like a pyramid. The base is composed of a collection of "observation reports" expressed in an observation language that is unbiased and free of any theoretical assumptions. These are generalized into mid-level "empirical laws" that describe natural regularities. At the top of the pyramid is the scientific theory, understood as an axiomatized set of theoretical statements connected to empirical laws via "correspondence rules" that partially interpret theoretical concepts in terms of observable data. Scientific explanations take the form of arguments in which a statement of the explanandum (the thing to be explained) is deduced from statements of universal laws or implied by statements of probabilistic laws, in conjunction with statements of the initial conditions.

A new scientific theory typically replaces an existing theory by incorporating it—in the sense that the existing theory proves to be a "special case" of the new theory and can be logically derived from it. (Galileo's law of falling bodies is incorporated by Newton's dynamics, which in turn is incorporated in relativity theory.) Entities invoked in one science are "reduced to" entities at a lower, more fundamental level—so that biology is seen as nothing but chemistry, for example. Progress in science occurs through an accretion of theories of increasing scope, precision, or primacy.

Science is rational by virtue of the logical and evidential relations between the statements that make up successful scientific theories and the statements in the observational base. Scientific theories and other statements can never be known with certainty, and a major aspect of the positivist program was to devise a rigorous formalism in which one could express the *degree of confirmation* enjoyed by a theory in terms of its "logical probability."

Over a period of several decades beginning in the mid-1950s, almost every facet of the positivist portrait of science would be questioned, transformed, or widely rejected. The notions of theory-as-axiomatic-system and explanation-as-argument lost ground to a "semantic" conception, which places emphasis on constructing *models* or abstract replicas—mathematical, visual, and otherwise—of the causal processes responsible for the phenomenon under investigation and demonstrating a close fit between the models and the available data. The concept of a neutral, unbiased observation report was replaced by a more complex account of the relationship between evidence and theory, in which observations are partially "theory-dependent" or "theory-laden" and hypotheses are not tested in isolation, but as part of a more holistic body of information that includes other theories and background knowledge: a view known in general as the "Duhem-Quine Thesis" (for Pierre Duhem and W. V. O. Quine). The image of the positivist pyramid, with justification flowing from rock-bottom upward, is replaced by a "web of belief" in which no statements are free from theoretical content or immune in principle from adjustment.

Perhaps the most controversial break with received views came in the areas of conceptual change in science and the rationality of theory choice. The project of devising a precise quantitative measure of confirmation encountered severe technical difficulties, as did the attempt to actually perform any complex reductions of upper-level to lower-level theories. Karl Popper's "falsificationist" philosophy of science, while in many ways in line with positivism, rejected completely the notion that scientific statements can be confirmed at all. Under falsificationism, science is rational not by virtue of the logical support of theory by evidence, but in virtue of the *critical attitude of its practitioners*—their willingness to subject their proposals to rigorous testing. In his *Structure of Scientific Revolutions* and subsequent works, Thomas Kuhn famously drew on the history of science to argue that conceptual change is often extremely discontinuous rather than cumulative, and that theory choice cannot be made solely on the basis of rational, cognitive criteria such as evidential support, explanatory scope, or predictive accuracy. In a period of "revolutionary science," communities of researchers are confronted with a choice between competing "paradigms," or ways of seeing the world and doing science in it, and each paradigm can claim its own criteria of theory choice. Just as in social revolutions, in which normal political procedures give way to extrapolitical means of resolution such as mob rule or violence, so too in scientific revolutions communities of researchers resort to extrascientific strategies in the contest for intellectual supremacy. Especially in *Structure*, Kuhn gave pride of place to nonrational factors such as shared education, loyalty to peer groups, institutional power struggles, personal ambition, and rhetorical persuasion.

The collapse of positivism occasioned a proliferation of diverse new perspectives on science, and none of the succeeding ideas mentioned above was without trenchant critics. Nevertheless, one theme that became dominant in the scholarship after Duhem-Quine and Kuhn is the **underdetermination thesis**, the claim that "the evidence" alone often does not suffice to justify the acceptance of one theory over its alternatives. From Kuhnian philosophy of science came the idea that the scientists in different traditions lack a common understanding of the evidence and its relevance to theory choice. From Duhem-Quine considerations came the realization that numerous different theories can be made consistent with the same empirical base.

The preoccupation with underdetermination fueled the creation of the new field of "science studies" or "sociology of knowledge" in the 1970s. Sociologists of knowledge point to cases such as the debate between the eighteenth-century chemists Joseph Priestley and Antoine-Lavrent Lavoisier, who fundamentally disagreed about what occurs when certain metals are burned. Lavoisier's understanding of the situation was based on his belief in phlogiston, an invisible substance released by combustion. Although it is now obsolete, phlogiston chemistry was widely accepted in Lavoisier's day.

> Both Priestley and Lavoisier were looking at samples of (what we would call) lead oxide and mercuric oxide. . . . Nevertheless Priestley and Lavoisier believed totally different things: they gave sharply conflicting accounts of the nature of the substances they observed and their properties and behavior. . . . Lavoisier denied that there was such a substance as phlogiston and postulated the existence of something called "oxygen." Priestley . . . insisted on the existence of phlogiston, identifying it with certain samples of gas agreed by both to be present in the experiment. . . . Clearly the effect of "the facts" is neither simple nor sufficient to explain what needs explaining, viz. the theoretical divergence. It is because the effect of "the facts" is so different that the sociology of knowledge has a task.[15]

A sociology of knowledge is meant to uncover the local, extrascientific causes that explain why people adopt one underdetermined theory rather than its alternatives. Other writers on science—sometimes identified as social constructivists—have taken the implications of underdetermination further, concluding that science is governed by no distinctively rational methods, or that science has no more authority as an arbiter of fact or truth than does religion, folklore, or superstition. In the words of Paul Feyerabend, in science "anything goes." At the extreme, social constructivists embrace the view, earlier called conceptual relativism, that our conceptions of reality actually *make reality* the way we conceive it.[16]

SCIENCE WITH A SMALL "s"

Radical doubts about science have led some to reject the very idea that scientific discourse is true or false by virtue of its relation to an underlying reality with an existence independent of us, a position known generally as **scientific realism**. The chief rationale for realism comes from the observation—known as the "Miracle Argument"—that the extraordinary success of science would be entirely baffling and unexpected unless we assume that it is getting something right about a mind-independent reality.

Nevertheless, there may be something problematic about the strong version of scientific realism, which remains a part of the commonsense view of science. According to this strong version of realism, an ideal piece of science is like an ideal police report: an unbiased and uniquely accurate account of the facts. The police investigator sifts through the evidence, including the various and sometimes conflicting perspectives of the victim, suspect, and bystanders, in order to arrive at "the truth"—not any one person's view of things ("just the facts ma'am"), but *the* view of things, a "view from nowhere." Similarly, science is supposed to go beyond partial and imperfect individual perceptions to disclose the facts about *the way the world is*. The problem with this picture is that the world does not speak for itself. Only people can speak for it. To do so we must use categories, vocabularies, and models—and as the underdetermination thesis suggests, there are many scientific categories, vocabularies, and models open to us. Moreover, our representations of the world are shaped by the cognitive and perceptual capacities and limitations peculiar to the human organism.

To many people, considerations such as these are consistent with a more modest version of realism. According to this realism, science is less like ideal police reporting and more like mapmaking, or cartography. The sort of map one constructs depends on one's interests and the constraints peculiar to the representational system one selects. There are geological maps, natural resource maps, political maps, city street maps, regional maps, and so on. Some features of a map are idealizations and shortcuts imposed by the map's particular media. For example, maps of the globe introduce distortions into the relative size of the continents because they must project the surface of the three-dimensional Earth onto two dimensions. Mapmakers must decide among these projections. In addition, every map sacrifices certain features by modeling a terrain at a particular scale. Therefore, in cartography there can be no "view from nowhere." Try to imagine a map of Asia with *no particular* scale, purpose, classificatory scheme, projection, or orientation. It would not be a map of Asia at all, or of anything else for that matter. There is no such thing as *the* map of Asia. For similar reasons, there could be no scientific view from nowhere of the universe.

All views are from somewhere, from within some conceptual framework and set of sensory powers. However, this does not mean that conceptually mediated knowledge is not knowledge of an independent reality (a political map of Asia is no less a map of Asia). Like maps, scientific thought uses certain categories and vocabularies to represent an independent reality, and it is by virtue of this reality that scientific claims are made true or false. The representations may be mind-dependent, but that does not prevent them from being *representations* of a mind-independent reality. In general, this more modest understanding of science and truth is sometimes termed **internal realism**.

On the questions of conceptual change and theory choice, post-Kuhnian discussions, and Kuhn himself in subsequent work, have significantly modified the arationalism of *Structure*. Scientific "paradigms" are not as all-encompassing, monolithic, and mutually exclusive as Kuhn depicted them to be, so that rational interparadigm communication and piecemeal conceptual change are typically possible. For example, the scientific acceptability of invoking unobservable entities emerged gradually between 1800 and 1860, and did so independently of any other major paradigm or theory shifts. Imre Lakatos devised an attractive synthesis of Kuhn with Popper's falsificationism in what he called the "methodology of scientific research programs." Lakotos's system distinguishes the *progressiveness* of a research program on the basis of its ability to account for the empirical successes and failures of its theoretical predecessors and to formulate and corroborate predictions of new facts. Building on Kuhn and Lakatos, Larry Laudan developed a view centered on the "problem-solving effectiveness" of theories.

In the main, scholars and observers of science have rejected the more radical Kuhnian and social constructivist themes while welcoming certain aspects of their historicist orientation. The first is more careful attention to the sociological details of scientific practice. What post-positivist philosophy of science sacrifices by way of logical precision, formal system-building, and black-and-white division between science and nonscience, it gains in fidelity to the behavior and beliefs of actual scientists working within flourishing research traditions. The second historicist element is that assessments of whether a research tradition is a science or good science cannot be made by looking at its structure as a snapshot in time. Rather, one must look at how the tradition performs over time—for example, the manner in which its practitioners respond to novel problems, recalcitrant data, and rival traditions.

Although debate on almost all of the above issues continues in contemporary philosophy and history of science, significant schools of thought continue to assert the rationality, objectivity, and realism of science, albeit in modest forms that may not satisfy the science booster.

THE AUTHORITY OF SCIENCE

Animating the debates about the nature of science are deep questions about its proper place in society and people's lives. The Enlightenment humanist tradition has insisted on a privileged position for science, yet there are plenty of other putative sources of beliefs—everyday sense perception, one's emotions, the testimony of other people, the arts, religion. How is science supposed to relate to these sources? Is it the only "real" source of knowledge? The notion that the only legitimate knowledge comes from science is sometimes called **scientism**. Clearly, scientism is inadequate, for we know many facts that are not scientific facts. For example, you know that you are reading this book, that you are supposed to tip cab drivers, and that your friends care for you, although none of these things figure in any scientific theory. But what happens when some piece of scientific knowledge conflicts with some piece of nonscientific knowledge? Why should science always prevail, as naturalism would have it?

To investigate this question it is helpful to first ask why anyone should care about what science says in the first place. Perhaps we should care about science because, unlike other forms of inquiry, it tells us *the way things really are*. But that answer presupposes the "view from nowhere," which, as discussed previously, has fallen on hard times. Perhaps we should care because science discovers exceptionally useful truths about the world: They are unequaled in helping us navigate through our environments and achieve our purposes, whatever they might be. Science is distinctive in its all-purpose, instrumental value. This point is indeed powerful in light of the tremendous potential of science and technology to improve human health, well-being, and material conditions, the evidence of which can be seen throughout affluent societies. Of course, not all scientific research discovers truths of direct practical significance. Consider the observation and cataloguing by astronomers of long-extinct stars in other galaxies.

Perhaps apart from its pragmatic worth, scientific truth has superior value for its own sake, or intrinsically. In view of all the possible descriptions of reality, there are innumerable facts about the world. Most of them are not intrinsically worth knowing, in our estimation, nor is it easy to imagine them being intrinsically worth knowing. For instance, one could discover the number of alphabetic characters contained in this text—but why? Presumably science seeks truths that possess special *significance*. Describing this significance that is above and beyond practical usefulness—what Philip Kitcher calls "epistemic significance"—has been a perennial concern in the study of science:

> Prominent efforts to understand the notion of epistemic significance, embodied in the writings of philosophers during the last three centuries and in the rhetoric of public paeans to scientific inquiry, attempt to show that inquiry is directed towards discovering a particular kind of truth, a kind scientists seek at all times, whatever practical projects they (or their contemporaries) may favor. The disciplines we pick out as *sciences* count as part of science because they aim at, and sometimes deliver, truths of this special kind.[17]

Various candidates for one overarching, "context-independent" sort of epistemic significance have been proposed: achieving objective explanation, identifying the laws of nature, constructing a unified picture of reality, discovering fundamental causal processes. The problem with these proposals, Kitcher argues, is that scientific practice is in fact quite heterogeneous, so that it is not plausible to construe all types of inquiry as aiming at the same generic kind of significance:

> [S]ometimes we are interested in triggering events, sometimes with enduring features that are taken to constitute the "natures" of the things under study, sometimes with the intentions of agents, sometimes with conditions that maintain an equilibrium, sometimes with factors that are to the advantage of an organism. Frequently, relevance relations reflect our interest in the covariation of properties we find salient or in factors that we can manipulate and control. Objective explanation goes on in the sciences, then, but only against the background of our questions and our interests.[18]

Science, at its best, is a search for truths of significance, but this does not mean that there is one kind of significance at which all scientific research aims.

If this pluralistic perspective offers the best way to think about the value of doing science, what are the implications for the authority of science? It seems there would be no overarching aim, such as "identifying the laws of nature," that all inquirers are rationally obliged to value. Instead, it will fall to the defender of the authority of science to show why people should care about *this* kind of truth with respect to *this* research on *this* subject matter—for instance, theoretical physics or the mapping of the human genome. The superiority of science in pursuing certain aims of inquiry—such as discovering causal processes relevant to prediction and control—is demonstrated by its outstanding success in those inquiries, and in this sense science can claim a privileged position. However, whether this privilege can be traded in for social authority also depends on the match between these scientific aims and the aims and interests that find favor in the society. The sciences may have the final word on the things that they talk about, but no purely scientific argument can compel everyone to want to talk about those things. Instead, the arguments will be pragmatic, historical, philosophical, and moral—in addition to scientific.

In this connection, it is interesting to note that many of the first champions of modern science appealed to precisely such extrascientific grounds in order to commend to their audiences the value of this new experimental and quantitative mode of inquiry. Early scientific societies were preoccupied with the application of the new techniques to practical, even economic affairs. For example, in the eighteenth century, England's Royal Society threw its resources into tackling a navigation problem confronting the shipping industry.[19] As the great publicist for the scientific revolution, Francis Bacon, said, "Human knowledge and human power meet in one."[20]

CONCLUSION

Twentieth-century philosophy of science has undermined many of the commonsense and received notions of the nature, structure, and rationality of science, giving credence to a more modest conception of science with a small "s." Nevertheless, if the extraordinary success of science is best attributed to its accuracy in apprehending a mind-independent reality (as the Miracle Argument for scientific realism suggests), then science must command a degree of epistemic privilege. The debate about the authority of science will then focus on the importance of the particular kinds of truth that a given scientific research tradition pursues. Similarly, if naturalism is taken to be an interrelated body of research projects in philosophy, ethics, social science, and so on, then the rational warrant for naturalism will depend on the success of those projects.

SECTION 6.2

Sky's The Limit? Science and Theology

In December of 1869 a large audience gathered in a New York City lecture hall to hear news of a conflict "with battles fiercer, with sieges more persistent, with strategy more vigorous than in any of the comparatively petty warfares of Alexander, or Caesar, or Napoleon." The speaker was Andrew Dickson White, the controversial first president of Cornell University in New York and author of the influential book *History of the Warfare of Science with Theology in Christendom* (1896). The conflict was between science and theology.

Observers of science and religion have long noted a pattern in which the advance of scientific knowledge encroaches on some territory that was formerly left to theology. Newton once postulated the periodic intervention of God to adjust the orbits of the planets, but when physical science progressed sufficiently, the divine assistance was no longer deemed necessary. The process has been particularly dramatic in biology, where evolutionary theory unsettled theological and religious doctrines of creation. In 1949, a leading evolutionary scientist wrote:

> Although many details remain to be worked out, it is already evident that all the objective phenomena of the history of life can be explained by purely naturalistic or, in a proper sense of the sometimes abused word, materialistic factors. They are readily explicable on the basis of differential reproduction in populations (the main factor in the modern conception of natural selection) and of the mainly random interplay of the known processes of heredity. . . . Man is the result of a purposeless and natural process that did not have him in mind.[21]

Because of their history of going obsolete, attempts to fill in the cracks of advancing scientific knowledge with supernatural agency are now usually met with suspicion, and referred to pejoratively as a "god-of-the-gaps" argument. The pattern has prompted many humanists to assume the following:

> 12. Science undermines supernatural religion.

However, in recent decades, new scholarship in theology, religious studies, philosophy, and the history of science challenged the historical accuracy and rational credibility of the conflict model. Some have argued that science and theology are properly seen as independent, while others have argued that they take part in mutually constructive engagement.

HISTORICAL AND COMPARATIVE STUDIES

One way to approach the relationship between the sciences and theology is by investigating the actual historical interconnections between the various practices and doctrines. In this vein, some intellectual historians claim it is no accident that modern science originated in cultural contexts of monotheism—namely, in the world of the medieval Islamic Enlightenment and in early modern Christian Europe. According to this view, educated people ensconced in the intellectual environment of monotheism tended to think in ways especially congenial to the scientific enterprise. In particular, specific theistic doctrines formed a set of presuppositions that made science possible.

> A world which is created by the Christian God will be both contingent and orderly. It will embody regularities and patterns, since its Maker is rational, but the particular regularities and patterns which it will embody cannot be predicted *a priori*, since he is free; they can be discovered only by examination. The world, as Christian theism conceives, is thus an ideal field for the application of scientific method, with its twin techniques of observation and experiment.[22]

This fascinating and important historical research can be distinguished from another, more distinctively philosophical, task of exploring the *epistemological relationships* (of logical implication or presupposition, evidential or rational support, and so on) between the sciences and theology. For example, one might be able to document how certain scientists were in fact drawn to adopt a certain practice because of the theological assumptions they embraced. But such an explanation would not in itself show that the scientists were *justified* in adopting the practice on this basis, or that no alternative basis for the practice is available. In other words, it is one thing to demonstrate that the sciences historically were influenced by a monotheistic metaphysics; it is another thing to demonstrate they *rationally presuppose* a monotheistic metaphysics.

Other lines of scholarship on religion and science draw attention to certain similarities or equivalencies between the methodologies of the sciences and the methodologies of theology. For example, Ian Barbour has accepted a model-based view of science and sought to "delineate some parallels between the use of scientific models in the interpretation of experience and the use of religious models in the interpretation of experience. Theoretical models in science, he says, are "mental constructs devised to account for observed phenomena in the natural world. They originate in a combination of analogy to the familiar and creative imagination in the invention of the new . . . theoretical models, such as the 'billiard ball model' of a gas. . . . [S]uch models are taken seriously but not literally."[23]

According to Barbour, models are crucial to religion as well, where they also arise from analogies. Religious models are "organizing images used to order and interpret patterns of experience in human life. Like scientific models, they are neither literal pictures of reality nor useful fictions. One of the main functions of religious models is the interpretation of distinctive types of experience: awe and reverence, moral obligation, reorientation and reconciliation, interpersonal relationships, key historical events, and order and creativity in the world."

Nancey Murphy, who argues that Lakatos's notion of a scientific research program applies to theological investigation as well, has conducted another comparative study.[24] Studies such as these often suggest that a religion shares in the rationality, objectivity, and authority of the sciences insofar as it shares in the methodology of the sciences, or something relevantly similar. Of course, the matter is somewhat more complex since a methodology might be appropriate to one domain of inquiry but inappropriate to another.

It is worth noting that comparative analyses typically refer to the purported structure of scientific knowledge in order to illuminate the structure of theological knowledge, not to illuminate apparent tensions or constructive engagement among these bodies of knowledge. For instance, one does little to substantiate or dispel the appearance of conflict between evolutionary theory and religious creation narratives by pointing out that theological and scientific theories have some structural features in common. To do that, one would have to carefully investigate the epistemological relationships between these bodies of knowledge. It is this epistemological approach that preoccupies much of the current scholarship on religion and science. Arthur Peacocke, a physical biochemist, expresses the motivation for this approach:

> [B]oth science and theology are engaging with realities that may be referred to and it is therefore entirely appropriate to ask how what scientists believe about the natural world and religious people believe about God and nature, including human nature, should be related. . . . Moreover, on theology's own presuppositions, if God's own self has given the world the kind of being and becoming it has, then it must in some respects reveal God's nature and purposes.

> So theology should seek to be at least consonant with those scientific perspectives on the natural world that are well-established, as far as can be reasonably judged.[25]

Historical and purely comparative studies of science and religion may be interesting and worthwhile in their own right, but they typically do not address the kind of epistemological questions that are the main subject of this chapter.

INDEPENDENCE

Some theologians, philosophers, and scientists who take the epistemological approach conclude that science and theology are independent of each other. On this view, these modes of understanding differ in their aims, objects of study, and methods, and so they share no points of contact where one could impact the other either constructively or destructively.

Recently, the paleontologist Stephen Jay Gould defended a model of independence he calls "non overlapping magisteria," or NOMA.[26] The magisterium of religion, he claims, is "to define meaning in our lives and a moral basis for our actions," while the magisterium of science is "to understand the factual character of nature."[27] Under this definition, religion contains no claims or knowledge about the world, at least, no nonmoral claims. By implication, it cannot even include the statements "There is no god but Allah," or "Jesus healed the sick." It is difficult to see how this understanding of religion could be acceptable to a sincere and reflective believer. Critics charge that Gould prevents the overlapping of the magisteria by relying on an implausibly narrow understanding of "religion," restricting it to the domain of ethics and values only.

Gould attains independence by taking a strong *antirealist* stance about religion. Antirealist philosophies of religion deny, in one way or another, that religious statements are objectively true or false propositions about the world. One sophisticated antirealism especially popular in the middle of the twentieth century is associated with Ludwig Wittgenstein, whose later work inspired the school of linguistic or ordinary language philosophy. Linguistic philosophers of religion followed Wittgenstein in describing religious devotion as fundamentally an attitude of trust or commitment to a certain way of life rather than an affirmation of a set of beliefs or creeds. The believer makes a commitment to the life of faith in much the same way we might say someone is "committed to" or "believes in" a spouse or loved one. This "belief in" need not entail or reduce to "belief that," such as in the beliefs that there is a God and that our souls exist forever. Therefore, the "language game" of religion is entirely different from the language game of science, whose purposes center on referring to and manipulating natural objects. Although religion and science may sometimes sound as though they are in contradiction, they are in fact *talking past each other*. One common complaint against such Wittgensteinian views is that "belief in" is logically dependent on "belief that." It is conceptually impossible, for example, to believe in one's family or friends without believing that they exist.

Other attempts to achieve independence through antirealism can be found, to lesser and greater extents, in the work of twentieth-century existentialist and neo-orthodox theologians such as Martin Buber, who tend to characterize religious life in terms of an irreducibly first-person and subjective confrontation between the finite individual and the divine person of God. However, most theologians and philosophers of religion have sought to avoid antirealism, in part because it flies in the face of the experience of actual religious believers who think their religious statements do make assertions about what exists and what happens.

Perhaps a more modest, realist form of independence might be suggested: Both science and theology aim at producing knowledge, but they aim at knowledge of entirely dissimilar objects. Sciences produce knowledge of the natural or finite, while theologies produce knowledge of the supernatural or "ultimate." Thus, they are independent so long as they concern themselves with their proper respective objects. Nevertheless, theological statements could be objective and truth-apt in their own domain: as descriptions of supernatural or ultimate reality. Science is in principle "naturalistic": It invokes no supernatural processes or entities, such as the intentions of a divine person existing outside of space-time, but neither does it cast doubt on the existence of such things. They lie outside its proper scope.

It is not beyond dispute that the sciences are necessarily naturalistic in this sense. Sciences seek to understand a number of regularities that characterize our world, and they do so by invoking causes and causal laws thought to provide the best explanation of those regularities. But suppose for the sake of argument that theism is true, and—as most theists believe—the intentions and actions of a personal deity explain a number of interesting things about our universe (why the actual universe exists rather than another kind of universe, or rather than "nothing," why humans possess consciousness, and so on). If sciences were barred on principle from postulating the intention or behavior of supernatural persons, then they would be incapable of explaining those things. But surely we should desire a science that can help us understand such interesting things, *even if theism is true*. In fact, the history of scientific inquiry suggests no a priori limits on the *kinds of things* it may invoke.

For example, when it was first introduced by quantum physicists, the notion of a "nonlocal cause" violated fundamental, centuries-old assumptions of modern physics, which had regarded causation as local, almost by definition. Nevertheless, scientists have been

No Wonder?

In his poem "Lamia," English poet John Keats (1795–1821) lamented that science had destroyed the wonder and poetry of the rainbow by analytically disassembling it with the tools of prisms and optical theory.

> Do not all charms fly
> At the mere touch of cold philosophy?
> There was an awful rainbow once in heaven:
> We know her woof, her texture; she is given
> In the dull catalogue of common things.
> Philosophy will clip an Angel's wings,
> Conquer all mysteries by rule and line,
> Empty the haunted air, and gnomed mine—
> Unweave a rainbow.

For discussion, see Richard Dawkins, *Unweaving the Rainbow: Science, Delusion, and the Appetite for Wonder* (Boston: Houghton Mifflin, 1998).

willing to accept the reality of nonlocal causation in light of the extraordinary experimental success of quantum theory. There is nothing about the *nature* of science that would, in principle, prevent its practitioners from legitimately invoking the activity of supernatural persons. The question is whether doing so would ever be necessary for the best explanation of a given phenomenon under scientific investigation.

It may be the case, as many physicists and cosmologists believe, that the cosmos is a "causally closed system," admitting of no "external" causal influences from beyond space-time. But presumably this is an empirical claim that must be defended through scientific inquiry, and not a ground rule for what counts as proper scientific inquiry. Otherwise, the sciences would be vulnerable to the charge, leveled by some intelligent design theorists, that their nontheism is a mere prejudice or a presupposition rather than a conclusion founded on an accumulated body of well-established empirical evidence and theory.

ENGAGEMENT

Even if one thinks, despite the above argument, that science is in principle neutral as to the supernatural, there will be much more to say about the epistemic connections between science and religion. Consider, for example, the relationships between the physical sciences and the theistic notion of divine creation—that the universe is brought into being and sustained by a supernatural person.

Some argue that the physical sciences provide evidence for theism. In the last twenty years, a number of physicists have begun discussing a very interesting realization. Current research into the basic features of the physical universe—its initial conditions, or the fundamental particles of matter and energy—has revealed that if these features had not possessed precisely the quantitative values that they in fact do, then the emergence of human life, and all life as we know it, would have been impossible. Similarly, astrophysicist Stephen Hawking points out that the universe is expanding at just the rate necessary to avoid collapse: "[W]e know that there has to have been a very close balance between the competing effect of explosive expansion and gravitational contraction which, at the very earliest epoch about which we can even pretend to speak (called the Planck time, 10^{-43} sec. after the big bang), would have corresponded to the incredible degree of accuracy represented by a deviation in their ratio from unity by only one part in 10 to the sixtieth."[28]

Such features that are preconditions for life are called **anthropic coincidences**. Educated opinions as to the number of genuine anthropic coincidences vary, but most agree that at least a dozen such features characterize the universe as we now know it. If any one of them had been altered even minutely (for instance, the number one in 10^{40}—ten followed by forty zeros—is unimaginably small), life would have been precluded. Some now argue that the best explanation for this fact is that somehow the anthropic coincidences are there *in order that life could emerge*. The universe, it is said, is exquisitely "fine-tuned" for life.[29] We would expect such fine-tuning if theism were true, because the creator would design a universe friendly to life. The fine-tuning argument for theism is examined, along with other arguments for theism, in the next chapter.

Although the anthropic coincidences have attracted a great deal of attention, a growing number of theologians reject the whole strategy of using scientific findings as evidence for certain theological views. Some propose instead that theology should speak about the "boundaries" or "limits" of scientific understanding. It is often observed that science may be able to trace the origins of the universe to a Big Bang or other first event, beyond which point science yields to theology. Similarly, it is suggested that science supplies an account of the operation of natural forces in the universe, while theology adds the further, complementary claim that these forces depend on a necessary Being for their ongoing contingent existence. According to John Polkinghorne, theology is "no rival to science but it seeks to complement it. It does not purport to answer questions that rightly lie in science's domain (such as how life originated on Earth) but it looks to the ground of science's explanation and goes on to ask whether the laws of nature are sufficiently self-contained to afford a fundamental basis for understanding the world, or whether they do not point beyond themselves to a deeper Ground of explanation."[30]

Contemporary thinkers see this "limit questions" style of theology as distinct from the discredited "god-of-the-gaps" style. Limit-question theology insists that even when naturalistic science is *complete*, a deeper, "ultimate" understanding can be gained by systematically integrating it with religious beliefs.[31] Other theologians argue that their field should be informed and enriched by information from the sciences. This orientation is sometimes called the **theology of nature**.

Theologians who identify with the tradition of **process philosophy** go farther, attempting to construct an overarching metaphysical system that integrates science and religion (as well as ethical and aesthetic judgments). Process philosophy, a movement led by the work of Alfred North Whitehead and Charles Hartshorne, centers on conceiving of process or "becoming" as more fundamental than unchanging "being." Process thinkers attempt to produce a comprehensive metaphysics integrated with evolutionary views of biological nature and the cosmos. Among other things, they are led to some controversial theological conclusions—for example, that God is not all-powerful, with no unilateral control over what happens in the world. Many theologians and religious believers find such diminishment of the classical God unpalatable.

On the other hand, some thinkers believe that prevailing physical theories are incompatible with the alleged divine agency. According to one influential theory of the origins of the universe, the quantum gravity cosmology developed by Stephen Hawking and James Hartle, a law of nature called the "wave function of the universe" provides a very high probability (close to 100 percent) that a universe of our sort will come into existence uncaused. Philosopher Quentin Smith contends that the Hartle-Hawking cosmology implies that classical theism is false:

> [T]he probability that a Hartle-Hawking universe exists follows directly from the natural-mathematical properties of possible finite universes; there is no need for a cause, probabilistic or otherwise, for there to be a 99 percent probability that a Hartle-Hawking universe will exist.
>
> This is not consistent with classical theism. According to classical theism, if a universe is to have any probability of existing, this probability is dependent on God's dispositions, beliefs, or choices. But the Hartle-Hawking probability is not dependent on any supernatural states or acts. . . .
>
> Furthermore, according to classical theism, the probability that a universe exists without divine causation is 0, and the probability that if a universe exists, it is divinely caused, is 1. Thus, the probabilities that are implied by classical theism are inconsistent with the probabilities implied by the Hartle-Hawking wave function of the universe.[32]

Philosopher Adolf Grünbaum has suggested another proposed instance of incompatibility between contemporary physics and classical theism. He argues that the law of energy conservation, along with the assumption that the universe is physically closed, rules out the doctrine of continuous creation, the notion that the universe depends for its continued existence on the perpetual, sustaining action of the divine. Grünbaum considers a standard formulation of the law of energy conservation: "The mass-energy content of an isolated system remains constant. The energy can be converted from one form to another, but can neither be created nor destroyed." Grünbaum further observes:

> Hence, even if the system is open, a *change* in its energy content can occur only by the exportation or importation of energy, *not* by its creation *ex nihilo* or *annihilation*. . . . [S]ince the law declares the impossibility of the annihilation of the energy *tout court*, the energy *could* not *lapse into nothingness* in the absence of God. Therefore, contrary to the long theistic tradition of perpetual creation . . . God is clearly *not* needed to *prevent* such supposed spontaneous annihilation by creative intervention.[33]

Whether or not the arguments developed by Smith and Grünbaum are correct (neither is without critics), they serve to illustrate two general points. First, limit-questions theology faces a dilemma. Consider any given naturalistic explanation. To the extent that the explanation is said to be incomplete, theology is in danger of reverting to the god-of-the-gaps strategy. To the extent that the explanation is complete, the role for any "deeper Ground" is less apparent. For instance, if physical science does in fact account for the continued existence of energy, what kind of additional, "ultimate" piece is missing? Second, science and theology may enter into dialogue, even if science is neutral to the supernatural. For even if it is true that current science does not *invoke* or deny the existence of any supernatural entities or processes, this would not show that current science has no *implications* for the existence of supernatural entities or processes. With respect to both points, there is no substitute for careful attention to the details of the relevant science, and the theology as well.

What about the implications of theology for science? Could theological statements provide reasons to reject scientific statements? Many theologians believe, along with Peacocke, that theology "should seek to be at least consonant" with well-established scientific knowledge—which implies that it is always theology, rather than science, that must align itself. Not everyone accepts this limitation. Alvin Plantinga encourages theists to take their existing theistic beliefs into consideration when assessing the plausibility of scientific claims: "[I]n understanding the issues involved in sociology, or psychology, economics, or biology or whatever, we should use *everything* we know—what we know by faith as well as what we know in other ways. . . . We must approach a topic like evolution from the perspective of faith—of the deliverances of the faith—as well as that of current science; what faith teaches here is of crucial importance and must not be silenced."[34]

For example, the scientific evidence marshaled in favor of evolutionary theory makes it highly probable that human beings resulted from a blind, undirected, unsupervised process. But when people make up their minds about this and about other matters, they should do so on the basis of the total evidence available to them. For theists, the total evidence includes the propositions that God created human beings (in one way or another), and (therefore) that the process that produced us was not blind, undirected, or unsupervised. According to Plantinga, it is not unreasonable for the theist to reject the evolutionary conclusion even though she realizes that it is probable given the scientific evidence. It is not probable given her total evidence. If believers are to be true to their faith, they will not set aside their religious beliefs when doing science. Instead, they will engage in what Plantinga calls "unnatural science" or "theistic science."

Needless to say, Plantinga's proposal is controversial. For one thing, it is hard to see how these unnatural scientists could successfully engage in scholarly exchanges and collaborations with scientists who do not share their particular religious background beliefs. The Protestant scientist, the Hindu scientist, and the atheist scientist might often find themselves with hugely different appraisals of the evidence: a recipe for cognitive anarchy. No doubt, science could not flourish without heterodoxy, dissent, and free intellectual competition among mutually incompatible viewpoints. And yet, within a given research tradition, there is broad agreement on the criteria by which opposing viewpoints may be objectively evaluated. So, were "unnatural scientists" to enter the fray, they would be obliged to indicate how their views can be assessed on the basis of accepted objective criteria—or, if they cannot be assessed on the basis of accepted criteria, to show why some alternative criteria ought to be accepted. The next chapter surveys some recent attempts to construct an unabashedly scientific case for theism.

CONCLUSION

An abundance of new scholarship explores possible constructive engagement between theology and the sciences, eschewing the god-of-the-gaps model. However, it is important to distinguish comparative and historical claims from epistemological claims. The proposal that theological knowledge complements scientific knowledge takes the awkward position of supposing that scientific knowledge is complete (thus avoiding the god-of-the-gaps strategy) while still retaining a role for divine agency. Moreover, specific bodies of scientific knowledge do indeed seem incompatible with theism. Plantinga's proposal of unnatural science raises the controversial possibility that in the case of such conflicts, theology may sometimes prevail.

SUMMARY

As they have been characterized here, humanist ideas on science and religion include the notions that science is a privileged source of knowledge about the world and that science reinforces naturalism while undermining supernaturalism. This chapter points out the complexities and vulnerabilities of both notions while underscoring their overall plausibility.

STUDY QUESTIONS

1. Outline the key elements in the positivist account of science.
2. Explain the thesis that scientific theories are underdetermined by the evidence.
3. What is the Miracle Argument for scientific realism?
4. Distinguish between external realism and internal realism with respect to science.

5. Explain scientism and one objection to it.
6. Contrast comparative and historical approaches to religion and science with epistemological approaches.
7. Describe an antirealist independence thesis and one objection to it.
8. Describe a realist independence thesis and one objection to it.
9. What is limit-questions theology?
10. What is Plantinga's unnatural science?

DISCUSSION QUESTIONS

1. How does Thomas Kuhn's notion of a "paradigm" in science differ from the use of "paradigm" that has entered mainstream English speech?
2. Formulate an objection to radical social constructivism, the idea that inquirers alter reality merely by conceiving of it in a particular way.
3. In what sense is money a "social construction"? Would this imply that money is not "real" or that it cannot be known objectively? What about gender? Or race?
4. What scientific knowledge is important to Western society? Can you think of real or imagined human societies in which this knowledge would not be worth pursuing?
5. In Kitcher's sense, what kind of epistemically significant truths might be pursued in the following research areas? (a) Formulating string theory, which attempts to synthesize existing physics into a Theory of Everything, (b) mapping the human genome, and (c) interviewing victims of sexual abuse.
6. After grasping a scientific account of rainbows, are you less apt to marvel at them or appreciate them aesthetically? Can one alternate between scientific and aesthetic contemplation of the same object?
7. Is Plantinga's "theistic science" a viable model for the sciences? How would scientific institutions (like university degree programs and research laboratories) need to change in order to accommodate his proposal?
8. Is limit-questions theology difference from god-of-the-gaps theology? Relate your answer to the arguments by Smith and Grünbaum.
9. Is science methodologically naturalistic? Why or why not?
10. In light of the distinctions presented in this section, how would you analyze the creation-evolution controversy?

FIELD PROBLEM

Scan the news and current events for a debate or controversy that involves, directly or indirectly, the authority of science or challenges to scientific knowledge from some other purported source of knowledge. Analyze the debate in terms of the distinctions introduced in this chapter.

SUGGESTIONS FOR FURTHER READING

Barbour, Ian. *Religion in an Age of Science: The Gifford Lectures*. Vol. 1. San Francisco: Harper and Row, 1990.

Bloor, David. *Knowledge and Social Imagery*, 2d ed. Chicago: University of Chicago Press, 1991.
Churchland, Paul M., and Clifford A. Hooker, eds. *Images of Science: Essays on Realism and Empiricism*. Chicago: University of Chicago Press, 1985.
Cobb, J. B., and David Ray Griffin. *Process Theology: An Introductory Exposition*. Philadelphia: Westminster Press, 1976.
Curd, Martin, and J. A. Cover, eds. *Philosophy of Science: The Central Issues*. New York: Norton, 1998.
Davies, Paul. *The Mind of God*. New York: Simon & Schuster, 1992.
Gould, Stephen Jay. *Rocks of Ages: Science and Religion in the Fullness of Life*. New York: Ballantine, 1999.
Kitcher, Philip. *Science, Truth, and Democracy*. New York: Oxford University Press, 2001.
Kuhn, Thomas. *The Structure of Scientific Revolutions*. Chicago: University of Chicago Press, 1970.
Lakatos, Imre, and Alan Musgrave, eds. *Criticism and the Growth of Knowledge*. Cambridge: Cambridge University Press, 1970.
Laudan, Larry. *Progress and Its Problems: Towards a Theory of Scientific Growth*. Berkeley: University of California Press, 1978.
Murphy, Nancey. *Theology in the Age of Scientific Reasoning*. Ithaca, N.Y.: Cornell University Press, 1990.
Peacocke, Arthur, ed. *The Sciences and Theology in the Twentieth Century*. Notre Dame, Ind.: University of Notre Dame Press, 1981.
Peacocke, Arthur. *Theology for a Scientific Age*. Oxford: Basil Blackwell, 1990.
Pennock, Robert T. *Tower of Babel: The Evidence against the New Creationism*. Cambridge, Mass.: MIT Press, 1999.
Ruse, Michael, ed. *But Is It Science?* Amherst, N.Y.: Prometheus Books, 1988.
Weinberg, Steven. *Facing Up: Science and Its Cultural Adversaries*. Cambridge, Mass.: Harvard University Press, 2001.

NOTES

1. See L. W. Levine, *Defender of the Faith: William Jennings Bryan* (New York: Oxford University Press, 1965), 277.
2. "Clarence Darrow's examination of Williams Jennings Bryan at the Scopes trial," www.beliefnet.com/story/1/story_191_1.html.
3. Frederick Crews, "Saving Us from Darwin," *New York Review of Books,* 4 October 2001.
4. Michael Ruse, "Creation Science Is Not Science," in Martin Curd and J. A. Cover, eds., *Philosophy of Science: The Central Issues* (New York: Norton, 1998), 39.
5. Ruse, "Creation Science Is Not Science," 39.
6. Ruse, "Creation Science Is Not Science," 40.
7. Ruse, "Creation Science Is Not Science," 40.
8. Ruse, "Creation Science Is Not Science," 41.
9. David Papineau, *Philosophical Naturalism* (Oxford: Blackwell, 1993), 1.
10. Paul K. Moser and David Yandell, "Farewell to Philosophical Naturalism," in *Naturalism: A Critical Analysis*, ed. William Lane Craig and J. P. Moreland (New York: Routledge, 2000): 3–23.
11. Michael Rea, *World Without Design: The Ontological Consequences of Naturalism* (New York: Oxford University Press, 2002), 63.
12. See James Beilby, ed., *Naturalism Defeated? Essays on Plantinga's Evolutionary Argument Against Naturalism* (Ithaca, N.Y.: Cornell University Press, 2002).
13. This general approach is defended by Michael Rea, *World Without Design*, and Peter Forrest, *God Without the Supernatural: A Defense of Scientific Theism* (Ithaca, N.Y.: Cornell University Press, 1996), 89.

14. Some commentators view these as distinct schools of thought, some of whose expositors overlapped.

15. Barry Barnes and David Bloor, "Relativism, Rationality, and the Sociology of Knowledge," in *Science, Reason, and Reality*, ed. Daniel Rothbart (Fort Worth, Tex.: Harcourt Brace, 1998), 332.

16. This view must be distinguished from the clearly correct claim that some things, for example, money, exist simply because our ways of thinking lead us to *act in ways that bring about or sustain their existence*. This view has been called, somewhat confusingly, *social constructionism*, or realist social constructionism. It is another matter to suppose that we can bring about or alter the existence of something *merely by thinking about it* in a particular way.

17. Philip Kitcher, *Science, Truth, and Democracy* (New York: Oxford University Press, 2001), 65.

18. Kitcher, *Science, Truth, and Democracy*, 75.

19. See Herbert Butterfield, *The Origins of Modern Science* (New York: Free Press, 1965); Dava Sobel, *Longitude: The True Story of a Lone Genius Who Solved the Greatest Scientific Problem of His Time* (New York: Walker, 1995).

20. *Novum Organum*, ed. John Gibson and Peter Urbach (Chicago, Open Court Books, 1994), book I, aphorism III.

21. George Gaylord Smith, *The Meaning of Evolution: A Study of the History of Life and of Its Significance for Man*, rev. ed. (New Haven, Conn.: Yale University Press, 1967), 345.

22. E. L. Mascall, *Christian Theology and Natural Science* (New York: Ronald Press, 1965), 132.

23. Ian G. Barbour, *Myths, Models and Paradigms: A Comparative Study in Science and Religion* (New York: Harper and Row, 1974), 6–7.

24. Nancey Murphy, *Theology in the Age of Scientific Reasoning* (Ithaca, N.Y.: Cornell University Press, 1990).

25. Arthur Peacocke, *God and Science: A Quest for Christian Credibility* (London: SCM Press, 1996), 6. See also Peacocke, *Theology for a Scientific Age* (Oxford: Basil Blackwell, 1990).

26. Stephen Jay Gould, *Rocks of Ages: Science and Religion in the Fullness of Life* (New York: Ballantine, 1999).

27. Gould, *Rocks of Ages,* 175.

28. In John Polkinghorne, *Science and Creation: The Search for Understanding* (Boston: New Science Library, 1989), 22.

29. Since they are relevant to the conditions for carbon-based life as such and not human life per se, the coincidences might more accurately be called "biotropic coincidences" or maybe "carbontropic coincidences."

30. John Polkinghorne, *Faith, Science and Understanding* (New Haven, Conn.: Yale University Press, 2000), 204–5.

31. Ernan McMullin, "How Should Cosmology Relate to Theology?" in *The Sciences and Theology in the Twentieth Century*, ed. Arthur Peacocke (Notre Dame, Ind.: University of Notre Dame Press, 1981).

32. Quentin Smith, "Why Stephen Hawking's Cosmology Precludes a Creator," *Philo* 1, 1 (1998): 75–94.

33. Adolf Grünbaum, "Theological Misinterpretations of Current Physical Cosmology," *Philo* 1, 1 (Spring–Summer 1998): 15–34.

34. Alvin Plantinga, "Evolution, Neutrality, and Antecedent Probability: A Reply to Van Till and McMullen," *Christian Scholar's Review* 21, 1 (September 1991).

7

God, Humanism, and Philosophy

Lewis Vaughn

God is difficult to ignore. Sooner or later most people find themselves pondering the existence of a deity. Both believers and unbelievers can be dramatically affected by their own notions about God. They both have certain attitudes or opinions about the existence of a supreme being—and this perspective, in small or large ways, can guide their steps and change how they look at the world. Does life have meaning? Does the world have both natural and supernatural elements? Does the universe contain a supreme being who cares about you? Does this being expect you to behave in a certain way? Are there such things as divine justice, immortality, and miracles? The answers to all of these questions can hang on belief or nonbelief in God.

Modern humanists understand this point well, for their worldview is defined in large part by their attitude toward the concept of God. Almost all of them reject **theism** (belief in God or gods) and embrace either **atheism** (belief that there is no God), **agnosticism** (belief that there is insufficient evidence to accept existence of God), or strong skepticism toward religious doctrine of all kinds.

Humanists of the past, however, were often believers. The great humanists of the Renaissance—including Dante, Petrarch, Erasmus, and More—were theists and usually devout Christians. But they took the classics to heart and incorporated human-centered or secular ideas into their views. Enlightenment humanists went further, vigorously attacking religious dogma and practices and often replacing the traditional concept of God with **deism**, the view that God exists but is absent from the realm of human affairs. In the twenty-first century, however, most humanists do not accept even this barely existing deistic God, though a few may consider themselves to be "religious humanists."

Throughout history, ideas about God or gods have been plentiful. In fact, there have been—and still are—more gods than faiths, more concepts of a deity than religions to accommodate them. The ancient Greeks were **polytheistic** (believing in more than one god), and the Hebrews were **monotheistic** (believing in one God only). The Greek gods were finite—laden with limitations such as weakness, fallibility, and immorality—as was Yahweh, the Hebrew God. But Christianity, Judaism, and Islam, the dominant religions of the West, are monotheistic, and their God is thought to be infinite (unlimited or boundless in key attributes). God also has been defined in ways that make him (her? it?) more of an idealization than a being. God has been characterized as Nature itself, the infinite Universe, everything there is (**pantheism**), the Ground of Being, the essence of love or truth, and the Force for Good or Life.

Philosophy, however, is generally not interested in these diffuse, reductive conceptions of God—and neither are most believers and unbelievers. In the West, when philosophers and theologians examine the notion of God, when theists affirm the existence of God, and when atheists deny it, they are usually referring to what is called the "traditional concept of God." This is the idea of God as a single being who is omnipotent (all-powerful), omniscient (all-knowing), and omnibenevolent (all-good). This God, unlike the diffuse gods mentioned above, is a *person*: a being who is free to think, feel, know, act, and respond. As a person, he cannot be merely synonymous with the universe or some aspect of existence. His relationship with the universe is not as a component, but as the Creator. The Christian philosopher Richard Swinburne provides an expanded version of this conception. There is a God, he says, who is "A person without a body (i.e. a spirit), present everywhere, the creator and sustainer of the universe, a free agent, able to do anything (i.e. omnipotent), knowing all things, perfectly good, a source of moral obligation, immutable, eternal, a necessary being, holy, and worthy of worship."[1]

Most theists accept the traditional view of God, but they may differ on how involved this God is in the world. Many, probably most, theists believe that God is *provident*. If God is provident, he is involved in human affairs. He controls and directs lives, perhaps answers prayers, and looks after his earthly children. But some theists reject the idea of a provident God. They believe that God is a person but think that he has little or no involvement in people's lives. **Deists**, for example, believe that God established the universe but does not respond to human needs or prayers or tamper with worldly events. In **process theism**, God is thought to be almost inactive in human endeavors. God is restricted to *persuading* people to do what he thinks is best for them. He cannot interfere in human events, and there is much that he cannot control.

The existence of God (in the traditional sense) is one of the "Big Questions" of philosophy. Philosophers ask, "Is there a God?" and then investigate whether there is any justification (evidence or argument) for believing that there is (or is not) such a being. In this chapter we explore this issue in some detail. Before we begin, however, we should note that some people think that this philosophical enterprise is somehow illegitimate or irrelevant. They believe either (1) that all talk about God is literally meaningless, or (2) that belief in God does not require justification or evidence.

The charge that God-talk is without meaning implies that claims or beliefs about God can be neither true nor false and therefore cannot be submitted to philosophical argumentation and analysis. After all, if a proposition is meaningless, it is not the type of thing that can be true or false.

But in what way are claims or beliefs about God supposed to be meaningless? Here is one way, probably the strongest bid to show theism incoherent: Statements are meaningless, say some philosophers, because there is no way to test or confirm them. If statements cannot be verified, they have no meaning at all. Knowing the meaning of a statement requires knowing how to verify it. This claim is the core of a theory of meaning proposed by some twentieth-century philosophers who came to be known as **logical positivists**. They asserted that there are only two kinds of meaningful statements: (1) purely logical truths such as "two plus two equals four" or "no bachelors are married," and (2) factual statements that can be verified only through the senses as they are, for example, in science. If a statement does not fit in either category, it is meaningless.

On this theory, statements about the existence of God are neither logical truths nor facts that can be verified by some empirical test, so all talk about God must be meaningless. To say "God exists" or "God is omnipotent" is to make no truth claim at all. In fact, all religious claims fail the test of meaning.

This verification theory of meaning can be traced back to the philosopher David Hume (1711–1776). He says that if you pick up a book about God or about other things that cannot be verified (what he called metaphysics), ask yourself two questions: "Does it contain any abstract reasoning concerning quantity or number? No. Does it contain any experimental reasoning concerning matter of fact and existence? No. Commit it then to the flames: for it can contain nothing but sophistry and illusion."[2]

This approach can be used to dismiss whole libraries of theology, metaphysics, and anything else that fails the verification test. In this view, statements such as "God is omnipotent" and "Platonic ideas exist in a transcendent realm" are nonsense.

The logical positivist's theory of meaning, however, has fallen on hard times. Few philosophers accept this view now because its flaws have become obvious. For one thing, the theory says that the meaning of a statement is the same thing as its method of verification—but many statements have different meanings and still would be verified in the same way. Consider these two statements: "This pole is ten feet long," and "If this pole's length were doubled, it would be twenty feet long." They have different meanings, but they would be verified by the same empirical tests.

A much bigger problem for the verification theory of meaning is that it self-destructs—that is, the theory undermines itself. The theory applies to all statements, so it applies to itself. Thus the theory ("The meaning of a statement is its method of verification") is meaningful only if it can be verified. But there is no empirical test to verify this statement; it cannot be verified. So according to the theory, the theory itself is meaningless. If the theory is true, it cannot be true (or false).

Some think that statements about God are meaningless in another sense: God is *unknowable*, so any statements about him would be inadequate or pointless. If something cannot be known, we cannot talk about it in a meaningful way. God could be unknowable either because that is his nature (he is the Great Unknowable), or because he is far beyond our power to understand him—he simply transcends all human categories of thought.

God's unknowability, though, seems doubtful. If God has properties that make him literally unknowable, he cannot be worthy of our worship or respect. How can we worship or respect something about which we know nothing? If he is unknowable, for all we know he could be anything: weak, cruel, hateful, immoral, or foolish. An atheist could accept this "god" just as easily as a theist could. This deity—whatever it is—could not be the God of traditional theism.

In addition, there appears to be good reason to think that we, even with our frail faculties, could at least partially understand a transcendent entity. We may not be able to fully grasp the nature of a transcendent God, but we surely can know something about him—just as we can know something about other transcendent entities. We can know at least some facts about infinite sets and infinite series in mathematics; about infinite space and infinite age of the universe; and about the greatest of all islands (because we know what an island is like), the perfect being (because we know what a being is like), or most powerful of all persons (because we know what a person is).

The most robust attacks against the meaningfulness of theistic language have not fared well. Inconsistencies may or may not be embedded in the traditional God concept (we examine this possibility later in this chapter), but there seems to be no good reason to think that all talk of God is literally without sense, and that statements about religious or divine things are neither true nor false. On the contrary, our commonsense experience (and the presumption of most philosophers) is that we can sensibly say a great many things about God.

Regarding the notion that belief in God does not require rational justification or evidence—there are several ways to construe this view. One very influential idea is this: Religious beliefs are not subject to independent rational evaluation and must instead be warranted by faith. (Recall that faith is essentially belief without supporting evidence.) This dismissal of reason in favor of faith is known as **fideism**. Some fideists insist that faith claims are in conflict with reason. Other fideists maintain that such claims must be established through faith but may also be seconded by reason. Among the thinkers who have endorsed fideism are philosopher-theologian Søren Kierkegaard (1813–1855) and theologian Karl Barth (1886–1968).

Traditionally, the attempt to ground religious belief in the natural processes of reason or argument has been called **natural religion** (or **natural theology**). Philosophers who accept some version of natural theology include Thomas Aquinas (1225–1274) and John Locke (1632–1704). The contrasting term is **revealed religion** (or **revealed theology**), the attempt to warrant religious claims through divine revelation. Fideism, of course, has little to do with natural religion, but it may find a home in revealed religion.

The question, then, is whether faith can independently warrant or establish belief in God's existence—whether faith is a source of knowledge. As we pointed out in chapter 5, on knowledge and belief, most epistemologists (those who study the nature of truth and knowledge) reject the claim that faith can be a source of knowledge. They offer several arguments for this position, but their simplest one would probably be this:

1. Knowledge is true belief that is justified (supported by argument or evidence).
2. Unjustified beliefs cannot constitute knowledge.
3. Beliefs based on faith are unjustified.
4. Therefore, beliefs based on faith cannot constitute knowledge.

This is a valid argument; it rests on the commonsense view of knowledge as *justified true belief*. Rejecting this definition of knowledge in favor of one that accommodates faith would itself require justification.

Some people, though, would object to this approach, believing that it is improper to judge beliefs based on faith by the same criteria used to judge ordinary knowledge claims. Faith, they say, is a legitimate, alternative source of knowledge. But as we noted previously, faith may be a trustworthy source of knowledge—but then perhaps it is not. We cannot simply *take on faith* that faith is a reliable indicator of truth. That would be assuming that faith *is* reliable, which is the claim we are trying to evaluate. To check on the reliability of faith, we have to use procedures that we already know are trustworthy—namely, our everyday methods of logic and experience.

This conclusion seems difficult to escape, especially when we consider the relative status of faith and our ordinary knowledge-acquiring procedures. Everyone—theist and atheist alike—deems our ordinary means of attaining knowledge to be generally reliable. But not everyone expects that faith can be just as dependable. So we cannot simply presume the methods of faith to be trustworthy—at least not until we put them to the test.

If faith really is a source of knowledge about God or religious doctrines, then an odd problem arises: How do we choose between competing (and often conflicting) faith claims? There are many religions, many doctrines, many firmly held beliefs—all supported by appeals to faith. Which road of faith do we follow—and why? We cannot choose one arbitrarily; that would be absurd. We could have no confidence (faith?) in such a decision. Neither can we use one tradition of faith through which to examine all of the other paths of faith. That would be assuming at the outset which brand of faith is the right one. What is needed here is some neutral standard by which we can judge competing faith claims. There seems to be no plausible alternative to employing the rational procedures we all use.

There are other ways to try to show that belief in God does not need to be supported by evidence or argument. We looked at the most sophisticated attempt in chapter 5—Alvin Plantinga's view of "properly basic beliefs." In any case, we can still assess the merits of arguments for and against God's existence. Regardless of whether theistic belief can be independently warranted by faith or by some other extraordinary faculty, the question of whether theism can be justified through argument and evidence is still important and intriguing. In fact, both theists and nontheists have been examining and reexamining the question for thousands of years.

So in the following section (7.1) we investigate the arguments purporting to show that God exists. In section 7.2 we assess the main argument that allegedly demonstrates God does not exist.

SECTION 7.1

The Case for God: Trying to Prove God's Existence

Why do philosophers and theologians—or anyone else, for that matter—care about arguments that purport that God does, or does not, exist? People have been debating the question for thousands of years. Why do they persist?

They persist because the question matters and because they think philosophy can yield some answers. As we noted earlier, some people believe that philosophical inquiry is useless in matters of faith, but those who undertake this task disagree. Like Thomas Aquinas, many are theists who regard reason as a divine gift meant to be used in the search for truth. Others view rational inquiry as the best—and perhaps only—hope for gaining knowledge in religious matters. In any case, to these searchers the trip seems worth the trouble.

As we have seen, humanists have generally been skeptical of religious claims, yet they have seemed to be as preoccupied with philosophical arguments about God as inquiring theists have. They, of course, have arrived at opinions markedly different from those of theists. In particular, most modern humanists have concluded that all of the traditional arguments for God's existence have failed. They would probably agree completely with this proposition:

13. There is no warrant for believing in God, as traditionally conceived.

Here, "traditionally conceived" refers to the traditional concept of God mentioned earlier—God as omnipotent, omniscient, and omnibenevolent.

Now, what if these arguments purporting to establish that God exists *are* failures? That is, what if they offer no justification for theistic belief? Must we then conclude that God does not exist? No. Lack of supporting reasons or evidence for a proposition does not show that the proposition is false. It shows only that we have no justification for accepting the proposition. Also, even if the traditional arguments for God give us no good reasons for theistic belief, this does not rule out the possibility that someone might devise new arguments that do provide good reasons. The key point is that to be justified, both the belief that God exists and the belief that God does not exist require reason and evidence.

Let's take a closer look at the traditional arguments for God's existence. There are three main types: (1) ontological, (2) cosmological, and (3) teleological. There are a few weaker arguments that do not fit in these categories, and we mention many of these along the way. Let's begin with what many consider to be the most interesting and exasperating type.

ONTOLOGICAL ARGUMENTS

What if you could prove the existence of God simply from the definition of God? This is essentially the tack taken by those who put forth an **ontological argument** (ontology is the branch of metaphysics dealing with very basic questions about what exists). If successful, this type of argument shows that God exists by simply uncovering the logical relations among concepts. This approach is appealing because to prove God's existence, you would not need to muster evidence from any empirical facts—and no empirical facts could prove the argument wrong.

There are many versions of the ontological argument, too many to assess here. But we can try to evaluate the most famous and the most powerful ones. Let's start with the version that spawned all of the other versions—the ontological argument offered by St. Anselm (1033?–1109 C.E.), the medieval philosopher and theologian. Here's his argument in a simplified form:

1. By definition, God is the greatest possible being (or, as Anselm says, a being "than which nothing greater can be conceived").
2. If God exists only in our minds, then there must be a being greater than God—that is, a being that exists not only in our minds but in reality as well. (A being that exists in reality is greater than a being that exists in our minds.)
3. But then there would be a being greater than God (the greatest possible being), which is a contradiction.
4. Therefore, God must exist in reality, not just in our minds.

The point is that since God is the greatest being possible, he cannot possibly exist only in our minds. If he existed only in our minds ("in the understanding alone"), he would not be the greatest being possible because any being like God who existed in reality (not just in the mind) would be *greater* than God. But that situation gives rise to a contradiction—God, the greatest being possible, is not the greatest being possible! So God must not exist only in our minds—he must exist in reality. This is how Anselm states his argument:

> And whatever is understood exists in the understanding. And assuredly that than which nothing greater can be conceived, cannot exist in the understanding alone. For suppose it exists in the understanding alone: then it can be conceived to exist in reality, which is greater.
>
> Therefore, if that than which nothing can be greater can be conceived exists in the understanding alone, the very being than which nothing can be conceived, is one than which a greater can be conceived. But obviously this is impossible. Hence, there is no doubt that there exists a being than which nothing greater can be conceived, and it exists both in the understanding and in reality.[3]

Does this argument seem right to you? Many people suspect that the ontological argument is somehow a philosopher's trick, a shell game with logic. There is a grain of truth in this suspicion. The trouble seems to be that Anselm tries to show that God exists by defining him into existence! But we cannot make something real by the act of defining it.

For example, let's say that you define the term "marbach" as a married bachelor, meaning someone who is both married and not married. In one sense, marbachs do exist—but only as a concept, a mental description based on a certain definition. Your definition in no way guarantees there really are such things as married bachelors. In the same way, Anselm's definition of God as the greatest possible being may or may not make good sense as a definition specifying the properties of God. But simply stipulating such a definition does not ensure that such a being actually exists.

At the heart of Anselm's definitional problem is his apparent assumption that the "being than which nothing greater can be conceived" actually exists in some sense because existence is part of the definition. If such a being really does exist in some sense, then Anselm's argument goes through. But this assumption begs the question. It may very well be that Anselm's concept of God involves the idea of actual existence, but this fact does not mean that there is an existing entity to which the concept applies.

Another argument against Anselm's proof is that it can be parodied by substituting all kinds of absurd entities in the argument for the God concept. The monk Guanilo, a contemporary of Anselm, took this approach. He pointed out that if Anselm's argument were valid, anyone could put forth similar arguments to prove the existence of all kinds of unlikely things—including the greatest possible island:

> When someone tells me that there is such an island, I easily understand what is being said, for there is nothing difficult here. Suppose, however, as a consequence of this, that he then goes on to say: You cannot doubt that this island, more excellent than all islands, actually exists somewhere in reality, because it undoubtedly stands in relation to your understanding. Since it is more excellent not simply to stand in relation to the understanding, but to be in reality as well, therefore this island must necessarily be in reality. Otherwise, any other land that exists in reality would be more excellent than this island, and this island which you understand to be the most excellent of all lands would then not be the most excellent.[4]

The main point here is that if Anselm's argument can lead to such absurd conclusions, there must be something wrong with it.

One notable response to the island analogy is that it does not undermine Anselm's argument because God and islands are not analogous. Anselm's argument, for example, refers to the greatest possible being, but an island is not the kind of thing that can be the greatest possible. No matter how many palm trees and coconuts the island has, it is always possible to have more, which means that the *greatest possible* island is impossible.[5]

It is not obvious, however, that there never could be a greatest possible island. It is not clear, for example, that an island with an infinite supply of everything could not be the greatest possible island.

Things look even worse for Anselm's argument if, instead of the greatest island possible, we substitute the greatest devil possible (a being than which no worse can be conceived). If we do this, the form of Anselm's argument seems to prove that a greatest possible devil must exist!

Many other versions of the ontological argument have been offered, both by famous philosophers of the past such as Benedict Spinoza and René Descartes and by modern authors such as Alvin Plantinga and Norman Malcolm. Descartes's version presents us with an interesting twist on Anselm's argument. Here is one way to state Descartes's argument:

1. By definition, God is a supremely perfect being (he possesses all possible perfections).
2. Existence is a perfection (that is, a defining property).
3. Therefore, God exists.

For Descartes, it is impossible for a supremely perfect being to not exist: "Hence, it is just as much a contradiction to think of God (that is, a supremely perfect being) lacking existence (that is, lacking a perfection), as it is to think of a mountain without a valley. . . . I am not free to think of God without existence."[6]

Descartes's argument, though, has the same defect as Anselm's argument: Embedded in the argument is the apparent assumption that a supremely perfect being actually exists because existence is part of the definition of God ("a supremely perfect being"). Again, this assumption begs the question. If this assumption is not embedded in the argument, then the argument does not prove much of anything. This dilemma—either the argument begs the question or proves nothing—seems to infect all variations of the ontological argument.

In addition, Descartes assumes something else that is debatable: that existence can be a defining property of something. Many thinkers—most notably Immanuel Kant (1724–1804)—have argued that to say that something exists is not to ascribe to it any particular property or quality. It is just to assert that something is—without ascribing to it any properties at all. It seems that we can often specify a thing's properties without making any reference to whether or not it exists. We might say, for example, that a unicorn is a horse-like creature with a long horn protruding from its forehead.

But whether or not existence is a property, Descartes's argument involves a more obvious difficulty. It is not all clear that existence is a perfection. A perfection is something better for a thing to have than to not have. But is it really always better that a thing exist rather than not exist? Is it always better that a person exist rather than not exist—even when the person's existence is fraught with agony? On what grounds could we say that it is better for a stone to exist than not to exist? How about a one-celled creature living in a cave under the sea? What reasons could we possibly have for thinking it is better for this creature to be than to not be?

Descartes also assumes that something (namely, God) could possess all possible perfections. This raises the difficulty of conflicts among God's attributes. For instance, let's say that God does possess all possible perfections. Then he must be all-powerful as well as all-good. If God is all-powerful, he should be able to do anything logically possible for him to do. If he is all-good, he cannot possibly do anything wrong. Thus, there are things that God cannot do that even humans can do—that is, do wrong. So it seems that God cannot be both all-powerful and all-good.

Here's another example. God is supposed to be both all-knowing and all-good. But if he is all-good, there must be some things he cannot know—such as what it feels like to be jealous, lustful, gluttonous, and covetous. If he knows these things, he would not be all-good. If he does not know these things, then he cannot be all-knowing. Again, we have a conflict of perfections and thus a reason to believe that it is not the case that God possesses all possible perfections.

COSMOLOGICAL ARGUMENTS

Ontological arguments begin with the definition of God and move to the real existence of God. **Cosmological arguments** start from a general fact about the world (that the world exists, that change exists, that things in the world depend on other things to exist, that every event has a cause) and then try to derive the existence of God from this fact. Essentially, cosmological arguments attempt to show that the best explanation for a given fact is that God exists. A major appeal of these arguments is that they do not begin with a questionable definition, but with an empirical proposition, a statement that most people would readily accept.

There are several kinds of cosmological arguments, each appealing to a different fact or alleged fact to make its case. In various forms, cosmological arguments have been put forth by Aristotle, Plato, Averroës, Spinoza, Aquinas, Leibniz, and countless other philosophers and theologians. Here we will concentrate on a few of the most influential types.

The First-Cause Argument

Unlike ontological arguments, cosmological arguments are based on a style of reasoning most people find natural. We see this clearly in the case of the classic cosmological argument—what is known as the **first-cause argument**. Most people would quickly agree that every event must have a cause. This notion is difficult to deny because all of the events they are aware of have had causes or apparent causes. People observe long chains of cause and effect, with causes leading to effects, and those effects causing still other effects, and so on—like a falling row of dominoes. But sooner or later they may wonder: Who or what *started* all of these tumbling dominoes? Events cannot cause themselves, and surely the sequence of causes cannot be traced backward into infinity. Did God tip the first domino?

The first-cause argument tries to show that the answer to this question is *yes*. Here is a famous statement of the argument by St. Thomas Aquinas (1225–1274):

> In the world of sense we find there is an order of efficient causes. There is no case known (neither is it, indeed, possible) in which a thing is found to be the efficient cause of itself; for so it would be prior to itself, which is impossible. Now in efficient causes it is not possible to go on to infinity, because in all efficient causes following in order, the first is the cause of the intermediate cause, and the intermediate cause is the cause of the ultimate cause, whether the intermediate be several or one only. Now, to take away the cause is to take away the effect.

> Therefore, if there be no first cause among efficient causes, there will be no ultimate, nor any intermediate cause. But if in efficient causes it is possible to go to infinity, there will be no first efficient cause, neither will there be an ultimate effect, nor any intermediate efficient causes; all of which is plainly false. Therefore it is necessary to admit a first efficient cause to which everyone gives the name of God.[7]

We may restate the argument like this:

1. Everything is caused by something other than itself.
2. The series of causes for anything cannot be infinite.
3. If the series of causes cannot be infinite, there must be a first cause (an uncaused cause).
4. Therefore, there must be a first cause (an uncaused cause), which everyone calls God.

What shall we make of this argument? First, if it is sound, it demonstrates that there must be a first cause. But Aquinas seems to be pressing his case too far when he identifies the first cause as God. The first cause is God only if it has the properties of God—that is, only if it is all-powerful, all-knowing, and all-good. Aquinas, of course, gives us no reason to take this further step. It is logically possible that Aquinas's first cause has none of these traits. Indeed, for all this argument shows, this first cause may have very little resemblance to the God that Aquinas and other Christians expect.

The biggest problem with this argument is that it undermines itself. Premise 1 says, "Everything is caused by something other than itself." If this is so, this premise must apply to God. God must also have a cause. But if God has a cause, he cannot be the *first* cause. This means that if premise 1 is true, the argument's conclusion is false! So in its original form, Aquinas's first-cause argument self-destructs.

We could alter premise 1 so that God is indeed uncaused: "Everything except God is caused by something other than itself." This move, however, presents us with a puzzle. It shows that we are willing to accept the notion of uncaused things, but it also suggests that we have arbitrarily decided to elect God as the one uncaused thing. But why must we do this? Why not posit the universe as uncaused and forgo the complication of an added (mysterious) entity?

Many people would say, however, that the whole idea of something being uncaused does not make any sense—especially in our cause-and-effect world. But there seems to be good reason to think that uncaused things are not only possible but also actual. As noted in chapter 3, on free will and determinism, there is good evidence suggesting that some things really are uncaused. According to quantum mechanics (the science of the subatomic level), subatomic particles occur uncaused all of the time. Particles such as electrons and positrons regularly pop in and out existence randomly—meaning that they are uncaused. They emerge spontaneously out of a perfect vacuum—events that physicists call "vacuum fluctuations." Here's what three physicists have to say about this strange phenomenon:

> [T]he idea of a First Cause sounds somewhat fishy in light of the modern theory of quantum mechanics. According to the most commonly accepted interpretation of quantum mechanics, individual subatomic particles can behave in unpredictable ways and there are numerous random, uncaused events.[8]

> In the everyday world, energy is always unalterably fixed; the law of energy conservation is a cornerstone of classical physics. But in the quantum microworld, energy can appear and disappear out of nowhere in a spontaneous and unpredictable fashion.[9]

> [Q]uantum electrodynamics reveals that an electron, positron, and photon occasionally emerge spontaneously in a perfect vacuum. When this happens, the three particles exist for a brief time, and then annihilate each other, leaving no trace behind. . . . The spontaneous, temporary emergence of particles from a vacuum is called a vacuum fluctuation, and is utterly commonplace in quantum field theory.[10]

If vacuum fluctuations have no cause and they are a common feature of our universe, then premise 1 is false, even in its amended version.

We should note that some physicists contend that not only can subatomic particles randomly jump into existence from a vacuum fluctuation, but so can the whole universe. They suggest that there is good evidence to support the theory that the universe is the end product of a massive vacuum fluctuation. If this is the case, the universe is uncaused, just as some subatomic parties are.

What about premise 2 ("The series of causes for anything cannot be infinite")? It too seems like common sense. Aquinas says plainly that no series of causes can be infinitely long, and some modern thinkers also reject the possibility of an infinitely long chain of actual events. The issue is important to the cosmological argument because if a chain of events can be infinitely long, there can be no first cause, and no first cause is required.

The gist of premise 2 is that an infinitely long series of past events is *logically impossible*. Something is logically impossible if it involves a logical contradiction, and something that is logically impossible cannot possibly exist. Square circles, for example, are logically impossible because they would involve a logical contradiction—a circle that is and is not a circle. Married bachelors would also involve a logical contradiction—a male human who is and is not married. Because square circles and married bachelors are logically impossible, they cannot possibly exist. In addition, it is impossible to even conceive of something that is logically impossible. We cannot conceive of square circles or married bachelors, though we have no difficulty conceiving of a golden mountain. We can, of course, be mistaken about what we can and cannot conceive. But if something seems conceivable to us, we are justified in believing it to be conceivable unless we discover good reasons to believe otherwise.

Premise 2 says an infinitely long series of past events is logically impossible and therefore inconceivable. But is this true? It seems that we can readily conceive of an infinite series of events existing into the future. Likewise it seems that most of us can readily conceive of an infinite series of events in the past. Philosopher David Hume (1711–1776) agrees. He says that whenever we imagine the occurrence of an event, we can always imagine the occurrence of an earlier event. No matter how far down the infinite chain of events we go, we can still conceive of going a little farther. If we can conceive of such an infinite series, we are justified in believing it logically possible, unless we are presented with evidence to the contrary. So we must reject premise 2. A chain of causes can be infinite, and a first cause is not necessary.

The Big Bang Argument

Did the universe have a beginning? If so, when? For centuries, these ancient questions belonged to philosophy, religion, and myth. But now they also belong to science. The prevailing theory among scientists is that the universe formed a few billion years ago when an unimaginably powerful explosion—the Big Bang—took place, belching out the matter and energy that make up the cosmos. Several lines of research and a number of novel predictions back up the Big Bang theory. It is also the starting point of a cosmological argument designed to demonstrate the existence of God.

The basic chain of reasoning goes like this: Science shows that the universe had a beginning called the Big Bang, but this beginning could not have simply happened—something had to cause it. The cause could only have been an all-powerful entity—namely, God. The premises of this argument spelled out look like this:

1. Everything that had a beginning in time has a cause.
2. The universe had a beginning in time.
3. Therefore, the universe had a cause.
4. The only thing that could have caused the universe is God.
5. Therefore, God exists.

Unlike the first-cause argument discussed earlier, this argument does not imply that God has a cause, nor does it deny the possibility of an infinite causal chain. Remember, these two elements severely undermined the first-cause argument. However, several premises of the Big Bang are just as vulnerable.

First, premise 1 is in trouble because, as we have seen, quantum mechanics says that some things that have a beginning in time do not have a cause. We have scientific data suggesting good reason to doubt premise 1.

Second, premise 2 conflicts with Albert Einstein's general theory of relativity, which says that time and the universe came into existence jointly. Time and the universe are inseparable and coterminous. You cannot have one without the other. So *there was no time* before the universe appeared. If there was no time before the existence of the universe, the universe could not have had a beginning in time. So premise 2 is false.

As we saw in our discussion of the first-cause argument, evidence suggests the universe may not have had a cause. This fact raises doubts about premise 3, but another consideration counts against premise 3. If the universe did not have a beginning in time as premise 2 suggests, it could not have been caused. According to our normal conception of causation, causes come before effects in time. But if there was no time before the universe existed (because time and the universe are coterminous), no cause could have preceded the universe. *Nothing* could have preceded the universe in time, so the universe could not have been caused by anything.

Even if the Big Bang argument were sound, it would not demonstrate that God exists. It would show only that the universe had a cause. In other words, premise 4 is untenable. As we discussed earlier, if the universe had a cause, it would not necessarily be a cause with the properties we associate with the traditional God. In addition, even if the argument is sound and God caused the universe, it would not show that God *still* exists. That is, it does not show that God is the *sustaining* cause of the universe—the one who ensures that the universe continues to exist.

The Argument from Religious Experience

Some people contend that religious experience—whether mystical, transcendent, or otherwise extraordinary—constitutes evidence for the existence of God. The basic argument goes like this: (1) Religious experiences occur, (2) religious experiences constitute evidence for the reality or existence of God, (3) therefore, there is evidence that God exists. Often what's behind premise 2 is the idea that religious experiences must constitute evidence for God's existence because such religious experiences are analogous to our ordinary sense experiences. This argument from analogy is the backbone of most (or all) religious-experience arguments. The strength of the argument depends on how similar the two kinds of experiences are.

Proponents of the argument from religious experience note several relevant similarities. Some say, for example, that just as we have tests to show that our sense experience is reliable (such as consistency among the five senses and agreement with established empirical facts), there are tests to show that religious experience is reliable (such as whether religious experiences are similar among several "experiencers"). Others dispute the validity of such tests, arguing that with ordinary perception, we know what constitutes normal conditions in which proper sensory tests can be conducted—but we can never specify proper conditions for religious experiences.

Some have insisted that just as we can make accurate predictions about events based on our normal sense experiences, we can accurately predict that people who have religious experiences will be better people because of them. Critics can reply, though, that moral consequences from an alleged religious experience are dramatically unpredictable.

This is a small sample of the arguments for and against the idea that religious experience can provide good evidence for God's existence. In any case, the burden of proof is on those who wish to show that religious experience is somehow evidential. It's fair to say that thus far they have failed to do this.

Swinburne's Cosmological Argument

Not all cosmological arguments begin with premises about first causes or cosmic beginnings. Some make very *explicit* use of inference to the best explanation (hypothetical induction), which is the underlying form of all cosmological arguments. Without appealing to anything except the existence of the universe, these arguments try to show that the best explanation of the world's existence is that there is a God.

The most sophisticated version of such an argument comes from Richard Swinburne.[11] His argument says:

1. The universe exists.
2. The best explanation of the existence of the universe is that God exists.
3. Therefore, it is highly probable that God exists.

What makes Swinburne's argument special is that he deliberately uses hypothetical induction in the same way science does. (As we have seen, philosophy also makes extensive use of hypothetical induction.) This style of reasoning involves proposing possible hypotheses, or theories, to explain a phenomenon and using specific criteria (called "criteria of adequacy") to judge which hypothesis is best. The best hypothesis is the one most likely to be true. If the God hypothesis does well when tested against these criteria, its credibility will be difficult to dismiss. As Swinburne says, "The very criteria which scientists use to reach their own theories lead us to move beyond those theories to a creator God who sustains everything in existence."[12]

A plausible list of the criteria of adequacy includes: (1) *testability* (whether a hypothesis can be tested), (2) *fruitfulness* (whether a hypothesis yields novel predictions), (3) *scope* (how much a hypothesis explains or predicts), (4) *simplicity* (how many assumptions the hypothesis makes), and (5) *conservatism* (how well a hypothesis fits with existing knowledge). These standards provide a means for making objective judgments about the validity of theories, even though there is no quantifiable way to apply them. Let's take a moment to examine these criteria more closely.

Testability. Most of the theories we encounter every day and all the theories that scientists take seriously are *testable—there is some way to determine whether the theories are true or false*. If a theory is untestable—if there is no possible procedure for checking its truth—then it is worthless as a theory. A theory is testable *if it predicts something other than what it was introduced to explain*. Suppose your electric clock stops each time you touch it. One theory to explain this event is that there is an electrical short in the clock's wiring. Another theory is that an invisible, undetectable demon causes the clock to stop. The wiring theory predicts that if the wiring is repaired, the clock will no longer shut off when touched. So it is testable— the theory predicts something other than the obvious: the fact that the clock will stop when you touch it. The demon theory, however, makes no predictions about anything *except* the obvious, the very fact that the theory was introduced to explain. It predicts that the clock will stop if you touch it, but we already knew this. So our understanding is not increased, and the demon theory is untestable.

Fruitfulness. Imagine that we have two testable theories, T_1 and T_2, that attempt to explain the same phenomenon. T_1 and T_2 seem comparable in most respects when measured against the criteria of adequacy. Theory T_1, however, successfully predicts the existence of a previously unknown entity, say, a star in an uncharted part of the sky. What would you conclude about the relative worth of these two theories?

If you thought carefully about the issue, you would probably conclude that T_1 is the better theory—and you would be right. Other things being equal, theories that perform this way—that successfully predict previously unknown phenomena—are more credible than those that do not. The new insight yielded by such theories can open up whole new areas of research and discovery. All things being equal, a fruitful theory is more likely to be true than one that is not fruitful.

Scope. Suppose T_1 and T_2 are two equally plausible theories to explain phenomenon X. T_1 can explain X well, and so can T_2. But T_1 can explain or predict only X whereas T_2 can explain or predict X—as well as phenomena Y and Z. Which is the better theory?

We must conclude that T_2 is better because it explains more. That is, it has more scope than the other theory. The more a theory explains or predicts, the more it extends our understanding. In addition, the more a theory explains or predicts, the less likely it is to be false because it has more evidence in its favor.

A major strength of Sir Isaac Newton's theory of gravity and motion, for example, was that it explained more than any previous theory. Then came Einstein's theory of relativity. It could explain everything that Newton's theory could explain plus many phenomena Newton's theory could not explain. This increased scope of Einstein's theory helped convince scientists that it was a better theory.

Simplicity. Other things being equal, *the best theory is the one that is the simplest—that is, the one that makes the fewest assumptions.*[13] The theory that makes the fewest assumptions is least likely to be false because there are fewer ways for it to go wrong. Another way to look at it is that because a simpler theory is based on fewer assumptions, it requires less evidence to support it.

Conservatism. We are naturally reluctant to accept explanations that conflict with what we already know, and we should be. Accepting beliefs that fly in the face of our knowledge has several risks. First, the chances of the new belief being true are not good (because it has no evidence in its favor, while our well-established beliefs have plenty of evidence on their side). Second, the conflict of beliefs undermines our knowledge (because we cannot know something that is in doubt, and the conflict would be cause for doubt). Third, the conflict of beliefs lessens our understanding (because the new beliefs cannot be plausibly integrated into our other beliefs).

In everyday life we often use inference to the best explanation and the criteria of adequacy to solve problems or get to the bottom of mysteries. Often, when we try to understand something in the world, we construct explanations of *why* this something came to be the way it is. Devising explanations helps increase our understanding by fitting our experiences and background knowledge into a coherent pattern.

For example, say that you discover that your car won't start in the morning (this is the phenomenon to be explained). You would like to know why it won't start (the explanation for the failure) because you can't repair it unless you know what the problem is. You know there are several possible explanations, or hypotheses: (1) the battery is dead, (2) the fuel tank is empty, (3) the starter has malfunctioned, and (4) a vandal has sabotaged the car. As you try to determine which hypothesis is most plausible, you appeal to the criteria of adequacy. By applying the criterion of conservatism, you see that some of the hypotheses do not fit with the available evidence (such as indications of a full tank of gas and a full charge on the battery). You may also see that one of the hypotheses seems to explain more than the others (has more scope) or that it makes unfounded assumptions (is less simple).

Inference to the best explanation has a simple pattern and it works fine for simple states of affairs. But it is frequently—and successfully—brought to bear on situations with far more complexity. Physicians use it to pinpoint the cause of multiple symptoms in patients. Scientists use it to discover planets, viruses, and subatomic particles (that they can't even see). Police detectives use it to track down lawbreakers. Judges and juries use it to determine the guilt or innocence of accused persons. And philosophers use it to assess the worth of conceptual theories. In all of these situations, the criteria of adequacy are brought to bear.

On these criteria (or variations of them) Swinburne rests the whole weight of his case for the God hypothesis. He wants to show that this hypothesis is superior to all of the main competing hypotheses—that is, naturalistic hypotheses that try to explain the universe without reference to any supernatural entities. If he succeeds, he will have shown that premise 2 is highly plausible and that the conclusion (premise 3) is well supported.

Overall, Swinburne's method is impeccable. His formulations of the criteria of adequacy, however, are problematic. First, his formulation of the criterion of conservatism is almost identical to the formulation given above. But he insists that the criterion does not apply when a hypothesis is trying to explain everything, as the God hypothesis does. The reason, he says, is that when a hypothesis is trying to explain everything, there is nothing left for the hypothesis to fit with or not to fit with. There remains no background knowledge for comparison.

But this is implausible. Even theories that purport to explain everything must be judged against our most reliable background theories—that is, with what we already know about the world. Scientists who put forth theories to explain the properties of the whole universe, for example, must ensure that their theories fit with existing data and well-established scientific theories. When the God hypothesis is evaluated with a more plausible conception of conservatism, it seems to conflict with, among other things, scientific data suggesting that the universe is uncaused.

Swinburne's notion of the criterion of scope is also similar to the one stated above. He maintains that the God hypothesis has more scope (explains more) than any naturalistic total theory. He argues that naturalistic theories can only go so far. They can explain only so much, then they must stop with a vast array of "brute facts"—the basic properties, potentialities, and forces of the universe. Naturalistic theories do not explain why the universe consists of the brute facts that it does. To explain these additional data, we need the God hypothesis.

Many philosophers would disagree with this assessment. They would point out that Swinburne and other theists regard God's agency itself as a brute fact, the ultimate stopping point in a long line of naturalistic explanations. But then the question arises: What is the explanation of *this* brute fact? Why did God create the universe that he did? Why does God have the powers, intentions, and properties that he does? Because such questions go unanswered, it seems that the God hypothesis does not explain as much as Swinburne thinks it does. This point undermines any claim of superior scope for the God hypothesis.

Swinburne claims that the criterion of fruitfulness is a measure of whether a theory leads us to expect many observations, either observations already known or those that the theory predicts. He says that it does not matter whether "100 observations are made first and the theory then constructed to explain them, or whether the theory is constructed on the basis of fifty observations and it successfully predicts another fifty."[14] If this is a correct formulation of fruitfulness, theological theories do not have to make novel or testable predictions as scientific theories do. The God hypothesis then does not have to lead to new observations (predictions) to establish itself; old ones will serve the purpose.

But whether a theory predicts previously unknown phenomena surely does matter. The history of science illustrates that a theory's successful prediction of something new and unexpected often lends credibility to the theory.

Swinburne puts more weight on the criterion of simplicity than any other. He believes that simplicity is a matter of the number of components something has. The fewer the parts, the simpler it is. He says, "The 'simplicity' of a scientific theory is a matter of it having few component laws, each of which relates few variables by mathematically simple formulae (whose consequences for observation are derivable by mathematically simple steps.)"[15]

For Swinburne, naturalistic explanations are not simple because they consist of innumerable brute facts. Theistic explanations, though, are simple because they posit just one thing—namely, God.

Is this notion of simplicity plausible? Should we always prefer the theory that involves the fewest components, all things being equal? Probably very few philosophers of science would accept this formulation. In science, there are simply too many cases in which the correct theory turns out to be the most complex one, even by Swinburne's criterion. There was a time, for example, when scientists thought that the realm of quantum mechanics was fairly simple, inhabited by one or two kinds of particles. As we now know, the truth is far more complicated.

Granted, the criterion of simplicity has been difficult to define satisfactorily.[16] As noted above, though, a plausible formulation does exist: The simplest hypothesis is the one that makes the fewest assumptions. The theory making the fewest assumptions should be preferred (all things being equal) because it is less likely to be false. It is less likely to be false because there are fewer ways for it to go wrong. There is, of course, the difficulty of counting assumptions. But it is often possible to make broad distinctions, such as the difference between a theory based on many assumptions and a theory based on few,[17] or the difference between a theory postulating an unknown, disembodied entity or mysterious force and a theory that assumes no unknown entity or force.

When a more credible concept of simplicity is used, the God hypothesis seems not nearly as simple as naturalistic theories. The reason is that the God hypothesis assumes unknown entities and forces, and naturalistic theories do not.

Any theory—naturalistic or not—can be an inferior theory, but if it is judged inferior, it is because it does not fare as well as competing theories when measured against the criteria of adequacy. The God hypothesis seems inferior to naturalistic theories on several counts: It is not testable; it is doubtful that it explains more than naturalistic theories; it makes no testable predictions; it is not as simple as naturalistic theories; and it does not fit well with existing knowledge.

In light of all of this, we must conclude that Swinburne's argument fails because premise 2 is false.

TELEOLOGICAL ARGUMENTS

Some people find it difficult to believe that the world could exhibit such order and complexity without a supreme being as its creator. In many ways the world resembles an artifact—something made by a person. So, some would say, isn't it reasonable to conclude that it *was* made by a person, an omnipotent person known as God? The world looks *designed according to some purpose*, so doesn't this fact suggest that it must have a designer with a purpose?

Such appeals are known as **teleological arguments** (from the Greek word *telos*, meaning "end" or "goal"), or **arguments from design**. Cosmological arguments appeal to the universe's existence. Teleological arguments appeal to the universe's characteristics (its beauty, its precision, its intricacy, and so on), which are supposed to suggest the working out of some purpose or goal, which in turn is evidence for a supreme intelligence or mind.

Teleological arguments have a long history. Aquinas, for example, offered this one:

> The fifth way is taken from the governance of the world. We see that things which lack intelligence, such as natural bodies, act for an end, and this is evident from their acting always, or

> nearly always, in the same way, so as to obtain the best result. Hence it is plain that not fortuitously, but designedly, do they achieve their end. Now whatever lacks intelligence cannot move toward an end, unless it be directed by some being endowed with knowledge and intelligence; as the arrow is shot to its mark by the archer. Therefore some intelligent being exists by whom all natural things are directed to their end; and this being we call God.[18]

There are two main types of teleological arguments—those that try to make their case through analogy and those that use inference to the best explanation.

Analogical Version

Analogical arguments have this pattern:

1. Thing A has properties P_1, P_2, P_3 plus the property P_4.
2. Thing B has properties P_1, P_2, and P_3.
3. Therefore, thing B probably has property P_4.

The basic logic here is that because two things are similar in some ways, they must be similar in still other ways. For example,

1. People have memories, exhibit goal-directed behavior, have the ability to solve problems, and are self-aware.
2. Computers have memories, exhibit goal-directed behavior, and have the ability to solve problems.
3. Therefore, computers are probably self-aware.

The strength of an analogical argument depends on the extent of the similarities between the two things compared. The more similarities, the stronger the argument. The more dissimilarities, the weaker the argument. In the analogical argument above, the similarities between people and computers are clear, and these give us reason to think that there may be further likenesses. But there are also significant dissimilarities. People are extremely complex systems made of flesh and bone, able to carry out many cognitive and perceptual processes with countless neural pathways and highly developed brains that are the product of millions of years of evolution. A computer is none of these things. In this case there seem to be as many similarities as dissimilarities, so the argument is weak.

Here is an analogical design argument devised over two hundred years ago by the English theologian and philosopher William Paley (1743–1805):

> In crossing a heath, suppose I pitched my foot against a *stone*, and were asked how the stone came to be there, I might possibly answer that, for anything I knew to the contrary, it had lain there for ever; nor would it, perhaps, be very easy to show the absurdity of this answer. But suppose I found a *watch* upon the ground, and it should be inquired how the watch happened to be in that place, I should hardly think of the answer which I had given—that, for anything I knew, the watch might have always been there. Yet why should not this answer serve for the watch as well as for the stone? Why is it not as admissible in the second case as in the first? For this reason, and for no other; viz., that, when we come to inspect the watch, we perceive

> (what we could not discover in the stone) that its several parts are framed and put together for a purpose. . . .
>
> This mechanism being observed . . . the inference, we think, is inevitable, that the watch must have had a maker. . . . Every indication of contrivance, every manifestation of design, which existed in the watch exists in the works of nature; with the difference, on the side of nature, of being greater and more, and that in a degree which exceeds all computation.[19]

Paley argues that if we found a watch and saw how all of its parts fit together precisely to serve some purpose, we would have to conclude that the watch had a maker, someone who had crafted it. Likewise, Paley says, the whole universe seems to have the same kind of conjoining of parts for some purpose. Therefore, someone must have crafted the universe, and that someone must be God.

The key question here is: How good is the analogy in Paley's argument? That is, how closely does the universe resemble a watch (i.e., a machine)? If the analogy is strong, we have reason to believe that the universe has a designer. If it is weak, then it provides no reason to believe that the universe has a designer.

In some ways, the universe does resemble a machine, with countless events occurring in an orderly fashion, in accordance with known laws, with impressive regularity and precision. But, as David Hume pointed out, the universe also resembles a living organism—"an animal or organized body." Living organisms appear, evolve, reproduce, and change

The Argument from Miracles

Some people put great stock in this argument: (1) Miracles have occurred; (2) miracles require a miracle worker; (3) therefore, a miracle worker must exist, namely, God. In other words, the occurrence of miracles proves the existence of God.

Both premises 1 and 2 have been challenged. A miracle is more than something surprising or out of the ordinary. A miracle is a violation of the laws of nature by a supernatural being. Premise 1 is dubious because we can never be sure that a miracle is the best explanation for the occurrence of any event. If a miracle were the best explanation for a seemingly impossible event, we would have to accept that a miracle had indeed occurred. But a miracle can never be the best explanation for an event because it is always possible that the seeming impossibility of the event is due to our ignorance of the relevant laws of nature. Historically, countless events once thought to be miracles turned out to be explicable in terms of natural laws. Meteorites were once thought to be impossible because people were ignorant of the natural laws governing objects in space. We now understand the relevant laws, so meteorites no longer seem impossible. We can never exclude the possibility that a natural explanation will be uncovered for an event.

Premise 2 is problematic because it says only that miracles require a miracle worker. But a miracle worker need not be God—that is, an all-powerful, all-knowing, all-good being. The miracle worker could be Satan, an advanced alien civilization, or some other powerful entity.

through natural processes requiring no conscious design. Much the same can be said about the universe. The Big Bang gives birth to the universe, the universe grows and expands, stars and galaxies are born and evolve, aging stars contract into black holes, and—as some scientists say—the black holes engender new worlds.

The analogy between the universe and living things seems at least as good as the analogy between the universe and machines (or any other artifacts). If this is the case, Paley's argument does not go through. It does not show that the universe must have a designer.

What if the argument were successful in demonstrating that the universe has a designer—would this show that God exists? Not at all. The argument cannot establish that the designer is indeed the God of traditional theism. The analogical design argument gives us no reason to think that the designer is all-powerful and all-knowing. A truly all-powerful being would be powerful enough to create not only our universe, but also every possible universe. But our universe may be the only one that the designer could make. A truly all-knowing being would know everything there is to know about our universe and every possible universe, but the designer may know only about our universe

Even if the analogical design argument could show that the universe was designed, it leaves open the possibility that the designer was not one person but *several*. Reasoning by analogy, we could plausibly think that because big construction projects require several workers, the universe—the biggest of big construction projects—also requires several creators. As Hume says, "A great number of men join together in building a house or ship, in rearing a city, in framing a commonwealth: Why may not several Deities combine in contriving and framing the world?"[20]

Does God Need the Universe?

The philosopher John Stuart Mill (1806–1873) offers an interesting argument against the idea that God designed the universe for a purpose. He points out that if the universe were designed for a purpose, the designer must have been trying to achieve some end result. But an all-powerful being would not need the universe to achieve some purpose. If God had to rely on some means to achieve his end, he must not be all-powerful. In other words, any evidence of design-for-a-purpose in the universe is evidence against the existence of the notion of an all-powerful being. Mill makes the point like this:

> It is not much to say that every indication of design in the Kosmos is so much evidence against the omnipotence of the designer. For what is meant by Design? Contrivance: the adaptation of means to end. But the necessity for contrivance—the need of employing means—is a consequence of the limitations of power. Who would have recourse to means if to attain his end his mere word was sufficient?*

* John Stuart Mill, "Three Essays on Religion," *Essays on Ethics, Religion, and Society*, ed. J. M. Robson (Toronto: University of Toronto Press, 1969), 451.

Hypothetical Inductive Version

The design argument can take the form of an inference to the best explanation. Recall that this is the same style of reasoning used in Richard Swinburne's cosmological argument discussed earlier. In this case the meat of the argument is that the existence of God is the best explanation for the apparent design or purposeful structure of the universe.

Inference to the best explanation arguments have this pattern:

1. Phenomenon Q.
2. E provides the best explanation for Q.
3. Therefore, it is probable that E is true.

In the design argument, the phenomenon to be explained (premise 1) is the design of the universe, and the best explanation for this phenomenon is that it was designed by God (premise 2). The conclusion, then, is that the universe probably was designed by God (so God probably exists).

Recall that the success of such an argument depends on the quality of the explanation (compared to competing explanations) as judged by the criteria of adequacy. If the God hypothesis is indeed the best explanation for the design of the universe, then the argument succeeds, and the conclusion follows: God probably exists. But if alternative hypotheses can explain the design of the universe at least as well as the God hypothesis does, the design argument fails.

The leading alternative explanation for the design of the world—especially of living creatures—is evolution. After Charles Darwin (1809–1882) articulated a version of the theory of evolution, doubts about the design argument became much more common. For the first time, evolution seemed to provide a plausible and detailed answer to the question: How can the world look designed without having been designed?

Since Darwin, scientists have fine-tuned the theory in light of new evidence and various advances in related fields, such as genetics. But the central idea remains unchanged: Living organisms adapt to their environments through a process called "natural selection," which results in changes in the creatures over time. More precisely, individuals of a species inherit certain physical traits from their parents, and these traits often vary from individual to individual. Any inherited trait that increases an individual's chances of surviving long enough to reproduce is more likely to be passed onto the next generation. After several generations, this useful trait, or adaptation, becomes widespread among individuals. The result is genetic changes—evolution—in whole populations through successive generations.

Those who defend a hypothetical inductive argument for a designer need not and often do not reject evolution as an explanation for biological processes. They may simply insist that there are certain facts about the world that cannot be entirely accounted for by evolutionary principles.

So the crucial question is this: Which explanation of apparent design is best—the God hypothesis or the theory of evolution? To answer this, we need to see how each hypothesis fares when we measure them against the criteria of adequacy.

First, we can see that evolution is a *simpler* hypothesis than design by a deity because it can explain the apparent design of organisms without assuming the existence of a supernatural entity with supernatural powers, as the God hypothesis does. Second, evolution is a more *conservative* theory because it fits better with existing knowledge—that is, with well-established facts in biology, biochemistry, geology, genetics, and several other fields. Third, evolution is a more *fruitful* theory because it has successfully made several novel predictions (such as that living things should adapt to changes in environments and that chromosomes of related species should resemble each other). But the God hypothesis has yielded no novel predictions that can be backed by evidence. Fourth, evolution has far more *scope* than the God hypothesis. Evolution can explain the findings from several different branches of science. The God hypothesis, though, cannot explain any of these data. Evolution can explain how different species arose, for example, but the God hypothesis tells us nothing about the process of divine design or creation. In fact, it seems that any hypothesis that tries to explain a phenomenon by reference to unknown entities using unknown forces in unknown ways cannot be an adequate explanation.

Some people, however, would disagree with this analysis. On various grounds they would insist that the God hypothesis really is a better explanation than evolution. In effect, these detractors appeal to the criterion of conservatism, arguing that the God hypothesis fits better with certain important facts about the world than does evolution.

One such fact is that organisms seem to be "irreducibly complex." The argument here is that many biological systems are so complex that they could not have arisen piecemeal through natural selection. A complex system such as blood clotting can improve a creature's chances of survival—but only if the system works. But a blood clotting system cannot work if any of its parts are missing. So a blood clotting system could not have arisen by gradual incremental changes of a partial system, as natural selection would have it. Partial systems and partial organs have no survival value. The divine creation of biological systems in one stroke makes more sense. It fits better with what we know about the workings of biological systems.

Does it? Most biologists contend that partial systems and partial organs do have survival value and that the parts of a complex system can develop independently of the system. Here's how some scientists express these points:

> An irreducibly complex system can be built gradually by adding parts that, while initially just advantageous, become—because of later changes—essential. The logic is very simple. Some part (A) initially does some job (and not very well, perhaps). Another part (B) later gets added because it helps A. This new part isn't essential, it merely improves things. But later on, A (or something else) may change in such a way that B now becomes indispensable. This process continues as further parts get folded into the system. And at the end of the day, many parts may all be required.[21]

> The multiple parts of complex, interlocking biological systems do not evolve as individual parts. . . . They evolve together, as systems that are gradually expanded, enlarged, and adapted to new purposes.[22]

Biologist Richard Dawkins points out that partial biological systems are not just theoretical entities—we can actually see them in creatures today. For example, he says, "not only are animals with 'half a wing' common, so are animals with a quarter of a wing, three quarters of a wing, and so on."[23]

The upshot of this is that it is indeed possible for an irreducibly complex system to arise through natural selection. If this phenomenon is possible, then the argument from irreducibly complex systems does not work, and it gives us no reason to posit intelligent design as an explanation for the structure of existing organisms.

Another fact often used to show that the world must have a designer is the "fine-tuning" of the universe. The universe is the way it is because the laws and constants of physics are fine-tuned just right. If these factors had been different, the universe would not exist and we would not be around to think about whether it has a divine designer. As one physicist says,

> If the universe had appeared with slight variations in the strengths of the fundamental forces or the masses of elementary particles, that universe would be pure hydrogen at one extreme, or pure helium at the other. Neither would have allowed for the eventual production of heavy elements, such as carbon, necessary for life.
>
> Similarly, if gravity had not been many orders of magnitude weaker than electromagnetism, stars would not have lived long enough to produce the elements of life.[24]

These factors that seem poised just right are called "anthropic coincidences" because, as some would say, they appear to be arranged for the existence of humankind.

Some people take such fine-tuning as evidence that the universe was indeed designed. They say that the occurrence of this rare and exquisite balance of forces and constants—which just happens to make life (especially human life) possible—cannot be a mere coincidence. The best explanation for this improbable phenomenon is that it was the handiwork of an intelligent designer.

Notice that if someone wants to undermine this line of reasoning, all she would need to do is show one alternative explanation for fine-tuning that is at least as good as the anthropic explanation. One plausible candidate for an alternative hypothesis is this: Universes like ours are not so improbable after all. The anthropic argument depends heavily on the assumption that the probability of a universe like ours coming into existence is incredibly small because the number of possible combinations of forces and constants is incredibly large. But how many of these possible universes formed with different parameters could still give rise to living things? Physicist Victor Stenger investigated this question and came up with some surprising results:

> I have made some estimates of the probability that a chance distribution of physical constants can produce a universe with properties sufficient that some form of life would have likely had sufficient time to evolve. In this study, I randomly varied the constants of physics (I assume the same laws of physics as exist in our universe, since I know no other) over a range of ten orders of magnitude around their existing values. For each resulting "toy" universe, I computed various quantities such as the size of atoms and the lifetimes of stars. I found that almost all combinations of physical constants led to universes, albeit strange ones, that would live long enough for some type of complexity to form.[25]

If Stenger's results are accurate, the probability of a life-supporting universe occurring is not so low after all. This means that a universe like ours may not be so rare that we need to posit a designer. Our universe could have been a random occurrence—but not necessarily a rare occurrence.

Let's push this point a little further. What if the existence of our universe were not only not rare, but also virtually guaranteed? Some physicists think that the physical parameters of the universe could only have turned out one way: the way they are right now. If this is true, we have another explanation for the universe's fine-tuning that seems at least as good as the anthropic hypothesis.

Even if all of the above is true, some people may still insist that something is left unexplained: Where did the laws of physics come from in the first place? Can't we simplify everything by saying that the laws came from God and that the universe happened as it did because of the laws? We could say this, but then our assertion would have the same problem as Swinburne's cosmological argument. It assumes a supernatural being and thereby undermines itself because of its lack of simplicity. On these grounds alone, both of the nonsupernatural hypotheses discussed above are superior to the designer hypothesis.

CONCLUSION

We have examined some important examples of the major types of arguments for the existence of God. What can we conclude from our assessment? If we are right about the plausibility of these arguments, we can conclude at least this: The theistic arguments we have assessed are faulty; they do not give us good reason to believe that the God of traditional theism exists. But from the fact that these arguments have failed we cannot conclude that *all* arguments for God's existence are failures. Maybe the formulation of good theistic arguments is still to come.

Most professional philosophers reject the arguments for the existence of God. Perhaps the only thing we can infer from this is that demonstrating the existence of God is no easy trick. Even the famous, influential arguments can go awry. Even premises that at first glance may seem like common sense (such as those in the design argument) can prove to be unsound.

Demonstrating that God does not exist requires an argument that gives us good reason to believe that this is the case. In the next section we evaluate such an argument.

SECTION 7.2

The Case against God: Coming to Terms with the Problem of Evil

When philosophers talk about evil, they usually are not referring to evil in the theological sense—that is, as sins or transgressions against God's law. They most often use the term "evil" to mean bad things generally such as disease, suffering, pain, death, crime, injustice, natural disasters, and war. For everyone, evil is a fact of life, but for many theists, the existence of evil is more than that—it is a serious challenge to their belief in God's existence.

For centuries philosophers, theologians, and others have wondered: If there is a God in the traditional sense, why is there evil in the world? The question becomes even more pointed when it is fleshed out. Such a God would be all-powerful, so he could prevent evil. He would be all-knowing, so he would know about evil. He would be all-good, so he would want to prevent evil. If he is all of these things, how can he permit evil? Given God's attributes, there seems to be no good excuse available to him for the existence of evil. Even worse, this conflict between the traditional concept of God and the fact of evil seems to lead directly to the conclusion that there is no God of this description. This conflict is known as the traditional "problem of evil."

The problem of evil arises for many people when they are confronted with inexplicable and horrific examples of evil: unimaginable human suffering (e.g., the agony of people with incurable cancer or massive burns), horrendous loss of life (e.g., the deaths of twenty million people worldwide from Spanish influenza in 1919), and catastrophic natural disasters (e.g., the three million people killed by earthquakes in the twentieth century). Some people take such examples as clear evidence that God does not exist or exists as a deity with regrettable limitations.

Many nontheists have regarded the problem of evil as their strongest argument against theism. If nontheists manage to undermine arguments *for* the existence of God, what have they shown? As we saw in the previous section, such a move demonstrates only that those arguments provide no justification for traditional theism, but arguments from the existence of evil purport to do more—to show that there is good reason to *deny* the existence of God.

In standard usage, those who deny the existence of God are known as **atheists**. (Some people, though, prefer to define "atheist" as someone who simply has no belief in God.) Those who think that there is insufficient evidence to justify belief in God are known as **agnostics**. So the failure of the arguments for God can justify agnosticism. The success of the argument from evil can justify atheism in the strongest sense.

Another distinction that we should draw is the difference between two kinds of evil: *moral evil* and *natural evil*. Moral evil is the evil that humans inflict on other humans. Murder, slavery, and injustice are moral evils. Natural evil is evil that nature visits upon humans. Floods, earthquakes, and hurricanes are natural evils. There seems to be a significant amount of moral evil in the world, but there appears to be far more natural evil.

We also need to distinguish between *necessary evil* and *unnecessary evil*. A necessary evil is one that is needed to prevent a greater evil or to achieve a greater good. The amputation of a gangrenous leg, for instance, may be a necessary evil. It's evil because it causes great pain, but it's necessary because it will save the patient's life. The senseless torture of innocent children is both evil and unnecessary. The perpetrating of necessary evil can be morally justified; it can be excused. But the causing of an unnecessary evil cannot be justified; it can never be excused. This distinction is important in discussions of the problem of evil because the sticking point is usually not whether God allows evil, but whether God allows unnecessary evil.

Throughout history, humanists have held a wide range of beliefs regarding the existence of God. As we have seen, many early humanists were theists or deists, though there was also a fair share of atheists and agnostics. Most modern humanists, though, are skeptical of all supernatural claims, adopting either atheistic or agnostic views. A large portion of these humanists, then, would agree with this proposition:

14. There is good reason to deny the existence of God, as traditionally conceived.

In the following section we discuss the reasons for accepting or rejecting this view.

THE ARGUMENT FROM EVIL

Let's state the argument from evil more precisely:

1. If there is an all-powerful, all-knowing, and all-good God, there would be no unnecessary evil in the world.
2. But there is unnecessary evil in the world.
3. Therefore, an all-powerful, all-knowing, and all-good God does not exist.

This argument is valid (its conclusion follows from the premises). So if it is to be defeated, either premise 1 or premise 2 must be shown to be false. Both theists and nontheists, however, readily accept premise 1. They both believe that preventing unnecessary evil is a good thing and that God would always ensure that such good things become actual.

Premise 2 is the disputed premise. Theists believe that it is false, and nontheists believe that it is true. If it is false or dubious, the argument from evil fails. All of the most important efforts to defend theism against the argument from evil focus on premise 2.

Before discussing these attempts, though, we should mention that there are several tactics that theists could use to easily defeat the argument from evil—if they are willing to give up certain ideas about the nature of God or evil. For example, premise 1 refers to the traditional God as omnipotent, omniscience, and omnibenevolent, but if any of these attributes were downsized to a finite property (less than all-powerful, all-knowing, or all-good), the argument would be no threat to this reduced God. The reason is that such a lesser God would then have an excuse for permitting unnecessary evil. If God is really not all-powerful, all-knowing, or all-good, unnecessary evil could occur because God would not have the power, knowledge, or goodness to prevent it.

Some theologians take this finite God approach, denying that God is omnipotent and omniscient. Others have adopted **pantheism**, the notion that God is everything or that God and the universe are the same thing. In any case, the problem of evil is avoided, but only by giving up the traditional concept of God.

Also, a few theists take the drastic step of asserting that evil is somehow unreal. Augustine (354–430), for example, argues that evil does not exist on the grounds that there is only good, and what looks like evil is actually the absence of good. If evil is unreal, premise 2 loses its bite. But this claim conflicts with our moral experience. We have ample justification for believing that evil is a very real fact of life quite apart from good. Unless we have good reason to accept such an implausible view, we are justified in rejecting it. Besides, even if evil were an illusion that afflicts humans, the illusion itself would be an evil. In any case, most theists are unlikely to dismiss the reality of evil because evil is an essential doctrine of the three major religions.

Premise 2 can also be weakened by another radical approach: showing that humans have neither the knowledge nor the moral perspective that God has to judge whether an evil is really unnecessary or acceptable. God is omniscient and therefore has full understanding of any state of affairs, but humans possess only limited knowledge. So from God's superior point of view, apparent unnecessary evils may not be unnecessary evils at all. In the same vein, some people argue that God's moral standards are perfect and thus far superior to human moral standards. So God's appraisal of unnecessary evils may be completely different from human appraisals—and God's view would be correct. If true, these claims would make premise 2 an empty assertion.

The Greater-Good Defense

Some have argued that evil is necessary for spiritual growth—that is, for the improvement of individual human beings. The idea is that suffering can build character by helping us acquire important virtues such as courage and sympathy. Philosopher of religion John Hick (1922–) takes this view. As he puts it, "this world, with all its 'heartaches and the thousand shocks that flesh is heir to,' an environment so manifestly not designed for the maximization of human pleasure and the minimization of human pain, may be rather well adapted to the quite different purpose of 'soul-making.'"*

People, however, are not always ennobled by suffering. Sometimes they are crushed by it or made resentful, cruel, and bitter. In addition, Hick's explanation for evil is based on an assumption that is rejected by many religious people and that conflicts with basic ethical principles. The assumption is that it is morally permissible to treat people as a means and not an end—that is, to make people do things against their will for their own good. In many ethical theories (religious and nonreligious), this assumption is rejected.

Hick's view also implies that humans should never try to eliminate evil. If evil is necessary to build character, getting rid of evil must be morally wrong. We should not try to help others overcome evil because doing so may interfere with soul-making. Better to let them suffer. But this implication is implausible. It is in direct conflict with our experience of the moral life.

* John Hick, *Philosophy of Religion*, 3rd ed. (Englewood Cliffs, N.J.: Prentice-Hall, 1963), 40–46.

The theist, however, would pay a high price for undermining premise 2 in this fashion. Both claims above imply that humans can not trust any moral judgment they make because their knowledge and moral standards are seriously flawed and very different from God's. God's goodness is not our goodness.

Taking this view seriously would lead to some hideous judgments. For example, a million innocent people burned alive in a firestorm may seem awful to us, but according to the God-knows-best theory, such a loss of life is actually a good thing and part of the divine plan. If only God sees the "big picture," humans must be in the dark all the time. But the moral experience of humans conflicts with this view. We do seem, at least sometimes, to be able to make trustworthy, accurate assessments of the good and evil of states of affairs. We do think that we have justification for saying that the deaths of a million innocent people was a great evil and should not have happened.

Arguments such as these based on human ignorance are sometimes called "epistemic gap" arguments, referring to the alleged gap between what humans know and what God knows. Alvin Plantinga puts forth such an argument, and philosopher Richard Gale is quick to point out the core difficulty in the "epistemic gap" approach:

> Epistemic gap theology, if consistently applied, also has the consequence that we cannot ascertain what God's purposes are and thus cannot determine how we should conduct our religious life. The proper answer to Plantinga's rhetorical question, "Given that God does have a reason for permitting these evils, why think we would be the first to know?" is that we should

be the first to know, at least for those evils that directly affect us. For in a communal love relationship, each party should give the other some reason why she allows evils to befall the other.[26]

THE FREE-WILL DEFENSE

Probably the most important response to premise 2 is the **free-will defense**. It maintains that there is no unnecessary evil in the world; the evil that does exist is necessary for the existence of free will. Behind this defense is the assumption that free will is important to persons because it helps make morality possible. Without free will, people could not be held responsible for their actions because they could not do otherwise. Moral principles and judgments could not apply to people who had no control over what they did. Having free will gives people the ability (and the right) to choose freely—to choose both good and evil. So if God grants people free will (and the theistic assumption is that he does just that), then there must be moral evil in the world. In other words, it is impossible for God to create a world of free persons without there being moral evil in it.

The free-will defense tries to explain why premise 2 must be false: there is evil, but it is *necessary* evil—evil that even God cannot prevent. It is necessary because persons cannot have free will without moral evil.

Critics have responded to the free-will defense by trying to show that the evil that exists really is unnecessary. It is unnecessary, they say, because it is possible to have free will and always, or usually, choose good over evil. If God is all-powerful, all-knowing, and all-good, he could create creatures who can act freely and still choose the good.

But are free persons who always (or mostly) choose the good possible? Something is logically impossible if it involves a contradiction, such as square circles. People who freely choose the good, though, do not seem to involve a contradiction in terms. After all, angels are supposed to have free will but always do good. In heaven or in a future kingdom of God on Earth, people are supposed to have free will yet be without evil. God himself is supposed to have free will and yet always opt for good over evil. This is how philosopher J. L. Mackie states the point: "[I]f God has made men such that in their free choices they sometimes prefer what is good and sometimes what is evil, why could he not have made men such that they always freely choose the good? If there is no logical impossibility in a man's freely choosing the good on one, or several occasions, there cannot be a logical impossibility in his freely choosing the good on every occasion."[27]

Nevertheless, some people think the idea that God could have made people free but always good is incoherent. Mackie thinks this charge of incoherence is often based on a misunderstanding: "It would, no doubt, be incoherent to say that God makes men freely choose the good: if God had made men choose, that is, forced them to choose one way rather than the other, they would not have been choosing freely. But that is not what was suggested, which was rather that God might have made—that is, created—beings, human or not, *such that* they would always freely choose the good; and there is at least no immediate incoherence or self-contradiction in that."[28]

But what if humans are naturally so depraved that God could not possibly create a world in which humans never do evil? Philosopher Alvin Plantinga has suggested this line, claiming that in every possible world (with humans) that God could create, humans would commit evil acts. He calls this idea "transworld depravity."[29] It is possible, of course, that the basic essence, or nature, of humans is hopelessly depraved. But if so, then this fact would conflict with church teaching. Jesus is thought to have been human—yet sinless. The Catholic Church teaches that Mary, the mother of Jesus, was human—yet without sin. Church doctrine then assumes that humans can be created without evil in their natures, and this conflicts with Plantinga's notion of human depravity.

Suppose, however, that God really is unable to create humans who always freely choose the good. Suppose that in order for humans to have free will, God had to create a world in which humans choose freely, and therefore sometimes cause moral evil. This scenario is just what many theists say is the current state of affairs. But given that there must be some evil in the world to accommodate free will, why must there be *so much* evil? Couldn't God have made humans so that they commit evil less often or commit less horrible evils?

There seems to be far more evil in the world than is required for the existence of free will. God could have endowed humans with high moral character, or taught humanity how to do good, or configured moral evil so its impact on the world is less severe—none of these possibilities would diminish humanity's free will.

Philosopher William Rowe tells the story of a fawn burned in a forest fire and left alone to suffer agonizing pain for days before dying.[30] Rowe asks: What is the point of such suffering? There seems to be no greater good to come out of it, no lesson taught to others, no moral development. Often the suffering or death of humans seems to be just as pointless. How can free will, as important as it is, be worth such cost—especially since it can be acquired with far less sacrifice? There seems to be far more evil in the world than is needed to ensure free will.

As we mentioned earlier, it will not do to say that God's view of the amount, severity, and purpose of evil is different from the human view and that God knows best. This tack implies that humans cannot trust any moral judgment they make because their perspective is inferior to God's. On the contrary, we do seem, at least sometimes, to be able to make trustworthy, accurate assessments of good and evil.

Even if we believe that the amount of moral evil in the world is appropriate, there still seems to be more evil than necessary because there is also natural evil. There is a great deal of moral evil in the world, but there appears to be even more natural evil. This type of evil cannot be defended by an appeal to free will because people are generally not responsible for natural evil. Floods, tornadoes, disease, earthquakes—these are "acts of God." The argument from natural evil, then, is if God were omnipotent, omniscient, and omnibenevolent, he would not visit these troubles upon human beings. Therefore, there can be no supreme being with these attributes.

Alvin Plantinga says that natural evil is caused not by God or by humans, but by Satan: "But a more traditional line of thought is indicated by St. Augustine, who attributes much of the evil we find to *Satan* or to *Satan* and his cohorts. . . . Unlike most of his colleagues, Satan rebelled against God and has since been wreaking whatever havoc he can. The result is natural evil. So the natural evil we find is due to free actions of nonhuman spirits."[31] This supposition, however, does not solve the original problem: An all-powerful, all-knowing, all-good God would not allow this. Such a God would not allow Satan to cause so much pain and death in his human children. A man or woman who had the wherewithal to stop the massacre of thousands of innocent people—people who are the victims of pointless evil—would be morally obligated to do so. Walking away from such a situation would be an act of evil in itself. God certainly has the wherewithal to prevent the evils caused by Satan—but he does not. So there must be no such God.

CONCLUSION

We have not examined every argument that purports to dismantle the nontheist's case against the existence of God. But we have looked at the most important ones. Remember that the argument from evil tries to show that God does not exist; if it fails, however, it does not necessarily follow that there is a God after all. It just means that the nontheist's most powerful argument is ineffective. But if the argument from evil stands, then a serious attempt to show that there is no God has worked. It then provides good reason to reject belief in the existence of God.

So does the argument stand? We think so. We also think that there is *justification* for believing that it stands. But we realize that other people may disagree and argue their case strenuously. Such engagement in the process of philosophy is a good thing. In some ways, this leap into philosophical and critical thinking is more important than the conclusions that it leads to. If you take this leap, whatever your conclusion is will likely be clearer and stronger than any rush to judgment.

SUMMARY

Throughout history, ideas about God or gods have been plentiful. The traditional concept of God is that God is a being who is omnipotent, omniscient, and omnibenevolent. Many have tried to show through philosophical argument that such a God exists. Because they use the natural processes of reason, they are said to be doing natural theology or advocating natural religion.

Natural theology has proposed several arguments to establish the existence of God. Ontological arguments try to derive the existence of God from a definition of God. Cosmological arguments start from a general fact about the world (such as its existence) and then try to derive the existence of God from this fact. For example, the first-cause argument tries to show that because everything is caused by something other than itself, and the series of causes cannot be infinite, there must be a first cause—and this first cause must be God. Teleological arguments appeal not to the existence of the universe, but to its design or other characteristics. Critics have found fault with all of these arguments.

Philosophers have also argued against the existence of God. Their strongest argument is the argument from evil: If there were an all-powerful and all-good God, there would be no unnecessary evil in the world. But there is unnecessary evil in the world, so God does not exist. The strongest defense against this argument is called the free-will defense. It asserts that there is no unnecessary evil in the world; the evil that does exist is necessary for the existence of free will.

STUDY QUESTIONS

1. What is the meaning of these terms: *atheism*, *theism*, *agnosticism*?
2. What is logical positivism?
3. What is the difference between *natural religion* and *revealed religion*?
4. What is Anselm's ontological argument?
5. What is the first-cause argument?
6. What is the Big Bang argument?
7. What are the criteria of adequacy?
8. What is the hypothetical-inductive version of the teleological argument?
9. What is the problem of evil?

DISCUSSION QUESTIONS

1. How does Alvin Plantinga try to show that believing in God without any supporting evidence can be rational?
2. What are the main criticisms of ontological arguments? Are they successful in undermining such arguments?
3. Which explanation is simpler—Swinburne's cosmological explanation or the hypothesis that the world was born from the belly of a spider?
4. How is the universe like a purposely designed machine? How is it like an organism?
5. Which is a better explanation of how the universe came to exist—(1) God created the universe out of nothing, (2) the universe came into existence uncaused, or (3) the universe has always existed?
6. What is a finite God? Would a finite God be worthy of worship?

FIELD PROBLEM

Rabbi Harold Kushner, author of *Why Bad Things Happen to Good People*, believes that evil happens because God is powerless to prevent it. This finite God avoids the problem of evil, but he is not the God of traditional theism. Consider whether you would find this God worthy of worship. If so, why? If not, why not?

SUGGESTIONS FOR FURTHER READING

Gale, Richard M. *On the Nature and Existence of God*. Cambridge: Cambridge University Press, 1991.
Mackie, J. L. *The Miracle of Theism*. Oxford: Clarendon Press, 1982.
Peterson, Michael, et al. *Reason and Religious Belief*. Oxford: Oxford University Press, 2d ed., 1998.
Schick, Theodore, and Lewis Vaughn. *Doing Philosophy*. Boston, M.A.: McGraw-Hill, 1999.

NOTES

1. R. Swinburne, *The Coherence of Theism* (Oxford: Oxford University Press, 1977), 2.
2. David Hume, *An Enquiry Concerning Human Understanding*, ed. L. A. Selby-Bigge (Oxford: Oxford University Press, 1975), 165.
3. Anselm of Canterbury, *Proslogium*, in Anne Fremantle, *The Age of Belief* (New York: New American Library, 1954), 88–89.
4. Gaunilo, *The Many-Faced Argument*, ed. John Hick and Arthur Hill (New York: Macmillan, 1968).
5. Alvin Plantinga, "The Ontological Argument," in *God, Freedom, and Evil* (London: Allen & Unwin), 91.
6. René Descartes, *Meditations on First Philosophy*, trans. John Cottingham (Cambridge: Cambridge University Press, 1986), 46.
7. Thomas Aquinas, *Summa Theologica* (London: Burns, Oates, and Washbourne, 1920), 25.
8. Richard Morris, *Achilles in the Quantum World* (New York: Henry Holt, 1997), 19.
9. Paul Davies, *God and the New Physics* (London: J. M. Dent, 1983), 162.
10. Edward Tryon, "Is the Universe a Vacuum Fluctuation?" *Nature* 246 (14 December 1973): 396–97.
11. Richard Swinburne, *Is There a God?* (Oxford: Oxford University Press, 1996).
12. Swinburne, *Is There a God?* 2.
13. Paul Thagard, "The Best Explanation: Criteria for Theory Choice," *Journal of Philosophy* 75, 2 (February 1978): 86ff."
14. Swinburne, *Is There a God?* 33.
15. Swinburne, *Is There a God?* 31.
16. Carl Hempel, *Philosophy of Natural Science* (Englewood Cliffs, N.J.: Prentice-Hall, 1966), 40.
17. Thagard, "The Best Explanation: Criteria for Theory Choice."
18. Thomas Aquinas, *Summa Theologica,* 24–27.
19. William Paley, *Natural Theology*, 1802.
20. David Hume, *Enquiry Concerning Human Understanding*, 136.
21. H. Allen Orr, "Darwin v. Intelligent Design (Again)," *Boston Review*, December 1996/January 1997.
22. Kenneth R. Miller, "Review of *Darwin's Black Box*," *Creation/Evolution* 16 (1996): 36–40.
23. Richard Dawkins, *The Blind Watchmaker* (New York: Norton, 1987), 90.
24. Victor J. Stenger, "Intelligent Design: Humans, Cockroaches, and the Laws of Physics," www.talkorigins.org/faqs/cosmo.html (accessed 11 March 2003).
25. Victor Stenger, "Intelligent Design."
26. Richard Gale, "Alvin Plantinga's Warranted Christian Belief," *Philo* (Fall–Winter 2001): 144.
27. J. L. Mackie, "Evil and Omnipotence," *Mind* 64 (1955), 200–212.
28. J. L. Mackie, *The Miracle of Theism* (Oxford: Clarendon Press, 1982), 200–212.
29. Alvin Plantinga, *God, Freedom, and Evil* (Grand Rapids, Mich.: Eerdmans, 1974), 49–53.
30. William Rowe, "The Problem of Evil and Some Varieties of Atheism," *American Philosophical Quarterly* 16 (October 1979): 337.
31. Alvin Plantinga, *God, Freedom, and Evil,* 58.

8

Society and Politics

Austin Dacey

"Men are born, and always continue, free and equal, in respect of their rights," proclaimed the Declaration of the Rights of Man, adopted in 1789 by the National Assembly of France and read throughout the world. Its authors, participants in the French Revolution, aimed at bringing about a radically new kind of society, founded on reason, that would assert the preeminence of individual liberty over the authority of the monarchy, the clergy, and the nobility.

The ideas about society, religion, and politics expressed in the declaration emerged from some of the most turbulent periods in the history of the West: the Protestant Reformation and consequent religious wars and a series of political revolutions in the seventeenth and eighteenth centuries. The religious wars convulsed European civilization for nearly a hundred years and swallowed up millions of lives in a multinational struggle over the destiny of Christendom. Through the treaties and armistices that ended the clashes, emerging European states attained compromises that would determine their religious character without resort to conflict and secure some measure of toleration for those within their borders who dissented from the national sect. The revolutions opened up new civil and economic freedoms and spread institutions of consensual government.

Along with this social upheaval, the religious wars and political revolutions transformed political thought and tested the viability of the notions of individual rights and religious toleration developed by Renaissance and Enlightenment humanists. The summary of humanist ideas with which we began this book made mention of "the value, dignity, and rights of individual persons" and "the responsibility of humans . . . to promote the welfare of themselves and all people." Tracing these broad outlines in more detail leads one into the field of social and political philosophy, where debate over the tenability of the humanist tradition still continues.

The humanist tradition has tended to take a view of the person in society that is liberal, individualist, universalist, and secularist. A **liberal** holds that personal liberty has normative priority. Freedom is the default presumption in the ethical analysis of society, so that restrictions on freedom by other people or the community demand justification, rather than the other way around. This meaning of "liberalism" derives from the early modern period and is still used in contemporary political thought. Another sense of "liberal" is used to refer to certain parties and movements in contemporary politics (as in "liberals and conservatives"). But usually all such parties and movements are liberal in the more fundamental, early modern sense because they agree on the normative priority of freedom.

The priority of freedom insisted on by the humanist tradition is the priority of *individual* freedom. This individualist strand regards the individual person as fundamental—in order of analysis and in order of moral value—to the community. To understand the nature of a community, one understands it as a collection of interacting individuals whose identities are in some sense independent of the group. To examine the ethical status of a community, one examines the ethical status of its relationship to the individuals within it.

The humanist tradition has been *universalist* (to lesser or greater extents) by supposing that the moral standing of individuals holds across distinctions of creed, class, sex, race, and nationality.

Finally, the humanist view is *secularist* in that it regards religion as theoretically and structurally distinct from government and other public institutions.

Throughout this chapter, these humanist strands of social and political philosophy are explored in detail. Section 8.1 discusses liberal universalism and individualism, section 8.2 discusses secularism, and section 8.3 probes the underlying justification of liberal rights, focusing on liberties of conscience, expression, and public debate.

SECTION 8.1

The Community of Equal Respect: Liberalism and Rights

Shakespeare's comedy *The Merchant of Venice* centers on a financial and legal entanglement between Antonio, a merchant and a Christian, and Shylock, a despised and persecuted Jewish moneylender who is eventually outwitted and ruined by Antonio's friends. At one point, Shylock protests to two Venetian Christians and anti-Semites:

> He hath disgraced me, and
> hindered me of half a million; laughed at my losses,
> mocked at my gains, scorned my nation, thwarted my
> bargains, cooled my friends, heated mine
> enemies; and what's his reason? I am a Jew. Hath
> not a Jew eyes? hath not a Jew hands, organs,
> dimensions, senses, affections, passions? fed with
> the same food, hurt with the same weapons, subject
> to the same diseases, healed by the same means,
> warmed and cooled by the same winter and summer, as
> a Christian is? If you prick us, do we not bleed?
> if you tickle us, do we not laugh? if you poison
> us, do we not die?[1]

Although the character of Shylock is in many ways an anti-Semitic caricature, Shakespeare voices an important ethical insight through him. Addressing a mainly Christian audience, Shakespeare points out that despite Shylock's cultural differences, he shares all of those features—like the capacities for suffering and joy—relevant to how he morally ought to be treated. This prompts the question: If Shylock is the same, in all morally relevant respects, as the full members of the community, why does he not deserve the same moral consideration and respect?

Here the character of Shylock evokes the universalist impulse in morality, the impulse to belong to a community in which all members are moral equals. The theme of universal equal respect is central to humanistic strands of social and political philosophy, and can be expressed as follows:

15. All people have equal moral rights and deserve corresponding political rights.

The present section examines several aspects of this theme, including its focus on equal rights, on individuals, and on human beings as opposed to other beings.

LIBERALISM

Liberalism as a political philosophy takes the equal freedom of individuals as a normative presumption, so that any limitation on freedom imposed by the state and society stands in need of justification. Liberals have also concluded that the extent of justified impositions is relatively limited, so that the political upshot is broad individual civil rights, limited government, and often some form of democratic representation or participation.

The liberal stance in Western political thought has its roots in the "natural rights" doctrines of the eighteenth century, exemplified by the Declaration of the Rights of Man. In turn, these doctrines drew on the Scholastic natural law theory of the medieval period (which was more concerned with a person's moral duties than his "rights"), itself a complex synthesis of Aristotelian and Greek Stoicism with Christianity and Judaism. Aristotle linked justice to the proper ends of human life and society, which he saw as determined by human nature. Aquinas argued that the inclinations and capacities inherent to human nature are the expression in us of God's eternal law. We receive divinely authored moral guidance by looking to our nature. The Renaissance ideal of personal self-direction and self-expression contributed to a shift from natural *duties* to natural *rights*. Dutch jurist and humanist Hugo Grotius (1583–1645) separated natural and divine law more clearly, and the modern notion of natural rights gained wide acceptance through the political writings of John Locke and Thomas Hobbes. They maintained that the legitimate powers of government are derived from the consent of individuals who, in a "state of nature," agree to entrust their antecedent natural rights to the protection of the state. For Locke especially, the right to property was crucial. Eighteenth-century Enlightenment thinkers, especially the French philosophes, began to speak of the inalienable "rights of Man" discoverable by reason. European and American revolutionaries presupposed this political philosophy when they affirmed natural rights to "life, liberty, and the pursuit of happiness," or, as the Declaration of the Rights of Man put it, "liberty, property, security, and resistance to oppression."

Liberalism as political movement arose in Western Europe and colonial America in the seventeenth and eighteenth centuries in close connection with the rise of the middle class.

It served as the intellectual backbone of three of the most important political revolutions in Western history—the English, American, and French Revolutions. The English Revolution consisted of a series of power struggles between 1642 and 1688 that pitted the crown and royalists against the Parliament and its supporters, mostly Puritan merchants and lesser gentry. As members of a minority faith who had been alienated under the established national Anglican Church, these Puritans sought greater religious toleration. As landowning subjects, they sought greater security of person and property against arbitrary actions of the crown. With the American Revolution and the adoption of the United States Constitution in 1791, liberal practices were extended by an expansion of the voting franchise among male nonslaves and the establishment of a constitutional government designed to guarantee freedoms of religion, press, speech, and assembly. Finally, the French Revolution produced highly influential expressions of the ardent liberalism of the time.

Natural rights theories of the state were radically different from those that had gone before, both in their liberal implications and in their secular character. Medieval political thought inherited from classical civilization the idea that the aim or end of the political order is to produce virtue in its members, and defined "virtue" in Christian terms. The splintering of Christendom triggered by the Reformation destroyed the unity of ecclesiastical authority and theological interpretation that was presupposed by this model of politics. In addition, with the rise of new, powerful national monarchies in Europe, political philosophy increasingly turned to the question of whether a state's claims on its citizens are morally legitimate. Natural rights doctrines proposed to justify the authority of the state without direct appeal to religious authority, unlike the "divine right of kings" doctrine, which legitimized civil power by association with a paternal order ordained by God.

Even still, the monotheistic heritage of natural rights theories is evident in several ways. Most Enlightenment liberals were also Enlightenment deists who believed that our natural rights can in some way be attributed to the fact that we are the creation of a provident and rational deity or a benevolent Nature. This tradition lives on today, most notably in public rhetoric about freedom as "sacred" or the gift of a creator god. The Creator's role is not insubstantial in some liberal theories. For instance, Locke relied heavily on the claim that everyone owes a duty of self-preservation to God because, as his creation, we are his property. Nevertheless, the philosophical heart of the natural rights tradition, which continues in contemporary liberal "social contract" or "contractarian" theories, is secular. It is the thought that persons possess certain features (for example, rationality, autonomous decision-making, or the ability to suffer) that exist independently of government and that substantially constrain the morally proper exercise of political and social power over us.

LIBERALISM'S EXPANDING CIRCLE

Since its beginnings, liberal theory and practice has faced the criticism that it excludes many people, that it is not so much about equal rights *for all* as it is about equal rights *for some*—namely, certain white male Europeans. It is indeed historically true that in the minds of many liberal thinkers, women, indigenous peoples, slaves, and in some cases wage laborers and the poor were not truly free individuals, and so did not deserve the special respect and political rights associated with that status. At best these others were seen as accessories of the male free individual, and, at worst, as his possessions. The causes of such attitudes are complex and related to deep cultural currents of the time and before, such as the European belief in the inferiority of non-Europeans, and the much more widespread belief in the inferiority of women to men. Along with this racism and sexism, however, was a very distinctive concept of freedom, which excluded even most white male Europeans from liberal equality. For most of the politicians and theorists who championed the early liberal cause, a person's fundamental freedom was intimately connected with having a certain measure of economic independence, which in turn was connected with holding property. Hence, the condition, ubiquitous in Britain and the colonies, that to vote one must be propertied.

By and large, the liberal revolutions were led by men from the urban middle classes—property owners, merchants, and others involved in the new economies that had resulted from the growth in commerce and urbanization begun in the late medieval period. Given their way of life, they were especially sensitive to burdensome taxation, restrictions on trade, and religious intolerance, and they turned against prevailing civil and clerical powers on those grounds. The age of revolution largely left in place the basically undemocratic structure of Western societies, a fact that Marx would later use to argue for more radical, communist, revolution. It was not until well into the nineteenth century that liberalism became more fully democratic and universal male suffrage became the norm in Western Europe and America. And it was not until the middle of the twentieth century that most women and former slaves gained the right and the genuine opportunity to use the ballot.

Nevertheless, although most classical liberals themselves did not fight and die for the kind of inclusive liberalism we might aspire to today, the classical liberal *philosophy* they developed would come to inspire and serve many of those engaged in that struggle. The concepts of freedom and equality represented an authoritative historical tradition that reformers could draw on and reorient in egalitarian directions. For example, the authors of America's founding documents, the Declaration of Independence and the Constitution, did not intend these documents to give political equality to slaves and indentured servants. Yet, nineteenth-century abolitionists—particularly black abolitionists like the former slave and orator Frederick Douglass (1817?–1895)—reinterpreted the ideals expressed in the texts, aligning them with the antislavery cause.

> [T]he constitution of the United States—inaugurated "to form a more perfect union, establish justice, insure domestic tranquillity, provide for the common defense, promote the general welfare, and secure the blessings of liberty"—could not well have been designed at the same time to maintain and perpetuate a system of rapine and murder like slavery; especially, as not one word can be found in the constitution to authorize such a belief. . . . [T]he constitution of our country is our warrant for the abolition of slavery in every state in the American Union.[2]

Thus, the abolitionist movement reshaped America's understanding of its own affirmation of freedom and equality. In his famous debate with Abraham Lincoln, Stephen A. Douglas asserted that the United States was made "by white men for the benefit of white men and their posterity forever," and that citizenship should be confined to white men. Lincoln, who was deeply influenced by his friendship with Frederick Douglass, responded that the rights affirmed in the Declaration of Independence belong to "all men, in all lands, everywhere," not just Europeans and their descendants.

Similarly, some early feminists such as Mary Wollstonecraft, Frances Wright, Susan B. Anthony, and Elizabeth Cady Stanton developed the case that the scope of liberal rights must be extended to include women because women share in the morally relevant features possessed by men. Wollstonecraft (1759–1797) contended that like men, women are naturally rational, and so must enjoy all of the rights that flow from this rational capacity. Women must be seen as part of the "human species."[3]

Other traditions of feminism did not embrace liberalism and sought different philosophical means of attacking male supremacy. Indeed, we discuss later, many contemporary political theorists maintain that liberalism is frequently incapable of addressing the moral concerns of marginalized or minority groups. At the same time, those loyal to liberalism have tended to conclude that despite its historical exclusivity, the moral ideals of liberalism are properly inclusive when applied consistently and with a full appreciation of the facts about people.

HUMAN RIGHTS

How broad can the circle of rights and liberties become? On December 10, 1948, the General Assembly of the United Nations adopted the Universal Declaration of Human Rights and called upon all member nations to publicize the text of the declaration and "to cause it to be disseminated, displayed, read and expounded principally in schools and other educational institutions, without distinction based on the political status of countries or territories." The Universal Declaration Articles 1 and 2 proclaimed that equal rights to life, liberty, and security of person (among many other things) are the entitlement of "all human beings" without distinction "of any kind, such as race, color, sex, language, religion, political or other opinion, national or social origin, property, birth or other status."

The notion of human rights extends the community of equal respect until it is coextensive with humanity per se. This ethical universalism is anticipated in some respects by Western monotheisms in which people are invested with equal worth by their shared status as favored creations of God. A kind of universalism is also implied by the classical elements of natural law theory, with its project of grounding morality in a shared human nature. The worldwide horror at the atrocities of World War II and the Holocaust contributed to the rise of human rights discourse in the latter half of the twentieth century. Today, the notion of human rights in some form has gained considerable acceptance around the world, and the legitimacy of governments is increasingly evaluated on the basis of their willingness and ability to protect certain alleged basic rights.

Nevertheless, the philosophy of human rights is beset with numerous open questions and controversies. Within the international community, nations of differing political ideologies and histories disagree about the proper content of human rights. While some nations (typically liberal, developed, capitalist democracies) place more emphasis on liberal, civil rights such as freedom of religion and expression—the so-called first-generation rights—others (such as socialist, developing, or postcolonial nations) insist on the preeminence of economic interests and basic needs, or a community's collective rights to self-determination and political representation, rights of the "second" and "third generation," respectively.

Universal Declaration of Human Rights (excerpt)

PREAMBLE
Whereas recognition of the inherent dignity and of the equal and inalienable rights of all members of the human family is the foundation of freedom, justice and peace in the world,

Whereas disregard and contempt for human rights have resulted in barbarous acts which have outraged the conscience of mankind, and the advent of a world in which human beings shall enjoy freedom of speech and belief and freedom from fear and want has been proclaimed as the highest aspiration of the common people,

Whereas it is essential, if man is not to be compelled to have recourse, as a last resort, to rebellion against tyranny and oppression, that human rights should be protected by the rule of law,

Whereas it is essential to promote the development of friendly relations between nations,

Whereas the peoples of the United Nations have in the Charter reaffirmed their faith in fundamental human rights, in the dignity and worth of the human person and in the equal rights of men and women and have determined to promote social progress and better standards of life in larger freedom,

Whereas Member States have pledged themselves to achieve, in co-operation with the United Nations, the promotion of universal respect for and observance of human rights and fundamental freedoms,

Whereas a common understanding of these rights and freedoms is of the greatest importance for the full realization of this pledge,

Now, Therefore THE GENERAL ASSEMBLY proclaims THIS UNIVERSAL DECLARATION OF HUMAN RIGHTS as a common standard of achievement for all peoples and all nations, to the end that every individual and every organ of society, keeping this Declaration constantly in mind, shall strive by teaching and education to promote respect for these rights and freedoms and by progressive measures, national and international, to secure their universal and effective recognition and observance, both among the peoples of Member States themselves and among the peoples of territories under their jurisdiction.

Article 1.
All human beings are born free and equal in dignity and rights. They are endowed with reason and conscience and should act towards one another in a spirit of brotherhood.

Article 2.
Everyone is entitled to all the rights and freedoms set forth in this Declaration, without distinction of any kind, such as race, color, sex, language, religion, political or other opinion, national or social origin, property, birth or other status. Furthermore, no distinction shall be made on the basis of the political, jurisdictional or international status of the country or territory to which a person belongs, whether it be independent, trust, non-self-governing or under any other limitation of sovereignty.

Continued

Universal Declaration of Human Rights (excerpt) (*continued*)

Article 3.
Everyone has the right to life, liberty and security of person.

Article 4.
No one shall be held in slavery or servitude; slavery and the slave trade shall be prohibited in all their forms.

Article 5.
No one shall be subjected to torture or to cruel, inhuman or degrading treatment or punishment.

Moreover, political and ethical theorists dispute a number of questions about the nature and justification of human rights. If all people are the holders of human rights, who are the *addressees* (those who have duties that arise from the rights of others): governments, individuals, or governments on behalf of individuals? More fundamentally, what justifies us in asserting such rights? To put it another way, are there really such universal, pre-legal duties, or is talk of natural rights nothing more than "nonsense upon stilts," as the British philosopher Jeremy Bentham famously charged?

AGAINST UNIVERSALISM

Liberals and human rights theorists also face difficult questions about the appropriateness of "exporting" Enlightenment conceptions of rights and liberties to other, non-Western, societies. What measures may liberal democracies take to diminish what they see as unacceptable violations of universal rights by other societies—for instance, with respect to the status and treatment of women under conservative Muslim regimes or local African customs? Such questions are complicated by the long history of global colonial domination by Western nations and the continuing disparities in wealth and power between the North and South. Is it possible to defend and promulgate liberal norms crossculturally in a way that is consistent with due respect for non-Western peoples and their interest in a government that represents their cultural values?

Liberal economic and political rights are sometimes identified as necessary conditions for modernization and development in postcolonial and industrializing nations. However, the experience of some newly industrialized nations, especially in East and Southeast Asia, has suggested that different societies may pursue different, yet no less successful, paths to development. The industrialization of the first major European powers was propelled by various private export industries, and it benefited from the social conditions created by Western-style free markets and individual rights. A country like Malaysia, on the other hand, was able to develop at a phenomenal rate in the late twentieth century with the help of interventions in the economy by centralized and highly active government, and nonindividualistic social ethics such as Confucianism. In light of the urgent moral importance of industrialization for elevating the living conditions and meeting the basic needs of the citizens of the developing world, liberal universalists are forced to consider whether certain societies might not be better off without the preferred liberal values, at least during such crucial periods of their history.

While some have found fault with Enlightenment universalism for being too broad—for "imposing" its liberal values onto foreign cultures, others have critiqued it for being too narrow. The tradition has drawn the limits of the community of equal respect at the limits of the human community. Human rights discourse, for instance, often invokes the "dignity" that is peculiar to human beings. This focus on human beings per se has prompted the charge of speciesism. Speciesism, as was discussed briefly in an earlier chapter, is the error of according different moral consideration to members of another species *simply because they are members of a different species*. In his *Introduction to the Principles of Moral and Legislation* (1789), British social philosopher and legal reformer Jeremy Bentham wondered whether the expanding circle of liberal rights might in the future come to include nonhuman animals.

> The day may come when the rest of the animal creation may acquire those rights which never could have been withholden from them but by the hand of tyranny. The French have already discovered that the blackness of the skin is no reason why a human being should be abandoned without redress to the caprice of a tormentor. It may one day come to be recognized that the number of legs, the villosity of the skin, or the termination of the os sacrum are reasons equally insufficient for abandoning a sensitive being to the same fate.[4]

Against the charge of speciesism, one might attempt to point to the existence of certain unique and morally relevant characteristics of humans—perhaps higher cognitive processes such as language use, self-awareness, or autonomous decision-making—that warrant duties toward humans but not other animals who lack those characteristics. Surely respect for a creature—whether human or not—requires that when judging how we ought to treat it, we take into consideration the characteristics it actually possesses. One challenge confronting this strategy is that the characteristics one cites to accord special weight to human beings may in fact be lacked by many biologically human beings, such as fetuses and infants, the comatose, or the severely mentally handicapped. Ethicists such as Peter Singer have accepted this implication, maintaining that in certain cases, nonhuman animals will be more morally considerable than some "marginal" humans.[5] In so doing they have left behind the notion of special human dignity essential to the humanist tradition in moral and political philosophy.

AGAINST INDIVIDUALISM

The case of *Hofer v. Hofer*, heard before the Canadian courts, pitted the Hutterite Church against two of its former members. It concerned a dispute over their property. Hutterites live in agricultural communities called colonies in which no one holds private property. The philosopher Will Kymlicka describes the case:

> Two residents of a Hutterite colony, who had been members of the colony from birth, were expelled for apostasy. They demanded their share of the colony's assets, which they had helped

> create with their years of labor. When the colony refused, the two ex-members sued in court. They objected to the fact that they had "no right at any time in their lives to leave the colony without abandoning everything, even the clothes on their backs." . . . The Hutterites defended this practice on the grounds that freedom of religion protects a congregation's ability to live in accordance with its religious doctrine, even if this limits individual freedom.[6]

The Canadian Supreme Court sided with the Hutterites. However, one dissenting justice argued that the proper scope of religious authority is "limited to what is consistent with freedom of religion as properly understood, that is freedom for the individual not only to adopt a religion but to abandon it at will." To Justice Pigeon, the Hutterite congregation was violating its members' religious liberty by foreclosing to them any real option to opt out of its ranks.

The opposing responses to the Hutterite case point to a general dilemma for liberalism. Given the existence, within a larger liberal society, of communities that do not share all of its liberal values, what is the appropriate way to protect religious liberty: by protecting the rights of *individual* citizens to believe and practice as they chose, or by protecting the rights of *groups* to maintain their religious communities as they chose, sometimes through means that violate individual rights? In liberal political philosophy, this dilemma has been called "The Problem of Non-liberal Minorities." This problem is not just a philosophical puzzle. It has a tangible impact on the lives of countless people. Consider the governments of Native American tribes in the United States, which are not subject to the Bill of Rights; North American religious sects such as the Amish and Mennonites, who prefer that their children be exempt from mandatory education laws; Christian Scientists and Jehovah's Witnesses, many of whom assert that their religious liberty permits them to deny certain forms of potentially life-saving medical treatment to themselves and their children; or members of recent immigrant populations in Europe, especially Muslims, who seek to insulate their communities from certain liberal norms, for example, concerning gender discrimination and equal education, that conflict with their traditional practices.

The Problem of Non-liberal Minorities is related to a more general critique of liberalism, which is associated with the school of thought known as **communitarianism**. Communitarian critics of liberalism object to its model of the person. Liberalism, they say, asks us to evaluate societies and political systems from a point of view outside of any particular way of life, a presocial "state of nature" from which free and equal agents agree or "contract" to take on the obligations of social cooperation. Unfortunately for this way of thinking, persons are not like independent atoms that bond together to form collectives. Rather, we are in part constituted by our particular social relationships and the obligations they engender. The Hutterite's practice of communal religious rituals is not an ornament to his otherwise intact identity; the practice is part of *what makes him the person that he is*. Because liberalism takes the point of view of a self unencumbered by such attachments and duties, it cannot correctly address what is of concern to actual citizens. According to Michael Sandel,

> It fails to capture those loyalties and responsibilities whose moral force consists partly in the fact that living by them is inseparable from understanding ourselves as the particular persons we are—as members of this family or city or nation or people, as bears of that history, as citizens of this republic. . . . [O]bligations of membership presuppose that we are capable of moral ties antecedent to choice. To the extent that we are, the meaning of our membership resists redescription in contractarian terms.[7]

According to Sandel, this failure has real consequences for the justness of the laws and the ethics of citizenship in a liberal polity.

Liberals have responded to the communitarian critique of individualism in several ways. Some deny that the liberal model of the person is committed to atomistic individualism. Others argue that the liberal model is not a substantive philosophical or metaphysical theory at all, but rather a "political conception," a minimal set of assumptions about persons that can be shared by all citizens who seek a mutually acceptable framework for cooperation in a pluralistic society.

Debates over individualism, the justification and nature of universal liberal rights, and the proper scope of the liberal community occupy center stage in contemporary political philosophy. In many respects these debates concern the tenability of the humanist tradition in social and political philosophy.

CONCLUSION

In contemporary social and political philosophy, the kind of liberalism associated with the humanist tradition is under intense pressure from several directions, even as liberal institutions and human rights discourse continue to spread. It remains to be seen whether liberalism can remain intellectually viable.

SECTION 8.2

The Earthly City: Society, Politics, and Secularism

In the aftermath of the September 11, 2001, terrorist attacks in New York City and Washington, D.C., novelist Salman Rushdie wrote an editorial in the *New York Times* urging a "Reformation in the Muslim world." He argued that to counteract the global rise in Islamic fundamentalism, Muslims must undertake to make their religion a "personal, private faith."

> The restoration of religion to the sphere of the personal, its depoliticization, is the nettle that all Muslim societies must grasp in order to become modern. The only aspect of modernity interesting to the terrorists is technology, which they see as a weapon that can be turned on its makers. If terrorism is to be defeated, the world of Islam must take on board the secularist-humanist principles on which the modern is based, and without which Muslim countries' freedom will remain a distant dream.[8]

The original Islamic community, begun and led by Muhammad himself in the city of Medina, was at the same time a religious, social, and political community. In the single person of the prophet, the early Muslims had a spiritual, civil, and military leader. Muhammad's followers lived, ate, prayed, worked, and fought together. The explosive expansion of the movement effected by the military conquests of 632–750 C.E. was designed not to win converts to the faith per se, but to increase the power and territory of a new comprehensive way of life. The practices of the historical Muhammad and the community he created came to serve as a model for subsequent social organization and political thought.

In articulating and defending legal norms, Islamic political thinkers drew instructions, examples, and analogies from the traditional texts—the Qu'ran and the hadith (accounts of the prophet's words and deeds during the period of his preaching). The texts revealed the proper path to be followed in Muslim life, or *Shari'a*, which became thought of as a complete system of rules encompassing all aspects of human life, from etiquette, hygiene, and marriage, to commerce, law, government, and the conduct of war. The purpose of the Islamic state was to apply and enforce the *Shari'a*. Thus, Islamic political thought represented society as a fusion of religion and politics.

In Rushdie's estimation, the key to addressing Islamic fundamentalism is to replace this model of society with a *secular* model, in which government and religion are institutionally and theoretically separated; in which the life of faith is left to private individuals and organizations whose practice or lack of practice is protected within a framework of freedom of conscience. (Islamic law has historically included various provisions for religious toleration, so that the religious freedom of medieval Jews was far better under many Islamic regimes than under Christian regimes.) Modern Western societies began to experience secularization over four centuries ago. In America, a peculiarly strict "separation of church and state" has emerged as a central constitutional principle. After an analogous process of secularization in Islamic societies, Rushdie hopes, Islam will be less vulnerable to being "hijacked" by violent radicals.

16. Governments and other public institutions should not favor a religious faith or religion in general.

What reason is there to embrace this ideal? Can the secular impulse go too far? To what extent is secularism a model for all societies? Might there be alternatives?

CHURCH AND STATE IN WESTERN HISTORY

The contemporary notions of church and state as distinct entities are relative newcomers in Western political thought. For much of the history of Western civilization, its political thinkers regarded their way of life as a single social and political order. From the ninth century on, this order was called "Christendom." Christendom was divided into two main systems of authority. There was an ecclesiastical hierarchy of popes and clergy members, and there was a system of secular rulers, such as kings and emperors. According to a popular medieval metaphor, Christendom was ruled by two swords. One sword was wielded by the ecclesiastical powers; the other was wielded by the civil powers.[9]

These two systems of authority were roughly associated with two spheres of human affairs: the temporal and the spiritual. Temporal affairs were such things as the biological growth, life, and death of human beings, their manipulation of their surroundings, and various social interactions such as communication, cooperation, and conflict. Spiritual affairs were such things as alterations in souls such as sin and redemption, the interaction of souls with the divine, the communion of people for the purpose of religious worship or instruction, and the elaboration and justification of religious doctrines and conventions.

Broadly speaking, the "temporal kingdom" had jurisdiction over such things as the creation and enforcement of positive law, corporeal punishment or punishment by fine or imprisonment, authorization of civil officials, allocation of state revenues, and the conduct of foreign affairs. The "spiritual kingdom," on the other hand, had jurisdiction over such things as the determination of metaphysical and moral religious doctrines, worship, the qualifications for membership in the clergy or laity; church punishment such as excommunication; and the ordination of church officials.

Although the idea of two conceptually and institutionally distinct social domains may seem obvious, earlier civilizations, such as the ancient Israelites and Greeks, did not draw the distinction.[10] With the Edict of Milan in 313 C.E. and the later adoption by Theodosius of Christianity as the religion of the Empire, the persecution of Christians by Rome was dramatically reduced. Following Christianization, however, Rome began to assume more and more control of the Church's internal affairs. Many early Church leaders responded by developing political theories that diminished the role and moral significance of the civil order.

Against the classical view of politics as natural, early Christian thinkers argued that the civil order is a conventional device needed to cope with Man's fallen and sinful condition. Excellent human lives would not include politics because they would be free from the spiritual corruption that makes politics necessary. On this view, the central human calling, and the primary beneficiary of social organization itself, is not politics, but faith.

The clearest example of the early Christian attitude toward secular authority is found in the writings of St. Augustine of Hippo. In *City of God*, Augustine portrays all of human history as a struggle between two cities, a heavenly city of God, and an earthly city of the world. The cities are not simply identified with the Church and the Empire. Instead, they are communities of souls grouped together according to their state of spiritual salvation or damnation. Members of both cities intermingle in actual human institutions, to be sorted out only on Judgment Day.[11] To the extent that the Church carries out its spiritual tasks, it brings a part of the City of God to earth.[12] The civil order does so as well, to the extent that it protects and empowers the Church for these tasks. The ecclesiastical order is prior to the civil order in that it is the reason for the existence of the civil order. Yet, it is not charged with temporal affairs, except for correcting the civil rulers when they act unjustly.

The spiritual-temporal distinction left open the question of the precise relationship between existing religions and governments. In one theoretical model, the church and the state are interdependent but the state is ultimately subordinate to the church. This is **theocracy**. A classic statement of the theocratic view is found in the political philosophy of St. Thomas Aquinas. As in the political philosophy of Aristotle, the aim or end of the political order is to produce virtue, or happiness, in its members. However, true happiness cannot be attained solely through "natural virtue," or traits of character such as courage and temperance. Rather, true happiness requires a spiritual blessedness, an "enjoyment of God" made possible by knowledge of the true religion and an act of God's grace. But earthly rulers cannot bring people to true happiness because they lack the authority to determine the truth about religious matters. Rather, people are directed to virtue by the church. The state pursues the end of virtue by supporting the church in its spiritual ministry, and the church may intervene to correct the state whenever it acts contrary to this end.

Under theocracy, ecclesiastical power has some significant jurisdiction over temporal affairs along with its jurisdiction over spiritual affairs. For example, it is entitled to and responsible for determining certain positive laws. That the church intervenes to correct civil powers regarding the law suggests that the civil powers also have jurisdiction over it. Whenever these jurisdictions overlap, however, the claims of the church have precedence.

In short, theocratic doctrines hold that ecclesiastical powers have significant and superior jurisdiction over temporal affairs.

In another model of the relationship between the civil and ecclesiastical powers, the two are interdependent but the latter is ultimately subordinate to the former. Such arrangements are sometimes called **erastian**.[13] An erastian holds that civil powers have some significant and superior jurisdiction over spiritual affairs. An example can be found in the political philosophy of Jean-Jacques Rousseau.

Rousseau's *Social Contract* made famous the phrase "civil religion."[14] Rousseau argues that a civil religion is necessary to motivate citizens to follow the law and thus to maintain social order. This religion is a "purely civil profession of faith, the articles of which it is the business of the Sovereign to arrange, not precisely as dogmas of religion, but as sentiments of sociability without which it is impossible to be either a good citizen or a faithful subject."[15] The articles of civil religion are the "existence of a powerful, wise, and benevolent Divinity, who foresees and provides the life to come, the happiness of the just, the punishment of the wicked, the sanctity of the social contract and the laws." The Sovereign is entitled to enforce this civil religion by expelling from the state those who disbelieve its doctrines and putting to death those who publicly profess belief but fail to act accordingly. Only if the doctrines of a religion are consistent with civil religion, then the Sovereign may not meddle with it. (Rousseau believed that much of Christian ethics fails to satisfy the needs of the state.) Rousseau's government has a jurisdiction over significant spiritual affairs that takes precedence over the jurisdiction of the ecclesiastical order.

In the medieval period, political thought and practice was dominated by a conflict between theocratic and erastian impulses, which was manifested in a variety of political contests and controversies. After Augustine, the Church had become increasingly powerful and coherent as an institution while political communities became more and more weak and fragmented. Justinian the Great's attempt to reunify the Empire in the sixth century was defeated by fresh waves of barbarian invasions. Consequently, the Western Church found itself among a multiplicity of disparate barbarian kingdoms. This environment proved advantageous for the religion. By contrast with the immense Empire, the small kingdoms found it relatively difficult to defy the Church. Moreover, the barbarian societies invested special authority in the community's customary law, which even kings were expected to abide by and guard. The Church was able to take advantage of this regard for customary law by presenting itself as the guardian and voice of the community's conventional morality. In general, it was very successful at persuading the new kings that their power should be used to protect and advance the Christian way of life.

The most consequential advance of the Church during this period was its increased role in bestowing perceived legitimacy on secular rulers. During the seventh and eighth centuries, a custom spread to all Western kingdoms wherein ecclesiastical officials performed ceremonies of anointing, enthroning, and coronating secular officials. The crowning of Charlemagne by Leo III to inaugurate the new Western Roman Empire helped to crystallize the idea that the secular order is entrusted by the ecclesiastical order with the protection of the Christian world. This idea in turn prepared the way for the "investiture contest" of the eleventh and twelfth centuries, in which the imperial power and the Papacy laid competing claims to the authority to grant and remove the legitimacy of the other.[16]

Christianity had always been salvationist and expansionist, claiming to possess spiritual truths necessary for redemption and eternal life, and intending to bring everyone within its reach to accept these truths, or least come in contact with them. When the Protestant Reformation in the sixteenth century split Christianity into two salvationist and expansionist religions sharing the same nations and societies, confrontation was inevitable. The new religious tensions fueled the tremendously bloody and destructive rivalries, riots, massacres, and wars that beset Europe roughly between 1540 and 1650. The treaties and truces that ended these conflicts sought various compromises to provide for the peaceful coexistence of Protestants and Catholics.

In the shadow of religious strife, some political thinkers began to argue that the civil and ecclesiastical powers ought to be confined to temporal and spiritual matters, respectively, and consequently that the civil and ecclesiastical powers are more or less separate and independent of one another. This idea can be called **separationism**. The idea emerges most clearly in the seventeenth century in the writings of Benedict Spinoza, John Milton, John Locke, and dissident minority Protestants such as the English Baptists. Like theocratic and erastian views, separationism assumes the dichotomy of domains or kingdoms. But it asserts that the civil powers have little or no jurisdiction over spiritual affairs while the ecclesiastical powers have little or no jurisdiction over temporal affairs. In those cases where the jurisdictions do overlap, the claims of the civil powers usually take precedence.

In this sense, separationism takes a position on several different aspects of the relationship of religion and politics. First of all, it concerns religious liberty, or the extent to which people are permitted to attend temples, participate in worship service, perform ceremonies, observe holy days, and so on, without interference from others. Second, separationism concerns the "establishment" of an official state religion. This issue involves the extent of such things as tax support of religious organizations, religious qualifications for public office, and the presence of religious ceremony, symbolism, or rhetoric in state institutions and discourse.

Among Western societies, it was the United States that was to become most strictly separationist. Although many colonists were members of minority faiths fleeing persecution in Europe, the colonial governments they established were firmly, and sometimes brutally, theocratic. Yet following the tremendous proliferation of Protestant sects during and after the First Great Awakening, institutions of toleration became more and more robust. New England Baptists successfully petitioned England for exemption from taxes used to support the Puritan establishments. Roger Williams, the radical Puritan Separatist and founder of Rhode Island, pressed to exclude government from any role in religious doctrine, worship, or internal church policy, and to exclude the church from any role in the allocation of public funds, the authorization of civil officials, and the conduct of civil ceremonies and oaths. During the Revolutionary era, a popular movement led by James Madison and Thomas Jefferson in Virginia attacked the notion of an established church itself. Largely as a result of the Virginia movement, a provision against religious persecution and the establishment of a church by the federal government was included in the First Amendment to the U.S. Constitution (churches *established by the states* were another matter). In 1803, Jefferson described the First Amendment as having erected a "wall of separation" between church and state. Starting in the 1940s, the Supreme Court applied the constitutional idea of separation to the states and began to interpret this separation more and more strictly. The constitutional ideals of liberty and disestablishment of religion came to be understood by the courts as the ideal of state "neutrality" toward religion: that the state should not favor any one religion over others, or favor religion over irreligion.

Consequences

The most straightforward argument made on behalf of separation was based on the harmful social effects of theocratic and erastian arrangements, such as were all too apparent to early modern Europeans. "The purpose of separation of church and state," James Madison wrote in 1803, "is to keep forever from these shores the ceaseless strife that has soaked the soil of Europe in blood for centuries." He also referred to the effects on religions themselves. Making his case for disestablishment, Madison asks, "During almost fifteen centuries, has the legal establishment of Christianity been on trial. What have been its fruits? More or less in all places, pride and indolence in the Clergy, ignorance and servility in the laity, in both, superstition, bigotry and persecution."[17]

According to Madison, establishment also works to "weaken in those who profess this Religion, a pious confidence in its innate excellence, and the patronage of its author; and to foster in those who still reject it a suspicion that its friends are too conscious of its fallacies to trust it to its own merits."[18] On this view, establishment injures the health of the church by corrupting clergy with self-interest and self-indulgence and weakens the dedication and drive of the laity by undermining their confidence in its self-sufficient strength.

Madison's general point about the effects of establishment on the self-sufficiency and vitality of religion (leaving aside the anti-Catholic aspect of his observations) continues to have some force. Yet it would not be irrational for religious communities to prefer to trade certain sorts of self-sufficiency for a position of special authority and public recognition.

It is beyond dispute that the horror of the Religious Wars propelled European thought and practice toward toleration and separationism. The argument from bad consequences continues to be relevant, especially in societies still plagued by religious persecution or violent faith-based antagonisms: Iran, India, Nigeria, China, Indonesia, Palestine, Northern Ireland, and elsewhere. The divisive potential of religion is somewhat less compelling as an argument for separationism in societies with relatively little sectarian unrest, and where institutions of religious toleration and liberty are quite secure. Indeed, most of the advanced democracies of Europe maintain established or otherwise or state-funded religions, even while safeguarding the rights and dignity of religious minorities within their borders. From this perspective, the consequentialist argument falls short of justifying the kind of strict disestablishment found in the United States.

The recent history of tension and confrontation between the West and the Islamic world points out that public religiosity can also have potentially dangerous consequences for the relations between nation-states and their peoples. For example, in the midst of the American-led "war on terrorism" and the mass detainment of Arabs and Muslims in the United States, key members of the Bush administration and the U.S. Congress participated in a surge of public piety that had the effect of framing the conflict as a struggle between Christianity and Islam. President George Bush, an outspoken "born-again" Christian, repeatedly invoked God's blessing on the U.S. campaign, which he once inadvertently described as a "crusade." U.S. Attorney General John Ashcroft, a Pentecostal who was known for holding daily Christian prayer gatherings at Justice Department headquarters, publicly remarked, "Islam is a religion in which God requires you to send your son to die for him. Christianity is a faith in which God sends his son to die for you." Members of the U.S. Congress used the legislative chambers for an extended prayer and worship service led by two Christian chaplains. These shows of fervor were no doubt welcome to radical Islamists wishing to incite Muslims around the world to a holy war against Christians and Jews. Efforts to build constructive and friendly relations between Western and Muslim nations are not served by identifying any regimes with Christianity or Islam. Similar dynamics have fueled the conflict between predominantly Muslim Pakistan and predominantly Hindu India.

Voluntarism

Another very influential defense of separationism is what can be called the "voluntarist defense." The basic idea is that state promotion of religion can only operate by coercive force, yet genuine religious belief or practice cannot be (or cannot properly be) adopted under coercion: it is *essentially voluntary*. This kind of argument was not new to the early modern period. Before the Christianization of Rome, Church Fathers such as Tertullian had opposed persecution of Christians on the grounds that religious belief must be adopted freely. The voluntarist argument was popular among the much-persecuted seventeenth-century English Baptists, such as Leonard Busher, who in 1612 declared "as kings and bishops cannot command the wind, so they cannot command faith."[19] Locke's famous defense of religious toleration makes extensive use of voluntarism. He claims, "And such is the nature of the understanding, that it cannot be compelled to the belief of any thing by outward force. Confiscation of estate, imprisonment, torments, nothing of that nature can have any such efficacy as to make men change the inward judgment that they have framed of things."[20]

Locke also believed that the voluntarism of religion has an unavoidable consequence: "And upon this ground I affirm, that the magistrate's power extends not to the establishing of any articles of faith, or forms of worship, by the force of his laws. For laws are of no force at all without penalties, and penalties in this case are absolutely impertinent; because they are not proper to convince the mind."[21]

Because the tools at its disposal cannot "convince the mind," the government is incapable of producing religious beliefs that are sincerely held or religious practices that are pleasing to God.

> Neither the profession of any articles of faith, nor the conformity to any outward form of worship . . . can be available to the salvation of souls, unless the truth of the one, and the acceptableness of the other unto God, be thoroughly believed by those that so profess and practice. But penalties are no ways capable to produce such belief. It is only light and evidence that can work a change in men's opinions; and that light can in no manner proceed from corporal sufferings, or any other outward penalties.[22]

Despite its influence, voluntarism has limited force as an argument for secularism. The voluntarist can only object to the coercive religiosity of public institutions, not to the religiosity of public institutions as such. Locke considers the rejoinder to his voluntarist argument that civil official could use rational persuasion rather than force to lead people to the true religion. He replies that this is perfectly acceptable: "Every man has commission to admonish, exhort, convince another of error, and by reasoning to draw him into truth."[23] It is even compatible with Locke's voluntarism for a magistrate to actively endorse a faith, use his station to persuade others of its merits, or even compel tax support of it. As one of Madison's contemporaries pointed out to him, the voluntarist argument does not rule out the public funding of a religion as it was intended to do. It "rather contends against forcing modes of faith and forms of worship, than against compelling contribution for the support of religion in general."[24] Taxation to support religion may be coercion, but it is not coercion *of religion* in the sense Locke condemns.

Skeptical Theology

Notice that the argument from voluntarism and the argument from religious consequences are based on particular views about the correct nature of religious faith, worship, or the divine. They depend on certain *theological* assumptions. Often these assumptions were widely held in the audience to which the argument was addressed. For example, voluntarism was addressed mainly to Protestant Christians, and it presupposes a distinctly Protestant view of salvation that stresses inward persuasion, assent, and experience of God's grace. The assumptions would be much less palatable to members of traditions emphasizing salvation through outward behavior and participation in sacred rites.[25]

Other rationales for separationism depend on theological premises even more controversial to believers. Some are explicitly *atheological* or nonreligious. Karl Marx, for instance, believed that religious faith is a kind of delusion produced by adverse social circumstances. "Religious suffering is at once the expression of real suffering and a protest against real suffering. Religion is the sigh of the oppressed creature, the heart of a heartless world, just as it is the spirit of spiritless conditions. It is the opium of the people."[26]

Marx thought that human beings should transcend and abandon religion, and he advocated "the emancipation of the state from religion."[27] "The abolition of religion as the *illusory* happiness of the people is the demand for their *real* happiness. The demand that they should abandon illusions about their condition is the demand to give up conditions that require illusions."[28]

Some separationist arguments assume an *agnostic* stance. Locke asks: "For, there being but one truth . . . what hope is there that more men would be led into it, if they had no other rule to follow but the religion of the court . . . and blindly to resign up themselves to . . . the religion which either ignorance, ambition, or superstition had chanced to establish?"[29] Locke claims that following a government-established "religion of the court" offers no (or at least intolerably little) such hope of finding the true religion. This assumes that those responsible for establishing the state religion do not know what is the true religion (or at least that others cannot know whether or not they know). For a devout believer, it would be difficult to reconcile this assumption with one's conviction that one's own religion is the true religion.

Finally, some secularist arguments stop short of atheism or agnosticism, but deny significant portions of traditional theology. Benedict Spinoza's *Theologico-Political Treatise* (1670) argued against theocracy and for robust religious liberties. His position is based on the unorthodox theological doctrine that true religion (specifically its "outward observance" or manifestation in action) consists only in acts of justice and charity. On this basis he maintains that so long as a government compels justice and charity of its citizens, one cannot legitimately ask for any more of an establishment of religion: "[A] man best fulfills God's law who worships Him, according to His command, through acts of justice and charity; it follows, therefore, that wherever justice and charity have the force of law and ordinance, there is God's kingdom."[30]

What's more, civil authority is also the authority on religious matters (including, of course, the doctrine that outward religion consists only of acts justice and charity). "As, then, both reason and experience tell us that the Divine right is entirely dependent on the decrees of secular rulers, it follows that secular rulers are its proper interpreters."

In view of the relative weakness of the argument from consequences as a defense of strict separation, and secularists' historical reliance on liberal, skeptical, or otherwise controversial theologies, the question arises whether a robust defense of the secular society is possible without appeal to disputed religious and moral positions. If not, the best arguments for strict secularism may be unpersuasive to those believers who find secularist theological or ethical assumptions unacceptable. A related question reappears in the next section.

RELIGION AND POLITICS

It is often said that when arguing about political decisions in a public forum, one should not "impose one's beliefs" on others. Here "beliefs" often refers to sectarian religious beliefs. The preceding discussions explored whether public institutions should be secular. But what about the secularization of *public debate*? Recently this subject has been taken up by a number of political thinkers who maintain that arguments put forward in political debates should rely only on reasons that are or "could be" accepted by all citizens. This issue is discussed at length in section 8.3.

CONCLUSION

Over the last several centuries, Western societies have seen the triumph of secularism to lesser or greater extents. There remains some room for debate about the best rationale for strict separationism, particularly whether it must rely on controversial theological or religious assumptions.

SECTION 8.3

Getting Some Respect: Pluralism, Toleration, and Civil Society

Human societies are inevitably pluralistic, inasmuch as they comprise numerous distinct individuals whose histories, attitudes, and cognitive perspectives differ. But especially over the last five hundred years, global technological, economic, and cultural factors have led to the creation of enormously complex societies populated by multiple races, ethnicities, cultures, and nationalities. Such pluralistic societies are home to a great diversity of moral, religious, and philosophical outlooks. Often these outlooks are apparently inconsistent or in conflict with each other. For example, the chief aim in life might be worship of and communion with God, or self-fulfillment. Presumably it cannot be both, and yet both views attract sincere adherents, many of whom have reflected on the belief and are capable of explaining what makes it plausible. In the terms used by contemporary political philosophers, we are confronted by **reasonable pluralism**. Charles Larmore puts the idea of reasonable pluralism this way: "In modern times we have come to recognize a multiplicity of ways in which a fulfilled life can be lived, without any perceptible hierarchy among them. And we have also been forced to acknowledge that even where we do believe that we have discerned the superiority of some ways of life to others, reasonable people may often not share our view."[31]

How should governments and societies respond to reasonable pluralism? Common sense would seem to suggest that society should in some way try to encourage the true outlooks and best ways of life while discouraging the alternatives. When in our own lives we are faced with a number of alternative yet incompatible options, we normally try to consider the options carefully from all sides and then pursue the one that looks best. Why shouldn't a community collectively do something similar with regard to the alternative religious and moral views found among its members?

Such a community would be dangerous and wrong, according to the liberal and humanistic tradition in Western social and political thought. Instead, society should respond to pluralism by creating a framework of liberties, mutual toleration, and discussion so that its members may *decide for themselves* which alternatives to pursue:

17. A good society nurtures freedom of conscience, toleration, and open, critical dialogue.

Probably the most influential champion of such a society was the English philosopher and social reformer John Stuart Mill, whose argument from the classic essay *On Liberty* will now be examined.

FREEDOM OF CONSCIENCE AND EXPRESSION

In *On Liberty*, Mill lays out a detailed case that governments and social norms should permit robust freedom of opinion and freedom of the expression of opinion. He proceeds by considering any given expression that a state or social authority might wish to suppress because it is contrary to "received opinion." An opinion, Mill says, is either true, or partially true, or false. But in none of these cases are we justified in suppressing it. In the first possibility, "the opinion which it is attempted to suppress by authority may possibly be true. Those who desire to suppress it, of course deny its truth; but they are not infallible. They have no authority to decide the question for all mankind, and exclude every other person from the means of judging. To refuse a hearing to an opinion, because they are sure that it is false, is to assume that their certainty is the same thing as absolute certainty."[32]

People are naturally prone to error. Once we own up to our unavoidable fallibility, we cannot be confident in suppressing an opinion on the grounds that it seems false to us. "Secondly, though the silenced opinion be an error, it may, and very commonly does, contain a portion of truth; and since the general or prevailing opinion on any object is rarely or never the whole truth, it is only by the collision of adverse opinions that the remainder of the truth has any chance of being supplied."[33]

Again, protection of the received opinion runs the risk of missing some truth. However, Mill continues, even if the received opinion is entirely correct, it would be a mistake to shield it from criticism because

> unless it is suffered to be, and actually is, vigorously and earnestly contested, it will, by most of those who receive it, be held in the manner of a prejudice, with little comprehension or feeling of its rational grounds. And not only this . . . the meaning of the doctrine itself will be in danger of being lost, or enfeebled, and deprived of its vital effect on the character and conduct: the dogma becoming a mere formal profession, inefficacious for good, but cumbering the ground, and preventing the growth of any real and heartfelt conviction, from reason or personal experience.[34]

Even a truth stands to gain from exposure to scrutiny, for "if it is not fully, frequently, and fearlessly discussed, it will be held as a dead dogma, not a living truth."[35]

It may appear as though Mill is insisting that we give up all confidence in our own positions, even those we have carefully considered, something that hardly seems possible or desirable. In fact, he is careful to point out that confidence in our positions is not only compatible with an openness to criticism, it actually depends on such openness:

> Complete liberty of contradicting and disproving our opinion, is the very condition which justifies us in assuming its truth for purposes of action; and on no other terms can a being with human faculties have any rational assurance of being right. . . . The beliefs which we have most warrant for, have no safeguard to rest on, but a standing invitation to the whole world to prove them unfounded. If the challenge is not accepted, or is accepted and the attempt fails, we are far enough from certainty still; but we have done the best that the existing state of human reason admits of.[36]

Notice that Mill's defense of freedom of expression is based on its alleged valuable effects: the value of finding truth, or more fully, knowledge (where "knowing" a statement entails that it is a true or warranted statement), and (arguably) the value of persons who arrive at their views and behavior patterns through critical reflection and experiment, what we will later call **autonomous persons**. He favors a social system in which dissenting and unorthodox views are permitted because he believes that such a system will aid us in gaining knowledge and autonomy. In this way, Mill's defense is **consequentialist**.

Suppose we grant the importance of the values to which Mill appeals. Still, his defense of free expression has limits. It is not plausible to think that *every* position, no matter how absurd or morally noxious, will serve to stimulate or deepen one's understanding. For instance, progress in medicine requires the freedom to entertain and test potentially false conjectures, but nevertheless some conjectures (such as the conjecture that a mental illness is caused by demons, or a "wandering womb") no longer repay serious consideration. The challenge for the Millian is to provide some way of identifying such hopeless conjectures and to explain how they ought to be treated, in light of the rest of the Millian account.

Another limit to the Millian account results more directly from its consequentialism. If free expression is supposed to be cherished because of its link to particular values, then presumably this value can be *weighed* against other competing values, such as the values of civil stability, social equality, or individual well-being. For example, one might argue that the value of living in a society that accords equal respect to all citizens weighs against the Millian value of tolerating certain forms of racist or sexist "hate speech." Countervailing values such as these are especially hard to ignore if one shares Mill's overall political philosophy, according to which social and political norms should be arranged so as to maximize persons' autonomy. Mill aims to show that many forms of government and social restriction on liberty prevent or undermine persons' autonomy. However, he has left open the door to arguing that certain kinds of expression or inquiry can be justifiably discouraged or stifled on the very same grounds.

Neutrality

It is often said that in an open society, public institutions such as the government should be "neutral" with respect to controversial moral and political views. That is, they should attempt to act in such a way as to equally benefit or burden all views or their representatives. This notion has been called **neutrality of effect**. However, the concept of neutrality of effect is highly problematic.

One difficulty lies in trying to determine precisely what counts as equal benefits and burdens. Suppose that a quarrel has broken out between a member of your family and one of your close friends.[37] You wish to remain entirely neutral between them as long as their quarrel persists. What should you do or refrain from doing? You wish to act so as to equally benefit and burden both parties. But one party in the dispute already receives special treatment from you in virtue of your family relationship. There are a number of possible ways to deal with this. For example, you could (1) suspend your special treatment of the family member; (2) continue your special treatment of the family member but alter your treatment of the friend to match it; or (3) suspend all interaction with both. Options (1) and (2) would even out the prior inequality, but only by imposing new disproportionate burdens and benefits at present. Option 3 has the appearance of even treatment, but if it is practically feasible at all it would likely affect each party differently because of prior differences in treatment. All options would purchase equal treatment in one regard at the price of unequal treatment in some other regard.

The problem is that the question of neutrality often arises against a background of prior patterns of treatment, which may or may not be equal across the relevant parties. Such is certainly the case with the question of neutrality with respect to religion. Because of the nature of traditional religions and their historical prominence, they have unique relationships to social life for which there is no parallel among nonreligious traditions. As a result, the question of what counts as equal treatment of the religious and nonreligious is extremely vexing. This is reflected in the deep tension between the two religion clauses of the First Amendment to the U.S. Constitution. The establishment clause is interpreted to require strict neutrality among religions and among the religious and the nonreligious, while the free exercise clause is interpreted as guaranteeing special protection to citizens' practice of their religion.

Another problem with the notion of state neutrality is that a state that attempts to be neutral often has the effect of hindering some controversial positions, such as ideals of the good life, which demand a certain social structure or collective effort to realize some shared goals.[38] Thus, the attempt at neutrality is self-defeating. For example, consider a state that attempted to remain neutral with respect to musical art forms, and did so by refraining from subsidizing all of them, or subsidizing them in equal amounts. Since opera is very expensive and difficult to produce, it might languish or disappear from the society as a result, while folk singing might continue unaffected because it happens to demand few social and financial resources.[39]

PUBLIC REASON

The above difficulties with the ideal of neutrality of effect have prompted some thinkers, including the influential American political philosopher John Rawls (1921–2002), to devise an alternative understanding of neutrality, which can be called **neutrality of justification**.

One important part (although not the only part) of politics is the public discussion and justification of decisions about what governments should do—for example, concerning access to abortion or public education. In such discussions, citizens and public figures often present each other with reasons in support of this or that political decision. But in a society characterized by a pluralism of contested religious, moral, and philosophical positions, the reasons endorsed by one citizen may not be endorsed by another. Is there anything objectionable about these differences by the lights of liberal values?

Philosopher Thomas Nagel once argued that the reasons we give for political decisions must make sense to our fellow community members because government actions have a direct impact on their lives and behavior. Therefore, our reasons must meet a certain standard of "higher-order impartiality" or objectivity. One must be prepared "to submit one's reasons to the criticism of others, and to find that the exercise of a common critical rationality and consideration of evidence that can be shared will reveal that one is mistaken. This means that it must be possible to present to others the basis of your own beliefs, so that once you have done so, *they have what you have*, and can arrive at a judgment on the same basis."[40]

The standard of impartiality is not met, Nagel claimed, when "part of the source of your conviction is personal faith or revelation—because to report your faith or revelation to someone else is not to give him what you have, as you do when you show him your evidence or give him your arguments." When political reasons fail to achieve higher-order impartiality, political debate amounts to a mere "clash between irreconcilable subjective convictions" rather than a disagreement in "the common, public domain."[41]

Some political theorists have argued in a similar vein that political discussions in a pluralistic society ought to be guided by an ideal of "publicity": Participants may introduce only those reasons endorsable by all reasonable citizens. In a society in which reasonable people disagree over fundamental religious and moral positions, citizens must set aside their "private" convictions when seeking a secure grounding for the political order. Typically, private convictions include religious convictions. The focus on "public reason," which has been especially popular since the publication of the later work of the John Rawls, can be traced to Immanuel Kant. Kant's famous essay "What Is Enlightenment?" introduces the notion of a public use of reason as "that use which anyone may make of it as a man of learning addressing the entire reading public" or "the world at large."[42] A private use of reason is that which is directed toward a more limited audience. For example, when the clergyman addresses his congregation, his use of reason is "purely private." The norm of public reason is not intended to be legally enforced. Rather it is supposed to be a "principle of conscience," or a prima facie moral obligation observed by conscientious citizens in a pluralistic democracy.

Philosophers, theologians, and legal scholars have lodged several complaints against the doctrine of public reason, especially as it pertains to religion. First, it misconstrues religious thought as "private," denying its essentially public, political dimensions, which are evidenced, for example, by the existence of significant religious duties with social and political content, and by theologies that evaluate the authority of the state vis-à-vis a divine normative order. The doctrine of public reason "trivializes" religious devotion, in the words of Yale law professor Stephen L. Carter, spreading the false view that "religion is like building model airplanes, just another hobby: something quiet, something private, something trivial—and not really a fit activity for intelligent, public-spirited adults."[43]

Second, the reasons that might be endorsed by all in a pluralistic society—such as "the value of fairness"—are too few in number and too broad and indeterminate in content to resolve many pressing political questions. Third, the doctrine of public reason would significantly restrict the religious and political life of believers. It would unjustifiably diminish the scope of believers' religious liberty, which includes the liberty to draw on one's faith when engaging political issues in a public forum. Moreover, participants in certain morally sound social movements—such as the abolitionist movement in America—have achieved their goals in part by formulating explicitly religious arguments in the public sphere.

It is highly questionable that secularism should go so far as to discourage ordinary citizens from expressing and acting on their religious conscience in politics. However, if the arguments for some form of separationism (like those examined in section 8.2) are cogent, then special restraint may be appropriate for legislators, judges, ambassadors, military officials, heads of state, and other citizens insofar as they serve as representatives of government or other public institutions.

In response to such criticisms, public reason theorists have qualified the norm of public reason by saying that it is satisfied in cases like the abolitionist arguments—so long as the appropriate public reasons are introduced "in due course" and that it is a prima facie obligation whose strength varies according to the gravity of the political decision at hand and the social position of the political actor (supposing that the obligation to avoid "private" reasons falls more heavily on public official than ordinary citizens). In response to the criticism about indeterminacy, some have asserted that private reasons may be welcomed when public reasons alone are incapable of resolving an issue. It is questionable whether what remains of the principle of public reason after such qualifications is robust enough to be of any real theoretical and practical significance.

Indeed, the concepts of publicity and privacy have numerous meanings, and discussions often slide back and forth between them, creating confusion, inviting misleading conclusions, and impeding intellectual progress. For example, in discussing a religious position, writers illicitly shift from the claim that it is private in the Kantian sense of not universally endorsed to the claim that it is private in the sense of "personal" or "nonpolitical." The dichotomy may not be the best conceptual tool with which to address the various issues raised by the use of religious reasons in political discourse.

Surely we should want our political debate to rise above the mere clash of "irreconcilable subjective convictions." But that does not imply that religious reasons must be precluded in principle. Rather, it implies that they must abide by the same standards of public discourse by which all serious contributions to politics are judged—such as civility, mutual respect, rationality, consistency, and cogency. Malice, ridicule, manipulation, and deceit belie the character of deliberation in a democratic society. But just as important is the need for shared application of logic and interpersonal criticism. If we are unwilling to present others with reasons for what we say that are open to critical analysis by them, then we are engaging in monologue, not dialogue. This goes for religiously based political proposals as much as for any others.

LIBERALISM: PERFECTIONIST OR POLITICAL?

At this point, one might raise the following question, as have many critics of contemporary liberalism. Pluralism of "reasonable" yet contested religious, moral, and philosophical positions is said to necessitate a government stance of neutrality (whether of effect or justification) with respect to those positions. But what about that stance itself? Is neutrality a *neutral stance* toward pluralism? Or should one expect that when a government takes a particular stance toward a set of contested religious, moral, and philosophical positions, that stance will itself be contested? To put it more vividly, does pluralism go *all the way down*?

Some liberals have met this concern head-on by attempting to construct a neutral justification of neutrality. In Larmore's words: "Controversy about ideals of the good life and the demand that the state remain neutral toward them have been the central ingredients of the liberal vision of politics. This means that if liberals are to follow fully the spirit of liberalism, they must also devise a neutral justification of political neutrality."[44] Roughly, this means that the liberal ideal of state neutrality or public reason must be supported without relying on any of the positions that are the subject of controversy. Rawls has called this kind of liberalism "political liberalism"—"political" because it attempts to provide a basis for liberal neutrality by drawing on notions, such as the basic idea of fairness, that are supposed to be implicit in the "public political culture," and so form part of an "overlapping consensus" among the views of reasonable citizens. By drawing only from shared views, political liberalism hopes to avoid any controversial moral or religious stance. By contrast, *perfectionist* liberalism argues that liberal politics helps citizens to approximate the ideal of the good life, the life of autonomy, toleration, and so on.

Consider again John Stuart Mill's liberalism. He argues that social institutions should be arranged so as to encourage the development of unique and autonomous persons. The creation of such persons is valuable in itself but also contributes to the intellectual and material progress of civilization. Governments best encourage this creation when they refrain from actively endorsing or forcing their citizens to adopt any particular way of life and instead allow them to conduct "experiments in living," freely exploring and assessing the possibilities. This way, people in general are more apt to discover those modes of human existence most worthwhile and fulfilling. Millian liberalism is perfectionist because it rests its case on a substantive ideal of the good life. The same can be said about Kant's liberalism, which is based on the purported moral worth of individuals realizing their freedom by directing themselves with their own reason.

Of course, many reasonable citizens of a pluralistic society reject the liberal ideal of the good life. They deny the value of freely adopting and revising ways of life according to one's own reason. So perfectionist liberals are faced with the challenge of demonstrating, as Kant and Mill tried to do, that their ideal is superior. Political liberals, on the other hand, must demonstrate how the values on which there is an "overlapping consensus" lead one to a liberal politics, without recourse to the perfectionist value of autonomy.

CONCLUSION

While there are important complexities and disagreements regarding the details, political theorists widely concur on the general desirability of an open, tolerant society that permits dissent and critical discussion of contested positions. Whether the open society should be thought of as a "neutral" society remains in dispute.

SUMMARY

Humanist ideas about society and politics have traditionally tended toward liberalism, individualism, universalism, and secularism. Each of these strands continues to be the focus of dispute and discussion in contemporary social and political thought, especially in the English-speaking world. The escape of the Western world from religious persecution and sectarian violence was made possible by a thoroughgoing transition from theocracy to secularism as the ideal for society. However, many European states enjoy civil peace and toleration despite continuing the tradition of an established church. This raises questions about what considerations might justify the strict separation of religion and government as found in the United States. Questions have also been raised about whether the ideal of secularism ought to include not only public institutions but also the public discourse of citizens. The implicit and explicit universalism of humanist social ethics has been enlisted in democratic and liberation movements, and is increasingly presumed in the human rights discourse that has arisen since the middle of the twentieth century. Humanist universalism faces charges of imperialist arrogance from some critics and speciesism from others. Likewise, the individualist model of the person has been attacked by communitarians, while other critics claim that individualism prevents liberals from protecting important group rights, especially those of tolerated nonliberal minorities. Late twentieth-century political philosophy has framed liberal theory in the context of "reasonable pluralism," generating questions about whether liberalism and secularism can be justified without appeal to controversial religious, moral, and philosophical premises.

Despite—or perhaps precisely because of—the triumph of secular liberal political philosophy in the West, it continues to be the source of considerable disquiet, dissent, and debate. The Austrian-born philosopher Karl Popper remarked on a similar phenomena in 1945. In his *The Open Society and Its Enemies*, Popper defended the ideal of the liberal, individualist, tolerant, humanist society against what he called "collectivist" and totalitarian alternatives. But the way of the open society, he wrote, is not free of risk or difficulty. Because of its openness to change, variation, and heterogeneity, the open society is subject to "the strain of civilization": "This strain, this uneasiness, is a consequence of the breakdown of the closed society. It is still felt even in our day, especially in times of social change. . . . We must, I believe, bear this strain as the price to be paid for every increase in knowledge, in reasonableness, in co-operation, and in mutual help, and consequently, in our chances of survival."[45]

The strain must be endured, Popper said, because for us there can be no turning back to the closed society. "If we turn back, then we must go the whole way—we must return to the beasts. We can return to the beasts. But if we wish to remain human, then there is only one way, the way into the open society. We must go on into the unknown, the uncertain and insecure, using what reason we may have to plan as well as we can for both security and freedom."[46]

STUDY QUESTIONS

1. Describe the "natural rights" tradition.
2. What is liberalism as a political philosophy?
3. In which ways was liberalism exclusive historically?
4. What is individualism? Describe The Problem of Non-liberal Minorities.
5. How is contemporary liberalism universalist? Describe one challenge to universalism.
6. Contrast theocratic, erastian, and separationist arrangements.
7. How did the Reformation and religious wars contribute to the growth of separationism in political history?
8. Describe the argument from bad consequences and one objection it.
9. Describe the argument from voluntarism and one objection to it.
10. How have separationist arguments relied on skeptical theologies? State an example.
11. Explain John Stuart Mill's argument against the suppression of opinions that are contrary to "received opinion." State one challenge to the argument.
12. Describe "neutrality of effect" and one difficulty with it.
13. Describe "neutrality of justification," or the norm of public reason.
14. In political argument, how is critical intersubjectivity different from publicity in the liberal sense?
15. Contrast perfectionist liberalism with political liberalism.

DISCUSSION QUESTIONS

1. Do all human beings have equal rights, simply by virtue of being human? If not, where do we draw the line?
2. What measures may Western societies take to affect the observance of human rights around the world?
3. Is liberalism guilty of an objectionable form of atomistic individualism? Why or why not? If so, could it do without this form of individualism?
4. Is the humanist tradition speciesist? Why or why not? If so, is this a telling objection against it?
5. Construct an argument for a universal right to freedom of conscience or belief.
6. How tightly connected are secularism of institutions and secularism of public debate? Could a society properly have one with the other?
7. How might someone reply to the Madisonian argument that theocratic and erastian regimes are bad for religion?
8. Can you think of a case in which a norm of antiestablishment comes into conflict with a norm of religious liberty? Is there a general principle that could be used to resolve such conflicts?
9. Must an argument for separation be acceptable to all reasonable citizens, or could different arguments be addressed to different citizens?
10. What sorts of institutional arrangements would Lockean voluntarism rule out? What sorts would it not rule out?

11. Can religion be political? In what ways? Cite specific examples.
12. Using specific examples, explain the senses of "private" in which religion is private. In which senses is religion nonprivate?
13. Do you think that in your own society there is a Rawlsian "overlapping consensus" favorable to liberalism?
14. Are you persuaded by perfectionist liberalisms based on the value of individual autonomy? Why or why not?
15. When engaging in political deliberation or debate, exactly what does respect for fellow citizens require of us?

FIELD PROBLEM

Secularism admits of degrees. Research four existing societies that represent a spectrum of strict to moderate separationism.

SUGGESTIONS FOR FURTHER READING

Goodin, Robert E., and Andrew Reeve, eds. *Liberal Neutrality*. New York: Routledge, 1989.
Greenawalt, Kent. *Private Consciences and Public Reasons*. Oxford: Oxford University Press, 1995.
Heyd, David, ed. *Toleration: An Elusive Virtue*. Princeton: Princeton University Press, 1996.
Larmore, Charles. *Patterns of Moral Complexity*. Cambridge: Cambridge University Press, 1987.
Locke, John. *A Letter Concerning Toleration*. Amherst, N.Y.: Prometheus Books, 1990.
Locke, John. *Political Essays*, ed. Mark Goldie. Cambridge: Cambridge University Press, 1997.
Mill, John Stuart. "On Liberty." In *On Liberty and Other Writings*, ed. Stefan Collini. Cambridge: Cambridge University Press, 1992.
Mulhall, Stephen, and Adam Swift. *Liberals and Communitarians*. Oxford: Basil Blackwell, 1992.
Nagel, Thomas. *Equality and Partiality*. New York: Oxford University Press, 1991.
Perry, Michael. *Religion in Politics: Constitutional and Moral Perspectives*. Oxford: Oxford University Press, 1997.
Pfeffer, Leo. *Church, State, and Freedom*. Boston: Beacon Press, 1953.
Quinn, Philip L. "Political Liberalisms and Their Exclusion of the Religious." In *Proceedings and Addresses of the American Philosophical Association* 69, 2 (1995): 35–56.
Rawls, John. *Theory of Justice*. Cambridge, Mass.: Harvard University Press, 1971.
Rawls, John. *Political Liberalism*. New York: Columbia University Press, 1996.
Raz, Joseph. *The Morality of Freedom*. Oxford: Clarendon Press, 1986.
Sandel, Michael. *Democracy's Discontent: America in Search of a Public Philosophy*. Cambridge, Mass.: Harvard University Press, 1996.
Weithman, Paul, ed. *Religion and Contemporary Liberalism*. Notre Dame, Ind.: University of Notre Dame Press, 1997.
Wilson, John F., ed. *Church and State in American History*. Boston: Heath, 1965.

NOTES

1. William Shakespeare, *The Merchant of Venice*, act 3, scene 1.
2. Frederick Douglass, *My Bondage and My Freedom* (1885) in *Frederick Douglass Autobiographies* (New York: Library of America, 1994), 392–93.

3. Mary Wollstonecraft, *A Vindication of the Rights of Women*, ed. Sylvania Tomaselli (Cambridge University Press, 1995).

4. Jeremy Bentham, *An Introduction to the Principles of Morals and Legislation* (1789), chapter 17, section 1, footnote to paragraph 4.

5. Peter Singer, *Unsanctifying Human Life*, ed. Helga Kuhse (Oxford: Blackwell, 2002).

6. Will Kymlicka, "Two Models of Pluralism and Tolerance," in *Toleration: An Elusive Virtue,* ed. David Heyd (Princeton: Princeton University Press, 1996.)

7. Michael J. Sandel, *Democracy's Discontent: America in Search of a Public Philosophy* (Cambridge, Mass.: Belknap Press, 1996), 14–15.

8. Salman Rushdie, "Yes, This Is about Islam" *New York Times*, 2 November 2001.

9. The introduction of the metaphor is often traced to King Henry IV in a letter to the bishops of Germany in 1076. The letter was part of an intense struggle with Pope Gregory over the extent of papal and royal authority. Henry traced the idea of the two swords to an enigmatic remark by Christ, as reported in the Gospel of Luke, that the apostles possess two swords. Henry intended to defend a strict division between the civil and ecclesiastical powers. But the doctrine of the two swords was ambiguous enough to admit of various interpretations. Henry had reasoned that two swords necessitated two swordsmen, or two hierarchies that exist more or less independently, without competing claims to authority over each other.

Later, Pope Eugenius III argued of the two swords that "the former (i.e., the spiritual) is to be drawn by the Church, the latter on behalf of the Church," suggesting that secular power is ultimately subject to ecclesiastical supervision. Long before Gregory, in 496, Pope Gelasius had described the "two powers by which this world is chiefly ruled" as "the sacred authority" and "the royal power." His formula was similarly ambiguous, and was used on all sides of the subsequent controversies.

10. Leo Pfeffer, *Church, State, and Freedom* (Boston: Beacon Press, 1953), 4–8.

11. John B. Morrall, *Political Thought in Medieval Times* (New York: Harper & Row, 1958), 21.

12. Anthony Quinton, ed., *The Oxford History of Western Philosophy* (Oxford: Oxford University Press, 1994), 292.

13. After Erastus (1524–1583), a Swiss doctor and Protestant theologian who argued, among other things, that the state should have the authority to punish sins.

14. Jean-Jacques Rousseau, *The Social Contract* (New York: Hafner, 1947 [1762]), vol. 4, 8.

15. Rousseau, *The Social Contract,* 123–24.

16. The struggle was not simply between secular and religious authorities. Provincial and feudal governments resisted the centralized imperial power, and a secularized episcopate resisted the control of the Papacy. Local secular authorities asserted the superiority of the pope when this would protect them from the interference of the emperor, while local ecclesiastical authorities asserted the superiority of the emperor when this would protect them from an intrusive pope.

17. James Madison, "Memorial and Remonstrance," in Robert Alley, ed., *James Madison on Religious Liberty* (Amherst, N.Y.: Prometheus Books, 1985), 58.

18. Madison, "Memorial and Remonstrance," 57–58.

19. Leonard Busher, *Religion's Peace: A Plea for Liberty of Conscience* (1614), cited in H. Leon McBeth, *A Sourcebook for Baptist Heritage* (Nashville, Tenn.: Broadman Press, 1990), 72.

20. John Locke, *A Letter Concerning Toleration* (Amherst, N.Y.: Prometheus Books, 1990), 20.

21. Locke, *A Letter Concerning Toleration,* 20.

22. Locke, *A Letter Concerning Toleration,* 20–21.

23. Locke, *A Letter Concerning Toleration,* 20.

24. Letter from Richard Henry Lee to Madison, 26 November 1784. In Alley, *James Madison on Religious Liberty,* 65.

25. Even within Protestant Christianity, the voluntarist assumptions are not universally held. For example, voluntarism often assumes that the individual conscience is incorrigible or at least highly

accurate as a guide to correct doctrine and practice. Otherwise, one would not attempt to perform one's duty of offering to God only correct forms of worship solely by consulting one's conscience. But according to orthodox Puritan doctrine of the seventeenth century, conscience is fallible and it must be augmented by consulting the Word of God. Furthermore, it is possible to be unaware of the voice of one's conscience. Thus, the Puritan could argue that the dissenter's conscience is mistaken or that he is mistaken about its judgment. In the first case, the dissenter should not worship according to conscience and should instead be encouraged to uncover its error by a correct reading of Scripture. In the second case, in order to worship according to his conscience the dissenter must be compelled to worship in a way that he thinks is misguided.

26. Karl Marx, "Contributions to the Critique of Hegel's *Philosophy of Right*," in *The Portable Karl Marx*, ed. Eugene Kamenka (New York: Penguin, 1983), 115.

27. Karl Marx, "On the Jewish Question," in *The Portable Karl Marx*, 100.

28. Marx, "Contribution to the Critique of Hegel's *Philosophy of Right,*" in *The Portable Karl Marx*, 115–16.

29. Locke, *A Letter Concerning Toleration*, 21.

30. Benedict Spinoza, *A Theologico-Political Treatise*, trans. R. H. M. Elwes (New York: Dover, 1954), 246.

31. Charles Larmore, *Patterns of Moral Complexity* (Cambridge: Cambridge University Press, 1987), 43.

32. John Stuart Mill, "On Liberty," in Stefan Collini, ed., *On Liberty and Other Writings* (Cambridge: Cambridge University Press, 1992), 20–21.

33. Mill, "On Liberty," 53.

34. Mill, "On Liberty," 53–54.

35. Mill, "On Liberty," 37.

36. Mill, "On Liberty," 24.

37. This is a variation on an example discussed by Joseph Raz in *The Morality of Freedom* (Oxford: Clarendon Press, 1986), chapter 5.

38. See Joseph Raz, "Liberalism, Autonomy, and the Politics of Neutral Concern," in *Midwest Studies in Philosophy, vol. VII: Social and Political Philosophy*, ed. Peter French, Theodore E. Uehling, Jr., and Howard K. Wettstein (Minneapolis: University of Minnesota Press, 1982).

39. This example is from Stephen Mulhall and Adam Swift, *Liberals and Communitarians* (Oxford: Basil Blackwell, 1992), 26–27.

40. Thomas Nagel, "Moral Conflict and Political Legitimacy," *Philosophy and Public Affairs* 16 (1987): 215–40, 230–31.

41. Nagel, "Moral Conflict," 231.

42. Kant, *Political Writings* (Cambridge: Cambridge University Press, 1995).

43. Stephen L. Carter, *The Culture of Disbelief: How American Law and Politics Trivialize Religious Devotion* (New York: Anchor Books, 1994), 21–22.

44. Larmore, *Patterns of Moral Complexity,* 53.

45. Karl R. Popper, *The Open Society and Its Enemies*, vol. 1 (Princeton: Princeton University Press, 1962), 200.

46. Popper, *The Open Society,* 201.

Index

About the Authors

Lewis Vaughn is the coauthor (with Theodore Schick) of the critical thinking text *How to Think about Weird Things: Critical Thinking for a New Age,* and *Doing Philosophy: An Introduction through Thought Experiments.* He is also the author of *Thinking Outside the Box: Thinking Critically about Ordinary and Extraordinary Claims* (Oxford University Press, forthcoming). For several years he served as the editor of *Free Inquiry*, a leading humanist magazine, and as the executive editor of the philosophy journal *Philo* and the medical journal *The Scientific Review of Alternative Medicine*.

Austin Dacey is visiting research professor of philosophy at SUNY–Buffalo and director of educational programs at the Center for Inquiry. He is executive editor of *Philo*, a journal of philosophy, and coeditor (with Quentin Smith) of *Naturalism and Theism* (forthcoming). In 2002, he received a doctorate in philosophy. He lives in New York City.